A JOURNAL OF CONTEMPORARY WRITING

IRISH PAGES

DUILLÍ ÉIREANN

IRISH PAGES is a biannual journal (Spring-Summer, Autumn-Winter), edited in Belfast and publishing, in equal measure, writing from Ireland and overseas. It appears at the end of each six-month period.

Its policy is to publish poetry, short fiction, essays, creative non-fiction, memoir, essay reviews, nature-writing, translated work, literary journalism, and other autobiographical, historical, religious and scientific writing of literary distinction. There are no standard reviews or narrowly academic articles. Irish-language and Scots writing are published in the original, with English translations or glosses. IRISH PAGES is a non-partisan, non-sectarian, culturally ecumenical, and wholly independent journal. It endorses no political outlook or cultural tradition, and has no editorial position on the constitutional question. Its title refers to the island of Ireland in a purely apolitical and geographic sense, in the same manner of The Church of Ireland or the Irish Sea.

The sole criteria for inclusion in the journal are the distinction of the writing and the integrity of the individual voice. Equal editorial attention will be given to established, emergent and new writers.

The views expressed in IRISH PAGES are not necessarily those of the Editors. The journal is published by Irish Pages Ltd, a non-profit organization.

Submissions are welcome but must be accompanied by return postage or an international reply coupon. No self-addressed envelope is required. Reporting time is nine months. If work is accepted, an electronic copy on disk may be requested.

Your subscription is essential to the independence and survival of the journal. Subscription rates are £16stg/€26/$45 for one year. Visit our website at www.irishpages.org for a subscription form or to order online. Credit cards are welcome.

IRISH PAGES
129 Ormeau Road
Belfast BT7 1SH

*IRISH PAGES is set in 12/14.5 Monotype Perpetua
and printed in Belfast by Nicholson & Bass.*

*This issue has been generously asssisted by Foras na Gaeilge, Northern Ireland
Community Relations Council and the Arts Councils of Northern and
Southern Ireland.*

ISBN 978-0-9935532-7-1

Supported by
The National Lottery®
through the Arts Council of Northern Ireland

COMMUNITY
RELATIONS
COUNCIL
Equity | Diversity | Interdependence

The Northern Ireland
Community Relations Council

Foras na Gaeilge

IRISH PAGES

CHRIS AGEE, *Editor*

CATHAL Ó SEARCAIGH, *Irish Language Editor*

KATHLEEN JAMIE, *Scottish Editor*

MEG BATEMAN, *Scottish Gaelic Editor*

JENNIFER KERR, *Managing Editor*

JACOB AGEE, RUTH CARR, STEPHEN DORNAN & RUTH PADEL
Contributing Editors

EDITED IN BELFAST
VOLUME 10, NUMBER 2

IRISH PAGES
DUILLÍ ÉIREANN

VOLUME 10, NUMBER 2

CONTENTS

The Belfast Agreement: Twentieth Anniversary Issue

*"'I get down on my knees and do what must be done
And kiss Achilles' hand, the killer of my son'."*

Michael Longley
from "Ceasefire"

PORTFOLIO

THE HUBERT BUTLER ESSAY PRIZE

The Patron of This Issue

ROBERT MCDOWELL

FRIENDS AND SUPPORTERS OF *IRISH PAGES*

Anonymous (Glasgow)

Gerry Bell

Vincent Browne

Paddy Bushe

John Cassidy

Manus Charleton

Charles Coventry

Donnell and Alison Deeny

Joe and Geraldine Duffy

Gandolfi Fish (Glasgow)

Elliot Duffy Garrett

Jack Gillespie

André Gumuchdjian

Philip Haughey

Marie Heaney

Brian Mac Call

Tom Mac Intyre

Enda McDonough

Robert McDowell and Manfred McDowell

John McGinley

John McMahon

Colette Ní Ghallchóir

Joe Prendergast

Gillian Reynolds

Carolyn Richardson

Tony Skelton

Anne Smith

Timothy Vignoles

David Woods

Subscribe online at www.irishpages.org

North
By Neil Shawcross

(See "Portfolio")

SONGS FOR DEAD CHILDREN: ON THE POETRY OF NORTHERN IRELAND'S TROUBLES

—

Michael Longley

Hauntings and shamings.

In August 1969, Patrick Rooney, a nine-year-old boy, was struck by a tracer-bullet fired by the RUC as he lay in bed in the Divis Flats in the Falls Road district of Belfast. He was the first child to be killed during the Troubles. In helpless response, I wrote "Kindertotenlieder" ("Songs for Dead Children"), its title borrowed from Mahler's great song cycle:

> There can be no songs for dead children
> Near the crazy circle of explosions,
> The splintering tangent of the ricochet,
>
> No songs for the children who have become
> My unrestricted tenants, fingerprints
> Everywhere, teeth marks on this and that.

Patrick Rooney haunts me to this day. In my new collection, *Angel Hill*, I remember him in a short poem called "Dusty Bluebells":

> Patrick Rooney, aged nine, was killed
> By a tracer-bullet where he slept.
> Boys and girls in his class resumed
> Their games soon after: *In and out go*
> *Dusty bluebells, Bangor boat's away*

The songs from the children's street games reverberate down the decades and sound, in my imagination, for the children killed in Manchester in May this year. The deaths of children – always "innocent victims" – epitomise the shame of political violence.

Northern Ireland is not a place apart. Its civil war, which killed more than three and a half thousand people, belongs to the dark history of

European conflict. In writing about the Troubles the poets of my generation took their bearings from Yeats and MacNeice, from the poems of Keith Douglas and Alun Lewis in the Second World War, from the Great War poets – Owen, Sassoon, Rosenberg, Blunden, Gurney, Edward Thomas. We read Brecht, Célan, Apollinaire, Montale, Akhmatova, Rózewicz and reached back to Homer's *Iliad*. But from the outset it has been (and still is) hugely difficult – impossible even – to find in poetry a voice, as Seamus Heaney put it, "adequate to our predicament." In a poem called "Wounds" which I wrote in 1972 I ask the ghost of my father what he makes of it all: he had joined up as a boy-soldier in 1914 and fought in the Trenches. Here is the poem's second section:

> Now, with military honours of a kind,
> With his badges, his medals like rainbows,
> His spinning compass, I bury beside him
> Three teenage soldiers, bellies full of
> Bullets and Irish beer, their flies undone.
> A packet of Woodbines I throw in,
> A lucifer, the Sacred Heart of Jesus
> Paralysed as heavy guns put out
> The night-light in a nursery for ever;
> Also a bus-conductor's uniform –
> He collapsed beside his carpet-slippers
> Without a murmur, shot through the head
> By a shivering boy who wandered in
> Before they could turn the television down
> Or tidy away the supper dishes.
> To the children, to a bewildered wife,
> I think "Sorry Missus" was what he said.

When the Bogside erupted in 1969 and West Belfast went up in flames, I was flabbergasted by the ferocity of it all. In the summer of 1969 Derek Mahon and I walked through the wreckage of the Falls Road. In a verse letter to him, I saw us as:

> Two poetic conservatives
> In the city of guns and long knives,
> Our ears receiving then and there

> The stereophonic nightmare
> Of the Shankill and the Falls.

As I recalled in an interview I gave in 2003: Part of me felt like an appalled outsider, another part – anti-Unionist, anti-establishment – felt exhilarated. The rest of me wanted to understand what I had hitherto ignored, the darkness and violence in my own community. From the beginning my poet-friends and I resisted the temptation to hitch a ride on yesterday's headlines, to write the poem of the latest atrocity. We learned from each other how complex the situation was, how inadequate the political certainties – Green Ireland, Orange Ulster. We knew there was no point in versifying opinion and giving people what they wanted to hear.

We believed that poetry, the opposite of propaganda, should encourage people to think and feel for themselves: it should appeal to their "generous instinct," as MacNeice said in the violent 1930s. We hated what we came to call "Troubles trash." We believed that, even when generated by the best of intentions, bad poetry about the sufferings of fellow citizens would be an impertinence; as part of an agenda it would be a blasphemy. We disliked the notion that civic unrest might be good for poetry, and poetry a solace for the broken-hearted. We were none of us in the front line.

So far as I can recall, we never discussed these dilemmas. We had no plans to face up to the crisis as a group, or to speak to the outside world about it. We continued to write the poems that presented themselves, no doubt hoping that one day we might produce something "adequate" about the Troubles. I find that I wrote in 1971: "Too many critics seem to expect a harvest of paintings, poems, plays and novels to drop from the twisted branches of civil discord. They fail to realise that the artist needs time in which the raw material of experience may settle to an imaginative depth, where it can be transformed into art."

We took our time. Paul Muldoon observed that if you didn't write about the Troubles you might be dismissed as an ostrich; if you did, you might be judged exploitative. Ciaran Carson said that his poems were not necessarily *about* the Troubles, but might be *of* them. Medbh McGuckian chose as the epigraph to her 1994 collection *Captain Lavender* what Picasso said in 1944: "I have not painted the war ... but I have no doubt that the war is in ... these paintings I have done."

Introducing his indispensable anthology, *A Rage for Order: Poetry of the Northern Ireland Troubles,* Frank Ormsby wrote: "It is arguable that any poem by a Northern Irish writer since 1968, on whatever subject, could be termed a Troubles poem, in that it may, consciously or unconsciously, reflect the context in which it was written."

A French writer once asked me: "Which side are the poets on?" But the true poets resisted demands to take sides. They listened to one another. In "The Hill Farm," a beautiful lyric written before the recent Troubles, John Hewitt recalls standing outside a Catholic neighbour's home in the Glens of Antrim, too shy to intrude as they say the rosary:

> At each Hail Mary Full of Grace
> I pictured every friendly face,
> clenched in devotion of a kind
> alien to my breed and mind,
> easy as breathing, natural
> as birds that fly, as leaves that fall;
> yet with a sense that I still stood
> far from that faith-based certitude,
> here in the vast enclosing night,
> outside its little ring of light.

Written *during* the Troubles, Seamus Heaney's "The Other Side" responds tenderly to Hewitt's poem and, reversing the situation, speaks from *inside* the house, from inside the Catholic community. Heaney evokes a Protestant neighbour standing outside their home as the evening prayers are being said. I shall quote the last ten lines:

> But now I stand behind him
> in the dark yard, in the moan of prayers.
> He puts a hand in a pocket
>
> or taps a little tune with the blackthorn
> shyly, as if he were party to
> lovemaking or a stranger's weeping.
>
> Should I slip away, I wonder,
> or go up and touch his shoulder
> and talk about the weather
> or the price of grass-seed?

These two poems explore the cultural intricacies of life in Northern Ireland. In "The Boundary Commission" Paul Muldoon wittily carries the question of "sides," of identity and allegiance, even further:

> You remember that village where the border ran
> Down the middle of the street,
> With the butcher and baker in different states?
> Today he remarked how a shower of rain
>
> Had stopped so cleanly across Golightly's lane
> It might have been a wall of glass
> That had toppled over. He stood there, for ages,
> To wonder which side, if any, he should be on.

There are delicate balancing-acts in this conversation between poems. Perhaps such open-heartedness, reflecting "generous instinct" elsewhere in the society, suggests why – despite the terrible violence – Ulster never quite descended into the nightmarish mayhem of Bosnia's civil war. Poetic conversations continue to this day. When the Good Friday Agreement was painstakingly achieved I felt it had – as it needed to have – an almost poetic complexity. To quote Heaney's metaphor, the Agreement was about "the price of grass-seed." In a poem of my own I called it "a fragment from some future unimagined sky." You might say that today Northern Irish politics more often resemble bad prose. But the Peace Process is a *process*. It is far from over. It will take generations.

In August 1994 it was rumoured that there might be an IRA ceasefire. At the time I was reading the passage in the *Iliad* where the old king Priam bravely visits the mighty Greek general Achilles to beg for the body of Hector whom Achilles has killed in combat. Priam in his fragility awakens in Achilles memories of his own father and rekindles the gentler emotions he has had to suppress in order to be a general. The *Iliad* is probably our greatest poem about war and death; and this episode is, for me, its soul. I wanted to compress its two hundred lines into a compact lyric and thereby make my own minuscule contribution to the Peace Process. I sent the resulting sonnet to *The Irish Times*. The then literary editor John Banville published "Ceasefire" on the Saturday of the week in which the IRA declared *their* ceasefire. Here is the poem:

i

Put in mind of his own father and moved to tears
Achilles took him by the hand and pushed the old king
Gently away, but Priam curled up at his feet and
Wept with him until their sadness filled the building.

ii

Taking Hector's corpse into his own hands Achilles
Made sure it was washed and, for the old king's sake,
Laid out in uniform, ready for Priam to carry
Wrapped like a present home to Troy at daybreak.

iii

When they had eaten together, it pleased them both
To stare at each other's beauty as lovers might,
Achilles built like a god, Priam good-looking still
And full of conversation, who earlier had sighed:

iv

"I get down on my knees and do what must be done
And kiss Achilles' hand, the killer of my son."

In my imagination I gave Priam the face of Gordon Wilson, the Enniskillen draper who was injured in the 1987 Enniskillen Remembrance Day IRA bomb blast. Trapped under the rubble, he had clasped the hand of his daughter Marie until she lost consciousness. With his arm in a sling, Gordon Wilson appeared on television a few days later and said he forgave his daughter's killers: he had prayed for them. Many people in the town and throughout Ulster were not ready to share these forgiving sentiments. After "Ceasefire" was published I was shopping on the Lisburn Road when an acquaintance approached me. "I admired your Achilles poem," he said. "But I'm not ready for it. My son was recently the victim of a vicious paramilitary punishment beating, and may never fully recover." This made me question "Ceasefire," its redemptive symmetries. I wrote a sort of lopsided corollary called "All of These People." Its eleven lines rehearse earlier elegies:

Who was it who suggested that the opposite of war
Is not so much peace as civilisation? He knew

> Our assassinated Catholic greengrocer who died
> At Christmas in the arms of our Methodist minister,
> And our ice-cream man whose continuing requiem
> Is the twenty-one flavours children have by heart.
> Our cobbler mends shoes for everybody; our butcher
> Blends into his best sausages leeks, barley, honey;
> Our corner shop sells everything from bread to kindling.
> Who can bring peace to people who are not civilised?
> All of these people, alive or dead, are civilised.

"Civilisation," "civilised." Earlier I called the Northern Irish conflict "civil war" – a term others might contest. "Civil war" is a kind of oxymoron, since it combines an idea of community with an idea of its fracture. It throws into question, to quote Derek Mahon's poem "Afterlives," "what is meant by home." Northern Ireland has only a million and a half inhabitants. So those who died in the Troubles are always in some sense intimately known, even across the divisions.

In 1999 four writers – David McKittrick, Seamus Kelters, Brian Feeney and Chris Thornton – compiled an extraordinary dossier of everybody who had been killed up to that date. This unbearably sad book is called *Lost Lives*. Reading over poems by myself and others, I realise that "lost lives" have always been at the centre of what we write: that the dominant genre of Troubles poetry is elegy – protest elegy, perhaps. To refer back to "All of These People:" "Our assassinated Catholic greengrocer" – I note I use the pronoun "our" – was Jim Gibson, murdered at Christmas by UDA gunmen who entered his shop on the Stranmillis Road and shot him because, I presume, he was a Catholic prospering in a predominantly Protestant area. My friend Sydney Callaghan, the Methodist minister in the poem, happened to be nearby, and was able to administer the Catholic Last Rites. Here is the second part of my elegy for Jim Gibson:

> Astrologers or three wise men
> Who may shortly be setting out
> For a small house up the Shankill
> Or the Falls, should pause on their way
> To buy gifts at Jim Gibson's shop,
> Dates and chestnuts and tangerines.

The first poem in the "Wreaths" triptych, "The Civil Servant," should really be called "The Magistrate." My friend Martin McBirney was a magistrate and well-known literary figure. As a barrister he had appeared in unpopular cases involving civil rights issues. The IRA shot Martin as he sat down to breakfast, at almost the same time on the same morning as Judge Rory Conaghan (a Catholic) was shot dead. Both men were liberals, a good advertisement for the law. The IRA claimed they had been killed for "collaborating with the British war machine." I disguised Martin McBirney as "a civil servant" because I didn't want to intrude on the family's grief.

The third poem in the triptych, "The Linen Workers," is about the Kingsmills massacre. In January 1976 ten workmen were taking their usual route home from the textile factory at Glenanne when their bus was stopped. The gun men asked each of them his religion. One man, a Catholic, was told to run away up the road. The other ten were lined up and machine-gunned. A policeman said the road was "an indescribable scene of carnage." That scene was viewed on television screens around the world. By pure chance I met in a Belfast pub the following day the English cameraman who had filmed the bloody aftermath. I asked him how he managed in such a nightmare. He replied: "I take out my light-meter, and I focus the lens." His stark honesty might provide a template for writers and artists.

After Bloody Sunday, Seamus Heaney and I drove to Newry to join the outlawed protest march. The roads and byways had been blocked by police and army. It took us an age to reach Newry and our fellow protesters. We had plenty of time to talk. If we were stopped by paramilitaries and asked our religion, what would we reply? We agreed we would sink or swim by what we were – in our eyes not so much Catholic and Protestant as honest and brave. In "The Linen Workers" I again enlist my father's ghost. Here are the last two stanzas:

> When they massacred the ten linen workers
> There fell on the road beside them spectacles,
> Wallets, small change, and a set of dentures:
> Blood, food particles, the bread, the wine.
>
> Before I can bury my father once again
> I must polish the spectacles, balance them
> Upon his nose, fill his pockets with money
> And into his dead mouth slip the set of teeth.

"Each neighbourly murder" – Seamus Heaney's devastating phrase – destroys family, poisons the futures of the bereaved, overwhelms small communities. On the Lisburn Road (where I live) the IRA murdered John Larmour who worked in his brother's ice-cream shop. I had been botanising in the Burren in County Clare, and had written into my notebook all the wild flowers I could identify in one day. On my return to Belfast I learned of the murder from my younger daughter Sarah who had bought with her pocket money some flowers to lay on the pavement outside the shop. I arranged the beautiful flower-names from my notebook into an aural wreath to place beside her bouquet. "The Ice-Cream Man" is addressed to Sarah:

> Rum and raisin, vanilla, butterscotch, walnut, peach:
> You would rhyme off the flavours. That was before
> They murdered the ice-cream man on the Lisburn Road
> And you bought carnations to lay outside his shop.
> I named for you all the wild flowers of the Burren
> I had seen in one day: thyme, valerian, loosestrife,
> Meadowsweet, tway blade, crowfoot, ling, angelica,
> Herb robert, marjoram, cow parsley, sundew, vetch,
> Mountain avens, wood sage, ragged robin, stitchwort,
> Yarrow, lady's bedstraw, bindweed, bog pimpernel.

I want that catalogue to go on forever, like a prayer. When the poem was published, I received a heart breaking letter thanking me and pointing out that there were, coincidentally, twenty-one ice-cream flavours in the shop and twenty-one flower-names. The letter was signed "Rosetta Larmour, the Ice-cream Man's Mother."

Several poems with their roots in the Troubles happen to be masterworks. I would name, for example, Derek Mahon's "A Disused Shed in County Wexford," Seamus Heaney's "Casualty," Paul Muldoon's "Gathering Mushrooms," Medbh McGuckian's "Drawing Ballerinas," Ciaran Carson's "Dresden." Colette Bryce, Frank Ormsby, Tom Paulin, Sinead Morrissey, Leontia Flynn, Peter McDonald, Gerald Dawe, Nick Laird have all extended our imaginative estate in troubled times. From across the Border, Paul Durcan has paid by far the closest and most pained attention to Northern Ireland's turmoil. And Alan Gillis has written a miracle poem called "Progress." It goes back over the nightmare ground I have been trying to cover in this lecture:

They say that for years Belfast was backwards
And it's great now to see some progress.
So I guess we can look forward to taking boxes
From the earth. I guess that ambulances
Will leave the dying back amidst the rubble
To be explosively healed. Given time,
One hundred thousand particles of glass
Will create impossible patterns in the air
Before coalescing into the clarity
Of a window. Through which a reassembled head
Will look out and admire the shy young man
Taking his bomb from the building and driving home.

This is an edited version of Michael Longley's PEN Pinter Prize Lecture, delivered in October 2017 in London.

Michael Longley was born in Belfast in 1939 and educated at the Royal Belfast Academical Institution and Trinity College, Dublin, where he read Classics. He has published ten collections of poetry, most recently Angel Hill *(Cape, 2017). In 2001 he received the Queen's Gold Medal for Poetry, and in 2010 was awarded a CBE. He was Ireland Professor of Poetry from 2007-2010, and continues to live in Belfast.*

DISTURBING WORDS

—

Evelyn Conlon

Minding our language.

I know you're wondering what I'm doing up here, not just up here, but here at all, the last you'd heard I was away out foreign someplace. So foreign that you don't even know the name of it, and that's a hard enough thing to achieve these days, when there is always some lurker beside you with infinite information on his telephone, as well as his entire life. Infinite does mean that there's no end to it, which is never a good thing. You mention a place, the strangeness of it lovingly on your tongue, its faraway mysteries tucked into the silence that you're trying to leave around it, and your man has whipped out his gadget, "how do you spell that?," he bellows. Perhaps not bellows, but it feels like it, the roaring cult of the amateur know all. Your youth was gloriously lived with the photographs kept in an album and only taken out if there was a reason to do so, something to check or an emigrant visiting, something to do with them when the talk of their grown children and their new fridge had run out of steam.

Actually, in all honesty, it's so long since you heard the last of me I could have been dead. And you're right, I have been away in a peculiar place, almost desert really, a place with red earth, spindly bits of mangy grass and heat that is laughable. And a neighbour whose job is building underground car parks in mosques.

But I had come home for my parents' funeral, naturally. And I say *home* when I'm here because it's easier. Demanding that anyone call my air-conditioned desert pad home would be a bit much. My parents had died within a day of each other and luckily enough the first funeral hadn't taken place so the two wakes were held together. In the passing around of the word it got mixed up which of them had gone first but it didn't really matter. Not to outsiders anyway. It did to me. But over the few days, the more I accepted condolences, even I got confused as to which of them had died of the broken heart. But I could have worked it out by trying to remember who was named when my phone went in Abu Dhabi. Because I was on my way home after hearing about the first when they rang me to tell me about the second. I had thought that they were just checking to see how my flights were going so far, no delays, that sort of thing.

On the first evening after the coffins were got and all the other essentials seen to, the neighbours came in with their manners and their good thoughts and after some sadness they proceeded to garden the memories so that there could be a shape put on the next few days. And a discreet map made for themselves, one to move on with next week. Before the day was up, between us we'd have looked at a lot of things about the lives of my parents, how they had met, and although we wouldn't say it, how love had changed them.

"They're pulling from our pen now," my father's oldest friend, John Moloney said.

He had meant it to be heard only over in the corner where the slagging men had gathered. But there had been a bit of quiet and it travelled further into the room. Brian Gallagher bristled. He wasn't too well himself at the minute. Mrs. Clancy jumped in with sandwiches and the talk took up again.

For as long as they could remember my father was a pernickety sort of man, particularly around language, and my mother seemed to follow suit. Although some of the women weren't sure if the following suit was a sleight of hand, they thought that it might have been her who started it. She was known as a reader. Serious reading hid in her very nerves. She got terribly annoyed about the man who had come walking here and lied about things she had told him. When she brought it up with the women they could see that it mattered more to her than it did to them.

"Imagine pretending to have been places that you weren't," she said indignantly.

"As if we wouldn't find out, as if we didn't read on the border."

They nodded their heads towards her. She spoke the truth.

And now they were gathered talking their ways through the shock of them both gone. "Remember the time he dressed you down for saying UK?" someone called to Gerry Moore.

And Gerry, who was a perfect mimic, brought my father's voice straight into the room.

"Let's not get lazy, it's England, or Britain if you want. United Kingdom of Great Britain and Northern Ireland? Not around here. And as for an Ulster Scot, that's a Monaghan woman in Edinburgh. Scotch Irish, that's how it goes. If we mind our language the rest will follow."

And we all stayed quiet in honour of the man who had thought that language mattered and the woman who liked the sound of the truth.

My father had been hurt young by the border, the line ran on the top of their ditch. His mother had mourned the loss of her friends, from both sides of the house.

"That's making them from a different country. How could that be."

She stopped to think about it some more.

"So if you were born in the six counties before now where will they say you were from? You can't have been from somewhere that never was."

She looked some more out over the imaginary divide, as people have always done, that is people who have lived on borders, who have heard the river running from one place to the other, not hesitating as it crosses the line.

"But you haven't lost them," my grandfather said, "you'll just have to go through a checkpoint to see them."

"You'd soon get tired of that," she said, looking out to the field, third from the window, that would now be in a different country.

Now that it had been mentioned I remembered the day that Gerry had got dressed down. They were moving cattle from the field that had all the grass eaten. This always caused a problem because they had to maneuver the cows over territory that had been disputed. In other places moving cattle caused problems because of cars coming around a bend too fast and landing on top of you, or a cow throwing back her head with the freedom of the road and making a run for it. They had all had a great weekend over at the Forkhill Singers' weekend. The pub had been lit up with sound. Singers had come from all over the country as well as England and Scotland. Funny enough there were none from Wales. The songs had happened, tied in with each other, ebbing and flowing all night. It could have been thought to be a funny thing, grown men and women hanging on to the words of songs. But if you were there you could see the sense of it. It would appear that at some stage Gerry had gone outside and found a soldier with his ear up to the back wall lost in an air from his own place. Those of us who know that can never forget it.

After the cattle had been successfully got into the new field and had disappeared in a cloud of joy to its far corners of shining abundant grass, the conversation slid into border things. It must have been the songs that did it, or Gerry seeing the soldier, and feeling sad for him, because they were usually careful to leave that sort of talk for behind their own closed doors. And somehow or another things got out of hand and descended into a shouting match and the evening became known as that time of the big row, a singular description, out on its own, the big row. Some of it carried across the fields, so we know about bits of it, but other things were said that passers by couldn't hear. My father came home quiet.

That shouting had been the end of something or the beginning of something else. My father left the modern world, stopped listening to the news. Funny enough my mother didn't, but then women can be like that, just in case there's the equivalent of a washing machine being developed, and they'd need to know. And in her case, something being written that might make sense of things. In time though she too said that there wasn't much of use going on and she retreated from the radio, back to her books. She did get a mobile phone though but she didn't charge it up that often. They ate their dinner quietly, making happy little remarks about the taste of things.

And I began to know that I would go away.

Around here they were all good at going away. The town down the road was so dead it didn't even know it. Gerry said that even Country and Western singers wouldn't darken the door of what passed for the pub, although mind you things were cheerful enough in the one on the actual border, the one where the singing had been. They had lots to laugh at there, the Traynor boys being caught smuggling a load of drink in an ambulance that they'd bought and converted, the Murtagh boys having their load taken off them by Customs men who turned out not to be Customs men at all, but maybe the Traynor boys dressed up. They concentrated on those bits, not serious things, only matters of money.

Yes, I had gone away. First to Dublin, where they couldn't stop hearing the headlines in my accent, and then to further away where it didn't matter. And as soon as the next plate of sandwiches was handed around maybe I'd go away again, slip out the door and up the lane. Or at least start packing my bag to the murmur of them in the kitchen.

Before I left for the faraway place my mother had said, *always live away from the border.*

On the second morning of the wakes, I took a breath and opened the desk in the back bedroom, I would take a very quick look. I had no notion of going through things, all that could wait. But the tidy bundle, strung together with a loose hessian bow, on the very top of all else, was clearly meant to be looked at. I was so glad that my brother hadn't come yet, not until this afternoon, my mother would have hated his suburban wife going through her things, not understanding what they meant, trying to put a value on them.

I undid the twine and spread out the papers. There were pages and pages of meticulous notes on all things border. All things to do with Partition. Who had mentioned it first. How it had come about that it was six and not four. And which six. There were notes on the Border Commission and chapters of books photocopied. There was a fortnights' reading in it, even for the first skim. One page had a large printing of the word *Gerrymander*. It was my mother's handwriting below it. It stated that *Gerrymander* was first used in the nineteenth century in the *Boston Weekly Messenger*, referring to the new voting district which Governor Elbridge Gerry had carved out to favour his own party, the map of which resembled a salamander. Behind that was a picture of my parents at the filling in of the cratered roads, those blown up by the British army. You could see them happening in the look they were giving each other. A split second of light between the trees, their futures hovering together. This was now where they wanted to be. They'd met apparently on the third day of the filling-in. My grandmother must have loved that. At least something good would come out of it. As they worked, some of the photographers caught shadows of soldiers passing along the hedges. They didn't hate them yet but they would if needs be. And in time they learned how to look out the car window, straight ahead, silent, as the camouflaged men with blackened faces examined their driving licenses.

And then there was my first letter to them from the desert. On the back of the envelope was a tiny map which I couldn't make out, the writing was so small, but there was our barn door, and all sorts of lines drawn down from it. It took me some time to find the larger version, which turned out to be a perfectly precise architectural flourish. My father and mother had drawn a plan to build a basement that would cross the border and thus they would live in two places. I wanted to believe that telling them about the underground car park in the mosque had helped. I really wanted to believe it. But in the meantime there was the tree. There was a picture of it, pinned to pages and more pages of horticultural notes. Clearly they had cultivated the tree to make sure that its roots, and now its branches, would spread across the line. I was struck still by the amusement of it all, who would ever have thought of it.

I heard movements begin as the morning started and I was needed downstairs but first I had to check the barn. I would slip out before the serious day began. I pushed open the door, multi-coloured in layers of new paints gone old. I fumbled my way to the far corner and there it was, a velvet curtain hanging as if on front of a stage, covering a large opening. Just for one second I heard a tapping sound, a small noise as the job was begun, and then a bigger one as the larger pick was used. I stared down into the darkness and wanted to see how far they'd got but heard my name being called, again. Later would do.

During the actual funeral, the parts that are said to remind us of the end, I thought of their beginning together and could dimly hear their laughs in chorus, as they drew to their hearts' content. So that's what they'd done when they left the News behind.

We were saying goodbye to some of the mourners when we saw the big yellow machine negotiate its way in the gap of the field on the other side, over the bog, up the hill. We watched as it stationed itself, belching out bad fumes. A cutting device unfolded and edged towards the tree. I don't quite know what got into me but I ran for it and made up through the branches as if I did this sort of thing every day. There was no thinking about how to get up a tree, no thinking about why, and what after. I had never known that I had such speed, nor that I could climb so high. The men roared at the machine and soon the driver saw me, perched up on the top, and he withdrew the blades. So here I am. With no plan.

I have plenty of time to think, although you'd be surprised how much there is to do. I have to organize the food, and other things, that they send up to me on a pulley that Gerry made in jig time. Eating takes a bit of work, it's not like I'm sitting in a kitchen. It's amazing what you can see from up here, how the people organize their days, how they move about, where they hide their scrap, how people sometimes break into dance in their kitchens. Although in the first few days it would be hard to know if perhaps they didn't change their routine, open their curtains earlier than normal. But that could have been to look at me. I'm also sure that George Wiggins never put out a flag every day before this.

Between myself and the people below we've decided that if I can manage to stay long enough the point will be made and they'll leave the tree alone. That's the general idea.

The big question now is, what is long enough, when do I come down. I do have a life waiting for me, with friends in it, and I will eventually need to be in a place where I am not known as the person who went up the tree that went over the border.

Epilogue

I did come down. And went back to the desert where we had a party and discussed borders we had crossed. And Famagusta, the sound of the name and the ghosts whistling through the deserted city. *Cancer*, *The Equator*, *Capricorn*. One of us had stood with women shouting to their relatives across to Jordan. The remark was made that the proximity of the border had a serious affect on Anselm Kiefer. What about Alsace-Lorraine, back and forth, back and forth. Korea, we said. Another of us, a tent-maker, had more truck than most with borders. He had seen a lot of people looking over lines. He told us that while the rest of us forget, get distracted by newer tragedies, the people forced to move often take excursions to look back. When the sun dropped down and the barbecue was over no one could remember how the conversation had got started. I get occasional cards from home and apparently the tree has not been touched and Gerry spends a lot of time in our barn.

A novelist and short-story writer, Evelyn Conlon was born in 1952 in Monaghan and lived in Australia in the early 1970s. She is the author of three collections of stories and four novels, most recently Not the Same Sky *(Wakefield Press, 2013) about the 4000 Irish Famine girls who immigrated to Australia under the "Earl Gray Scheme." She now lives in Dublin and is a member of Aosdána.*

WEATHER REPORT:
GOOD FRIDAY WEEK, 1998

Chris Agee

*Four years on, the author recalled
an historic Irish agreement at Stormont.*

*This essay appeared in "Inaugural Issue: Belfast in Europe"
(Volume 1, Number 1, 2002), the first issue of* Irish Pages.

Afternoon weather was the metaphor.

On the Tuesday before the talks deadline of Thursday April 9th, 1998, set by Tony Blair early in his premiership, it had cleared suddenly to a deep and flawless azure more like Provence than Ireland. Inside the talks, however, all was gloom. The unionists were declining to accept the draft Agreement – prepared by the British and Irish governments and presented through Senator George Mitchell, the American chairman of the talks – as the basis for a final constitutional settlement. Predicting Thursday's outcome would, clearly, be as chancy as prophesying the next hour's processional of cloud-laden, Turneresque moods.

Wednesday was the archetypical Irish "dirty day": wet, bleak, grey. The Belfast hills were topped by *tourbillons* of low mist. By late afternoon, the usual mizzle-mist or sporadic shower had turned to a heavy downpour. But at the talks, adjacent to the old Parliament at Stormont near Belfast, the mood was brightening. It was just possible that a settlement ending the Thirty Years Stalemate of the Troubles, and the most important political beginning since Partition in 1920, was on the cards.

Ireland has what meteorologists call an "oceanic" climate, particularly in the North. It is swept by the restless vagaries of North Atlantic isobars. Here the trade-winds, currents and tempests from the circumnavigations of the Gulf Stream make their far-western European landfall. The phosphorescent flares of New England trawler-nets and the smooth brown pods of the Caribbean bean litter the tidelines of Mayo. Year round, Irish weather is soft, clement, rain-drenched and fickle; whereas that of its latitudinal twin, Newfoundland, with its Arctic winter and fleeting summertime, is harsh and intemperate, a New World Siberia. Where one might dig deep in bog in Ireland, there is tundra and permafrost in Labrador.

Precipitation and changeability: therein lies the glory of Irish weather. Like the unique air of a culture or period, or some autochthonous ecology of light and wet, the island's weather is full of its own special blend of shimmerings and dazzles. Ireland lacks both the true wintriness that frequents Scotland and the continental warmth of the South of England at high summer. Sea-girt and sea-buffeted, it is shielded from the extremes of the great Eurasian landmass. It seldom freezes for long and is never sultry in the meridional sense. Snow is rarely more than a shallow icing. If it lacks the steady warmth and illumination of Mediterranean *claritas,* or the crisp resolutions of North American seasons, Ireland has its own its medicine-bag, its own Ariel, for meteorological enchantments.

Above all, Irish weather throbs and shines when sunlight meets the endless impressionism of ocean moisture. Cloud shadows mountain. Hailshowers in sunlight. A rainbow amid storm-darkenings over Belfast Lough. Dusk and rain-drops spangling the shimmy of a window like a bird's breast. Moon adrift in scud or rack, sunshafts fingering curtains of mist. Droplets on clover as tensile as the tremblings of quicksilver. It is an atmospheric dazzle you often glimpse in that Vermeer of sensation, Seamus Heaney: buffetings, dews, frosts, hail-stones, rinsings, lightenings, "glitter-drizzle, almost-breaths of air" and other "subtle little wets." Or even, on occasion, in Samuel Beckett, in the brightening recollection of blue skies knotting the grain of his parables.

Thursday, the decisive day, dawned oceanic. Cottony dirigibles arose in the East and steamed over. It shone, darkened, gusted, showered; a stream of cycles. When my late afternoon work-out finished and I stepped from the gym in the cloud-capped shadow of Black Mountain, a splatter of hail was falling in bright sunlight. It bounced and settled on a grass verge dotted with speedwell. Endgame time. Turning the ignition I looked forward to the evening's television.

On the news the consensus was that a deal, despite impediments, was in the offing. It was the beginning of an astounding moment: modern Ireland's psychic Appomattox, though – crucially – no one was surrendering. From then on the Irish channels – BBC Northern Ireland, Ulster Television, Raidió Teilifís Éireann – suspended scheduling and went more or less live. A succession of talking heads, politicians and pundits, propounded from Stormont, or studios in Belfast, London, Dublin,

Brussels, America. Downstairs to make a cup of tea, I found myself thinking of that moment, on the upstairs landing, when I had shouted to my wife that the Berlin Wall had fallen. The high drama of high politics.

Only towards midnight, however, did I twig the depth of the parallel. With each new assessment of the waxing prospects, the psychic partition of the country was being breached before our eyes. The actual brick and breeze-block wall that snakes for miles through the heart of West Belfast, whose euphemism is "the peace line," might stand for years. No jubilant crowds were gathering in the streets to deconstruct division. But just as surely, the inner Irish Wall was tottering, being chipped away by invisible, televisual legions: the spirit-troop of popular hope.

Then it happened. Perhaps there is a moment in every revolution, literal or psychological, when symbolism translates directly into the ebb or flow of power – whose momentousness lies in this very transmutation. Such was Ceausescu's speech from the balcony, Yeltsin mounted on a tank, or Mayor Daly haranguing the podium at the 1968 Democratic Convention. For it was around midnight that the panjandrum of extreme Protestantism, the Reverend Ian Paisley – high priest of bigots and homophobes, scourge of Christian charity, Jeremiah of Ulster's apocalypse – arrived at the gates of Stormont Castle to join a chanting crowd, aswirl with Union Jacks and St George's Crosses. Imagine a Cotton Mather unredeemed by humane learning; or an ignoramus instinct with charisma masquerading as Jonathan Edwards. Then imagine a party of ethnic "Protestantism" centred around such a figure. What you have, perforce, is a deformation of the Reformation.

He was let in the grounds and led his hundreds to the Soviet-style statue of Edward Carson, architect of Partition and first Prime Minister in Northern Ireland's old Parliament, prorogued in 1973 for the blatant Jim Crowism of unionist rule. It was instantly clear that despite the braggadocio of his protest against the imminence of compromise – a shot across the bows from a cunning wrecker – he was staring at a colossal miscalculation and, down the road, the political wilderness. From day one, he had boycotted the talks, a prime reason they were now succeeding against all easy expectation.

The crowd was held back, and he and a few lieutenants proceeded to the entrance of the perimeter fence surrounding the purpose-built building for the talks. Slyly, a few days earlier, the British Government had already denied him entrance, on no other grounds than astute politics, since he had long been invited and held a pass. It was a classic piece of political sharp practice within the rules of the game. He was made a gate-crasher at the moveable feast of peace. Thundering, Paisley adjourned to a Nissen hut next to the fence, there to hold forth at an *ad hoc* news conference: no doubt his intention all along.

Now, crying wolf for the umpteenth time, he was the true wolf at the door. The talks had overrun their midnight deadline, and though hope was escalating by the hour, it was still a close-run thing, and success might yet be tipped at the post by some unbridgeable gap. Although Paisley has always been careful not to sully his hands directly, no one person, within the structure of mindsets and forces in the North, had done more to foment years of violent unionist backlash and so pad the self-exculpations of the IRA. His "Province" may be small as the Baltic Oblast of Kaliningrad, but his certitude is an overweening and gargantuan as Stalin's.

A truly great totalitarian (and like many others, he hails from a borderland), he has built the hot gospel of his politics and church (an offshoot of an offshoot of Presbyterianism) on one-man ground so pinched and narrow that it affords his ego a perfect fastness from which to bellow, bully, rabble-rouse, threaten, instigate. (I come – two generations back – from a line of Tennessee Calvinists, and know whereof I speak). He is an adept at provoking, negatively, the inner mask of ethno-national identity that can either inflect or suppress the individual sensibility.

Nor is he simply some pre-modern dinosaur – like so much of twentieth century religious pathology, Paisley's specious revival of "old-time religion" is a wholly modern phenomenon. It means to cherish an ignorant caricature of old faith by papering over the cracks posed either by the paradigm of science or (most dangerously) by the contemporary revision of religious sensibility. It substitutes the ardour and imagery of doctrine for a true opening to the challenge of a living and lived experience of authentic faith. Postmodernism in reverse, you might say. But by ignoring the cracks, it fails also to address them and in a sense accepts them; so it, too, is a form of unbelief, and a most invidious sort, one that will plague this century as it did the last: *religious nihilism.* That is why the patent medicine of apocalypse always has the flavour of people who despair of life, and would soon enough give it up. In truth Paisley's is not so much a theology or a politics as a perennial politico-religious psychology, no less evident in Catholicism or Judaism or Islam, that calls down ire and hellfire on the Other due to some molten angst, flaw or wound in its own spirituality. Arrogance as the obverse of deficiency. Zeal masking aggression. In this way Paisley professes

Christian love even as he traduces its spirit though a tone-deaf fabulation of the letter.

Then, as I say, it happened. The hut was jammed with journalists, security officials, low-level politicos and sundry hangers-on. Outside, the night was Shakespearean – wind-tossed, lashed by bouts of rain. The cameras went live just as Paisley and his two main lieutenants seated themselves at the microphones.

"The Big Man" began to speak. It was the usual growling bellow that is slowly built up to paroxysms of high-pitched thunderings of contempt and betrayal. But no sooner had he gotten a few words out, he was being barracked by several unseen voices at the back. You could feel the whoosh of a collective televisual gasp: who *were* these noises off? In a flash it was obvious that they were *loyalists* – the Irish descendant of a term once also used for Americans loyal to the Crown during the Revolutionary period.

Incredible moment: Paisley stood down, in the full glare of mass theatre, by his own "side." Loyalism is a strand of unionism but with a more militant, working-class, secular and (dread word) *Irish* inflection; it stands to mainstream unionism as republicanism does to moderate nationalism. Paisley, who had always presumed to lead it, instantly intuited the political danger of being hoisted on his own media petard. Although it is doubtful whether he was fully aware of it, it was the man, rather than the politician, that was being rumbled by the uncut gaze of the camera.

Paisley was flummoxed by the brickbats. One expected him to recover from the stumble and, as usual, to override the adversity, but somehow he didn't manage it. Was he getting old? A voice floated up: "Where will you take us, Ian, if we follow you out the door?" Another sang through the growing commotion: *"The Grand Old Duke of York, he had ten thousand men..."*

With a sweep of the arm Paisley barked out to no one in particular: "Remove them!" He smiled inwardly, arrogantly; muttered a few words to himself, in the downward direction of the baize, with the bristling sarcasm and embattled brittleness of a fundamentalist autodidact; pursed and flattened his lips in a trademark tic of rectitude and intolerance shared by many of his Northern compatriots. He wanted a congregation, not an audience.

His tar-barrel theatricality – a Hibernicised descendant of the camp revivalism of the American Bible Belt – was malfunctioning. He who in a fog of self-righteousness had so often treated his interlocutors to extreme rudeness, was now getting a dose of his own medicine. Live coverage bore down like one of those all-seeing divine eyes, ensconced in a triangle, that adorn the Masonic regalia of Orangeism. In a few moments, with a few deft strokes, the Paul Bunyan of loyalism was outflanked, punctured like a helium float. Even many of his stalwarts must have found it difficult to suppress, as the Buddhists say, the truth of consciousness. If every dog has its day, this dog's was done, or at least ending... however much it might keep barking and snapping.

Weeks before the symbolism of dates had dawned on me. Happenstance symmetry, or the astuteness of those managing "the peace process" under the aegis of Anglo-Irish cooperation? The deadline for the completion of the talks was Maundy Thursday (8 April); since they were likely to run to the eleventh hour, the deal, if clinched, would be delivered to the world on Good Friday. In the first place, it seemed scheduling and political logic argued not for happenstance but astuteness. Yet, maybe it was one of those extraordinary coincidences, like Germany's 9th November, which has seen the end of the monarchy and the proclamation of the Republic (1918), *Kristallnacht* (1938) and the Fall of the Wall (1989)? And if a deal was indeed clinched, the Referendum would be held on 22 May; on that day two centuries before, the United Irishmen had launched, in Belfast and Dublin, their uprising for an Irish republic.

Then there was the special Irish resonance of Easter itself, evoking the republican iconography of the 1916 commemorations at Bodenstown and Milltown. It seemed extraordinary that the fracture that commenced with the Easter Rising had come full circle and begun to be annealed in a new light at the same season. On second thought, hadn't the Northern love of calendrical symbolism, and the aestheticization of violence attendant on the inevitability of such symbols – that special Ulster sense of fate, like the *wyrd* of Old English, lurking in the iconography – hadn't this love, in fact, been one of the prime sources of the glamour and ritualism of the "Troubles," so different, even in that homely label, from the true wars of the former Yugoslavia?

Of course the Easter Rising had happened not on Easter, but Easter Monday. Patrick Pearse, Gaelic scholar and aesthete that he was, would have well understood the symbolic distinction, whether or not it was factored into his calculations or his piety. In Irish "Dé Luain" means both "on Monday" and "on the day of judgment." The Irish language poet and novelist Eoghan Ó Tuairisc titled his 1966 novel on Pearse and his leadership of the Rising just that, *Dé Luain*. When the neoclassical GPO was seized and the

Republic descending from the Greeks proclaimed, it was a step into the historical dark and, for some of course, a rendezvous with the actual dark.

Still deeper in the background, there was the ancient pedigree of the seasonal meaning. The Anglo-Saxon for Easter, *Eastre*, was derived by the Venerable Bede from the name of a goddess whose feast was celebrated at the vernal equinox. Its ultimate root, harking back through Old Frisian and Old High German, was the Sanskrit for *morning* or *dawn*. As such it is cognate with the "aurora" of Latin and "tomorrow" of Greek.

With this image at the back of my mind, I had been hoping to take Jacob, my son, to watch the Easter dawn from the Giant's Ring at Ballyleeson, just outside Belfast. If we rose before first light, we might get there in time, perhaps, to catch, like a harbinger, the tail of Hale-Bopp. If it was clear, we could sit on the dewiness of the immense earthen embankment and watch the molten foil spill over the mountains round Belfast, lifting shadow from the great bowl of sward and illumining what Robinson Jeffers, who lived for a time in Belfast in the mid-twenties, called in a poem about the Ring "that great toad of a dolmen/Piled up of ponderous basalt that sheds the centuries like raindrops." (It is odd to think of the poet of the Big Sur domiciled amidst the mists and glooms of Partition, in a British backwater at the height of the Deep Freeze, a stone's throw from Yeats' "Meditations in Time of Civil War." Though, on reflection, perhaps not.) In the event, two days later, when I awoke in the morning dusk of Easter, it was wet and overcast, and I scuppered the outing without wakening Jacob.

Good Friday was bright and gusty, "through-other" with sun and cloud. I woke slightly later than usual, towards ten, and straight away switched on the Tube. Atmosphere electrified the scene beamed from the car park, where the world's media had established its caravanserai of trucks and dishes: it *had* happened, it seemed, bar the last push. A wind-buffeted microphone was swivelling between the sound-bites of pairs of politicians queuing to speak.

In my own satirical self-speak I had for some time been fond of seeing the North's lead players as either Antiques or Moderns. An Antique was a soul afflicted with the pathology of provincialism. A Modern was one who had missed or slipped it. The Division transcended age, culture, creed, class, education and politics. It was more a frame of mind, or an orientation of deep formation, than a matter of the surface of self-conscious belief. Some of the worst Antiques being, in fact, intellectuals. To use a culinary metaphor, it was the difference between a cholesterol-laden "Ulster fry" (bacon, egg, sausage, black sausage, potato bread and soda bread fried in fat) and a Continental breakfast. Antique Ulster was a secret monoculture with two colour-coded inflections that ate the same breakfast.

Over my Special K I watched the wind-jostled camera bring another pair into view: John Hume, the leader of the Social Democratic and Labour Party, the party of constitutional nationalism, and Davey Adams, one of the leaders of a small loyalist party affiliated with the Ulster Defence Association, a paramilitary organisation responsible for the random killing of hundreds of Catholics. A few years earlier, months of meetings between them, let alone a meeting of minds, would have been political pie-in-the-sky. Yet that is precisely where these two Moderns – one preeminent, one improbable – had now ended up, this very moment, stepping out of the marathon of the final all-night negotiations. Who was to be more admired, the one who had not changed, or the one who had changed?

Hume, always alert to the language of occasion, edged forward and took pole position to speak. He has always seemed to me to be cut from the same cultural cloth as his fellow Derryman Seamus Heaney. Both belong to the Redmondite tradition of constitutional nationalism, but the affinity strikes me as deeper than mere politics or even the traditional Catholicism of the upbringing of each. It is more a matter of cultural poise; of being at home in equal proportion in their *provincia,* on the island, within the wider world.

What the two make of background navigates the Scylla and Charybdis of Ulster's culture wars: the laager mentality of the unionists, and its gangrenous doppelganger, the martyrological imperative of armed republicanism. In distinct but overlapping spheres, politician and poet have fashioned a discourse of the optative Ireland where "hope and history rhyme," and where the parish is comprehended – as the great Irish essayist Hubert Butler once put it – from the vantage of the cosmopolitan: *"The interpreters will be those who can see the national life as well as live it. To acquire this detachment, they will need to have access to other forms of society, so that they can see their own lives objectively and in totality from the threshold."* And now, it seemed, was the crowning moment, when the optative had begun to transmute to the present continuous.

Visibly moved, Hume said simply, "This is a Good Friday gift to the people of Ireland," before giving way to Adams, who made to speak. But all that issued was the strangled beginnings of an opening *Uh*. He was choked up, near tears. You felt the moment in yourself, the camera lulling for a second on the silent pair, before being magicked up to the anchor-man in a Portacabin studio above the parking lot.

It was late afternoon when I drove home from the week's last workout. On the hills above West Belfast the whitethorn blossom of the hedgerows put me in mind of combers foaming down through the quilted fields. It was cloudy but lightsome, and the streets, emptying early before the long weekend, were spangled with showers. A pillar box painted green caught a sudden shaft of declining sun. By the time I reached South Belfast, the West had cleared to a deepening hue of cobalt, a last late sunshine bathing the brick of an old terrace district. The scruffy kerbstones of Primrose and Gipsy Streets were awash in a sudden preternatural glow. About this time, I would notice later on the news, the final Stormont plenary had convened for the cameras; Senator Mitchell announced "the new British-Irish Agreement"; and the eight delegations emerged successively onto the steps of Government Buildings to address the massed ranks of the global media – braving, over the next hour, and only a few miles away, a final meteorological fitfulness of gusts, drizzle, sun showers and sleet.

Towards eight I walked out with Jacob to see what was playing at the cinema a few blocks away. A last deep glaze of jade, darkling and translucent, lay on the horizon under a streak of stratus. The Moonrise has just lifted over the silhouette of the houses beyond the thoroughfare of the Ormeau Road. Among the innumerable images for its elemental presence, would I ever quite find the one that got the beauty, the minerality, the geometry of that bright alabaster disc, its Minerva's owl's-eye, light out of the dark, magnificence reflected in the void?

Easter came chill, fresh and sunny. It blustered, and the brilliant blue of Tuesday was brindled with puffs of cumulus. Even as sun warmed the skin, there was the smoke-scent and crispness of autumn. Mid-afternoon, a low wall of grey cloud agleam, interspersed with blue, trailed a sudden manna of hail across the street-scene in my bay, rattling the panes. Within minutes, it had laid an immaculate blanket of snowy catkins on the tarmac, cars, roofs, gardens and bins. The hailstones were light, dry, peanut-sized – the largest I had ever seen – and out front the clover-and-grass seemed coated in drifts of Styrofoam. Suddenly the air had the high-altitude freshness of a timberline.

Just as quickly, the downfall was changing to a slush the colour of mothballs. The sun shone on the steaming street's meltwater, and the last white on the facing roof was like fallen blossom. Soon nothing was left of the day's visitation of hail but a few white shadows in the green shade of hedges. An hour later, all was rinsed, the light crystalline. The large camellia five doors down, its fall of magenta daubing the footpath, reminded me of Chagall. Incontrovertibly, something new was in the air.

A poet, essayist and photographer, Chris Agee is the Editor of this journal. His third collection of poems, Next to Nothing (Salt, 2008), *was shortlisted in Britain for the 2009 Ted Hughes Award for New Work in Poetry. He recently edited* Balkan Essays *(The Irish Pages Press, 2016), the sixth volume of Hubert Butler's essays. His fourth collection of poems,* Blue Sandbar Moon *(The Irish Pages Press, 2018), has just appeared. He lives in Belfast, and divides his time between Ireland, Scotland and Croatia.*

THE GOOD FRIDAY AGREEMENT

Patricia Craig

Failed rhymesters.

It couldn't go on. The carnage, destruction, fear and chaos had to stop, the alternative being that two intractable forces, nationalist and unionist, would wipe one another out like a pair of Kilkenny cats. Peace initiative followed peace initiative, and all came to nothing. "The political talks collapsed," went the dismal refrain. So when the Good Friday Agreement was actually signed in 1998, there was general rejoicing, and a great collective sigh of relief: perhaps, at last, the life of the province could get back to normal, or what would pass for normal.

But the Agreement was not unassailable. Immense feats of negotiation, amendment, commitment and bending-over-backwards went into it, but every time it had approached a resolution, some disgruntled northern voice would pipe up complaining about a slight or an oversight. Take the question of "Ullans." (We are still in the early months of 1998.) "Ullans," a made-up Ulster equivalent of the Scottish Lallans, nearly scuppered the whole protracted, delicate, arduous process. Fortunately none of the disinterested parties involved – Tony Blair, Bertie Ahern, Alastair Campbell, Jonathan Powell, Bill Clinton, George Mitchell, Mo Mowlam and others – was willing to let the Agreement slip through their fingers, and further exorbitant exercises in fine-tuning ensued. In the end, it was miraculously steered through. When Tony Blair later compared the exhausting, exacting negotiations to "a very complicated trek through a very dense and dangerous jungle," he wasn't exaggerating. But the goal was reached, in spite of obstacles, and the consequent sense of triumph and euphoria was all the more overwhelming for having been so much a matter of uncertainty.

But "Ullans," in its later designation of Ulster Scots, hadn't gone away, and neither had innumerable other contentious issues, starting with the decommissioning of paramilitary weapons – not to mention the instinctive distrust and animosity between the Northern Irish parties. (I'll come back to "Ullans" in a minute.) An executive was put in place, after further delays, with David Trimble and Seamus Mallon as First Minister designate and Deputy First Minister designate. It lasted for precisely 72 days – but never mind; as Seamus Heaney put it with determined optimism, "the fact that the first executive bickered and faltered and fell was less important than the change it effected in the overall mindset." However, he then felt obliged to add: "The sectarian underlife is still there, of course."

So it was, and so it still is. A strange thing about unionism in general is the way it contrives to banish from public life every politician of its persuasion who veers, however slightly, in the direction of compromise, from Lord O'Neill to David Trimble and Mike Nesbitt. (Peter Robinson is perhaps an exception: under his and Martin McGuinness's stewardship, the province was actually beginning to work.) Power-sharing has been fraught with dissension and recrimination; and now, once again, it has come unstuck. A miserable and infuriating situation prevails – and it didn't have to. Only a short time ago, it seems a deal to reinstate Stormont was on the cards, before it fell a victim to DUP pig-headedness. (I'm not overlooking misplaced exulting on the part of Sinn Féin, or their wearisome repetition of the idiotic expression, "*Tiocfaidh ár lá*" – *droch-Gaeilge*, if ever I heard it, and *droch-polaitíocht* too, at a crucial moment.)

One of the issues engendering fear and loathing among current DUP supporters is the long-sought Irish Language Act. And this is where "Ullans"/Ulster Scots comes back to roundly assert its corresponding cultural importance. (Considering it nearly did for the original Agreement, it's as if a small prickly wheel has come full circle.) In fact, the putative (unviable) deal made provision for the official recognition of Ulster Scots, but it wasn't enough. It wasn't enough, though to most rational people it seems a rather large concession, given that Ulster Scots is not a language. Let me repeat: ULSTER SCOTS IS NOT A LANGUAGE. It is a dialect. (Indeed, it is only one of a number of dialects peculiar to the north of Ireland, though to be sure you find a good deal of overlap between them.) It is no more a language than a Yorkshire, Devonshire or Cumbrian dialect is. Like these, it contains intriguing, expressive and eccentric words and phrases. It has produced some striking, indigenous works of literature, including James Orr's "Donegore Hill" of 1817, and "The Lammas Fair (Belfast)" by Robert Huddleston (1844). It deserves to be cherished and preserved – though not, perhaps, to the point of absurdity. For example: when a public body like the Arts Council of Northern Ireland, in the interests of even-handedness, has to style itself "Airts Cooncil o Norlin Airlann," we know we are well on the way to making a total lachin-sport o' oorsels.

There are some further points to be made. Throughout the twentieth century, both rural and urban versions of an Ulster vernacular persisted alongside standard English, and these were not confined to one political/religious faction or the other. I would contend that every mode of speech that exists, or existed, in the North, is an asset of the entire population, irrespective of particular affiliations. Two outstanding works of fiction making full use of local speech patterns, respectively Co Armagh and Co Derry, are set against a Catholic/nationalist background. They are John O'Connor's *Come Day – Go Day* of 1949 ("I never seen such a pack of coul-rifed craythurs in my life") and *No Mate for the Magpie* by Frances Molloy ("… sure a didn't look like a catholic wain atall"). Then, it might be salutary for the DUP and their followers to bear in mind that the Irish language, against which they appear to have set their faces, was upheld and sustained, during the nineteenth century, by Protestants such as Sir Samuel Ferguson and Robert MacAdam (I'm averse to using these denominational terms, but there seems no way around it).

Unionists and loyalists should understand, moreover, that an Irish Language Act doesn't represent the thin end of a republican conspiratorial wedge, a plot to impose a difficult language on a hostile and deeply resistant populace (as English was once imposed on native Irish speakers, whether they liked it or not). It hasn't worked like that in Wales or Scotland, where comparable Acts have come into force without any compulsory element to them. And you have to laugh when you find Ulster loyalists fiercely declining to have street signs in Irish, without realising that, in many instances, they already do. The most obvious example is of course that heartland of loyalism, the Shankill Road, whose Gaelic origin could hardly be plainer: it's simply a transliteration of "Sean cill," meaning old church. (Cal McCrystal's very pertinent enumeration of place names all over the province – in a recent letter to the *London Review of Books* – underscores the point.)

The Good Friday Agreement of 1998 was a momentous achievement. But it should be remembered that the DUP took no part in the proceedings; in fact it boycotted them. And Sinn Féin at the time came up with some impossible demands. Now these two parties have overtaken the UUP, on the one hand, and the SDLP, on the other. And between them, they have made a hames of power-sharing. (To make my own position clear: I hold the DUP entirely responsible for the most recent collapse of talks to bring back Stormont.) Is it a sorry case of everyone reverting to type, adhering to tribal imperatives for which there is no place in the modern world? I hope not. I believe that progress must be maintained, despite everything that has gone wrong, despite irremovable bones of contention, despite the disintegration of good will, despite the lunacy of Brexit and its implications for the Irish border. I believe that, sooner or later, those involved in the political process will come to their senses. But for the moment, you would have to say that hope and history have failed to rhyme.

One of Ireland's foremost critics and essayists for over 40 years, Patricia Craig was born and grew up in Belfast, and lived for many years in London before returning to Northern Ireland in 1999. She has written biographies of Elizabeth Bowen and Brian Moore, and edited many anthologies including The Oxford Book of Ireland, English Detective Stories, Modern Women's Stories, The Belfast Anthology *and* The Ulster Anthology. *Her celebrated memoir* Asking for Trouble *(Blackstaff Press) was published in 2007, followed by* A Twisted Root: Ancestral Entanglements in Ireland *(Blackstaff Press, 2012), and a collection of critical prose is forthcoming. She is a regular contributor to* The Irish Times *and the* Times Literary Supplement.

MAKING AND IMPLEMENTING
THE AGREEMENT

—

Monica McWilliams

Floating papers.

The snow was coming down in flurries that Easter of April 1998. Huddled journalists from all over the world were reduced to interviewing each other to justify the wait for smoke of any hue to emerge from Castle Buildings where the peace talks were on a roller coaster towards their end point. Even the trees looked uncertain as to the season or the outcome of the talks. It was Holy Thursday. The catering staff had closed up as they had been told to go home for the Easter holidays whilst the political parties grumbled they were being starved into submission. Talks chairperson, George Mitchell, was muttering threateningly about a promised family holiday that he had vowed to uphold. The Prime Minister was looking longingly at the flight tickets for his own family break. A number of figures, including Jeffrey Donaldson, left the building, deserting the acrimonious Ulster Unionist Party debate on whether or not to support the proposals being put forward for agreement. Mo Mowlam looked exhausted, with an intravenous drip in her arm to stymie on-going pain – not caused by the long hours of the talks but from a pre-existing health condition. The final draft of the Agreement was circulated with everyone being summoned into the plenary session. The tedium was over and the deal had been done. Joe Cahill was on hand to legitimise Sinn Féin's position, while the regulars from the Shankill Road's Rex Bar seemed to be clustered around the room.

Despite my warning to the Women's Coalition members not to break down and cry since the cameras would be on us, when I turned around and saw that grown men beside me had begun to cry, I threw my arms in the air and didn't much care who was crying. At 5.30 pm, the drama of Good Friday was finally over. What a roller coaster of emotions we had been through – one minute it was on, then off, then on again. We had to stay awake all through the previous night and, with more and more drafting to be done at the last minute, I begged my colleagues to go to the toilet when they could and not when I needed them.

It was in that same toilet that we held a meeting with Mo Mowlam to encourage her to insert new words into the document on victim's rights. We had been told by the NIO that we were getting too much access to her so we decided that the only way to have a private meeting was to do so in the toilets. And it worked. We had orchestrated for Pearl Sagar to stand outside the one and only ladies toilet in the building and give us the heads up when Mo appeared. Convincing Mo of the need for the new clauses turned out to be prophetic as we learned later that some believed the peace agreement was nothing but a terrorist's charter. We were able to point to both the dedication and the declaration addressed to victims. It still haunts me though that what was promised back then has taken so long to deliver.

After the sign-off, I did the round of press interviews going from camera to camera, with print and broadcasting journalists from all around the world wanting a sound bite. They already loved Tony Blair's "I feel the hand of history on my shoulder," followed by John Hume's "We have a new dawn" – but still, they were looking for more. I had promised Hervé, a French journalist, that I would give him a sign but since we had no chimneys, we couldn't send out smoke signals so we agreed that we would throw our papers in the air like the students do to signify the end of two torturous years. As protocol dictated, we were the smallest party and therefore the last in line to face the press. Most had put down their cameras and missed what one of them caught: a beautiful picture of us heartily laughing as we tried to catch the now redundant papers floating high above us. That became the image that went out on CNN that evening and for capturing that moment, that same journalist pocketed a very generous commission. And then as the calm descended on Castle Buildings, along with our papers, we gathered up the detritus and went home.

As I was making my way home, I met the younger of my two boys skateboarding down the street so I shouted over to him that we had made peace. He thought that was what I was supposed to be doing and skated away unimpressed. The older fella was watching the scene being played out on the TV and jumped up to hug me and to ask if it was true. When I told him that it was, he asked a very different question: "Does that mean all the killing will stop and will all the parades and protests get sorted out and the hateful things that go on come to an end?" "I am not sure about that son" was my only response. His reply "What did you sign today Mam if it doesn't mean that?" meant that the euphoria began to dissipate. When my neighbours poured in moments later, they brought their own euphoria for me to share in. It became another long night and when I finally got to bed,

I thought again about what my son had said and prayed that every Friday would be a "good" Friday from then on.

What Happened Next?

The preamble to the Agreement proclaimed that a new society could be built on respect for human rights, equality, inclusion (social and political) and mutual acceptance/esteem. The well-crafted sentences exuded hope of a new beginning, while leaving space for a menu of national aspiration and identity that circumvented narrow notions of state-specific citizenship. This was to be an Agreement guaranteed by both the Irish and the British Governments, under the benevolent gaze of the EU and the USA. It was to be an international beacon of what can be achieved when there is imagination, pragmatism and patience to the point of exhaustion. It was the entry to a win-win for a country that had so long been mired in political stalemate.

So once again we took to the streets to sell it to the people. The Women's Coalition and the loyalist parties, despite being the smallest in numbers, worked hard in every town and village around the country to ensure that it would be ratified. It needed to be a resounding *Yes* in both parts of Ireland and once again, everyone held their breath until that vote came in. We got the result we needed so it was time to start building.

So What Went Awry?

Once the spirit of goodwill lifted there were crucial issues that needed to be addressed, starting with the lack of attention to implementation and the absence of a validation committee. Subsequent crisis summits toured the gracious houses of England along with overnight sessions in Hillsborough Castle. Ulster Unionist leaders pushed Tony Blair for concessions, endlessly repeating the mantra that they had "lost" out by what was agreed. When they said it often enough, people from the Lower Shankill to Sion Mills began to believe them. Sinn Féin, for its part, spun out the ambiguities of decommissioning and negated the possibilities of police transformation until political will became frayed.

Friction and failure was once again on the horizon. The essential principles of human rights and parity of esteem, along with notions of a "shared future," were nuanced virtually out of existence. The UK Government delegated much of its responsibilities to the still bitterly divided Northern Ireland Executive, whilst the Irish Government lost its mojo and started promoting its ablest negotiators to ambassadorial positions in far-away countries. Since the Good Friday Agreement had concluded without any discussion on what constituted the seeds of the conflict, it was unsurprising that the legacy of the past turned up as a troubling spectre over its future.

2007 marked movement when Reverend Ian Paisley led the self-excluded DUP back into the fold by recognising the legitimacy of Sinn Féin's political mandate and agreeing to sit down with Gerry Adams at the infamous rectangular table. The photos would be able to show that he was seated alongside, rather than beside, his former opponent and the process was on the move once more. The smiles resulting from the most unlikely of friendships between Martin McGuinness and Ian Paisley, as First and Deputy First Ministers, were captured in pictures of the "chuckle brothers." By then there were too few spoilers on both sides to undermine this engagement and players from other conflict situations flocked to Northern Ireland to learn from this turnaround of events. Things worked and while they worked, there were people walking the streets who might otherwise have been in the graveyard.

But there was still the quagmire of frustrated expectations that flew in the face of this heady optimism. A "benign apartheid" was allowed to set in and became more acceptable than the politics of a shared society. Friction repeatedly arose over a "sharing-out" of favourite "political" projects. The British Government adopted a narrative of being a neutral referee for the warring sides. Victims/survivors of the violence were used to score a political point with their entitlements ignored or prevaricated. The proposals the Women's Coalition had inserted into the agreement on shared housing, integrated education, support for community development (rather than single-identity community contracts), and promotion of the representation of women were mostly parked. The advice on a Bill of Rights for Northern Ireland (which I later was responsible for drafting, along with my fellow Human Rights Commissioners) was handed to the Secretary of State in 2008 and has sat on the shelves of 10 Downing Street ever since.

What Now?

Twenty years is a long time in politics, particularly in the context of the destructive post-Brexit climate. The Good Friday/Belfast Agreement needs rejuvenated with its full implementation and the combined strength of the British and Irish Governments behind it, without cavil or caveat. If this Agreement that was ratified in both parts of Ireland is to be tinkered with, then what is the basis for trusting another agreement? The Civic Forum, also put in the agreement by the Women's Coalition, that was stood down by the NI Executive, should be reinstated. We could take lessons from the Citizens' Assembly that worked so well in the South of Ireland, taking people's views on previously contentious issues and finding consensus on the way forward. Such a Forum, as it was intended, could advise on the longer-term social, economic and cultural issues as well as deliberating on the potential outcomes of Brexit. The current vacuum cannot be filled by local councillors alone – or by the London and Dublin administrations. If narrow short-term party interest is put before the long-term challenge of conflict transformation in Northern Ireland, then it is clear that the hand of history will be both heavy and unforgiving.

Monica McWilliams was born in Kilrea, Co Derry in 1954 and has degrees from Queen's University Belfast and the University of Michigan. As one of the Women's Coalition representatives at the multi-party negotiations that culminated in the Good Friday (or Belfast) Agreement, she played a key role in this major political development in the Northern Irish peace process of the 1990s. Emeritus Professor at the Transitional Justice Institute, Ulster University, she is the author of Bringing It Out in the Open *and* Taking Domestic Violence Seriously *(both HMSO, 1993 and 1996). She lives in Belfast.*

THE WAY I REMEMBER IT

Ruth Carr

It was that knot in your chest
lodged so long its clench an integral part of you –

suddenly, unimaginably, loosening;
its fist daring to open.

It was black bird and yellow gorse blurting
their blossom of song across the lough.

It was that handshake making a pledge
for something better – from us all, for us all.

It was the beauty of something stirring
where the knot had been,

feeling that bird's heart beat within my own.

Ruth Carr was born in Belfast in 1953 and studied at Queen's University and the University of Ulster. She has published three collections of poetry, There Is a House *(Summer Palace Press, 1999),* The Airing Cupboard *(Summer Palace Press, 2008), and* Feather and Bone *(Arlen House, 2018). She organizes the "Of Mouth" poetry reading series at the Linen Hall Library, Belfast, and works as a freelance editor and tutor.*

TWENTY YEARS ON

Paul Arthur

Frogs back to coconut shells – and fearing the future.

During 1997-98 I was a Senior Fellow at the United States Institute of Peace in Washington, D.C. It was a wonderful opportunity to study the American input into the peace process. It meant a lot of time "on the Hill" giving my tuppence-worth on Irish politics. To get to USIP in the first place I had to deal with our fifteen-year-old who was reluctant to leave his friends at home. Negotiations were entered and one of the outcomes was a promise of a visit to Disney World. So it was in a motel in Orlando that I witnessed the signing of the agreement. In retrospect Disney is a good vantage point for surveying the surrealism of politics in Northern Ireland.

USIP placed a certain distance from the noises on the street and one's professional perspective. After all, I was a commentator on contemporary Irish politics who had also been a student radical in the civil rights movement. The latter could be overcome by applying Orwell's dictum that the "more one is conscious of one's political bias the more chance one has of acting politically without sacrificing one's aesthetic and intellectual objectivity." It was for others to judge whether I lived up to those high aspirations. But it is the former – the burden of contemporary history – that carries the most challenges. It is neatly encapsulated in R.G. Collingwood's *Speculum Mentis* (1926) when he says that contemporary history embarrasses a writer "not only because he knows too much, but also because what he knows is too undigested, too unconnected, too atomic."

And so to 1998, and interpreting all that flows from that. The first reaction is to recall Zhou Enlai's comment that it is too early to assess the impact of the French Revolution – although it's not certain whether he was referring to 1789 or 1968. Francis Fukuyama had declared already the End of History in 1989. (To be fair to him, he did insert a question mark). So distance is essential. The second is to be aware of the frog in the half coconut shell as understood by Benedict Anderson. That has been his entire universe and we are left with the image of the frog being "narrow-minded, provincial, stay-at-home and self-satisfied for no good reason" ("Frameworks of Comparison," 2016). We live partial and blinkered lives.

Thirdly we have to acknowledge Enoch Powell's conception of "pre-play." What induced the 1998 agreement? The blunt answer is thirty years of political violence and faltering attempts to staunch it. There were constitutional landmarks along the way. It is inconceivable that it would have been signed in 1998 had there not been the 1985 Anglo-Irish Agreement. The contours of 1998 can be found in that earlier document. It provided "institutional machinery for the cultivation of a mature diplomatic rapport between Britain and Ireland" (Richard Bourke, *Peace in Ireland: The War of Ideas*, 2003). It was a form of political blackmail foisted on the unionist community by the sovereign government. It was Westminster's revenge for the UWC strike in 1974; and a challenge to the IRA's armed struggle through closer British-Irish security co-operation. In the interim, there was the joint declaration launched by John Major and Albert Reynolds on 15 December 1993.

The 1993 and 1998 documents allow for an interesting linguistic comparison. The former was a (deliberate) piece of tortuous syntax that defied textual analysis. Indeed it was so bad that it was awarded, I think, the prize for the worst piece of official language for 1993. Its authors would have been so proud. Its essence is caught (by a diplomat): "a minor diplomatic masterpiece ... [which] is not a formal agreement or treaty setting the framework for a comprehensive constitutional settlement; it is a political statement of attitude and intent directed primarily at the IRA. The two heads of government have carefully shelved all the difficult longer term issues ... in order to make a bid for an IRA ceasefire" (David Goodall, "Terrorists on the Spot," 1994). They got it in August — and that of the loyalists in October — 1994. We had entered the territory of constructive ambiguity.

The 1998 agreement came on the back of a twin-track process of establishing an international decommissioning panel (chaired by George Mitchell) to establish the parameters for the negotiations. Mitchell delivered his report on 22 January 1996 but it was not enough to save the peace and the IRA ceasefire collapsed less than three weeks later. To move beyond the dominance of decommissioning, the Major government called elections for a Northern Ireland Forum for 30 May which his Minister of State, Michael Ancram, later described as "a one-off system for a one-off purpose." They were unique in the UK's electoral history and belonged to the surrealist school because they had to ensure that minor parties representing loyalists and others were part of the negotiations. Tony Blair's massive victory in May 1997 accelerated the process and the Belfast Agreement was the outcome.

One of the more perceptive comments on the 1998 agreement came from a literary critic who recognized that the genius of the 1998 agreement can be traced to how it deals with identity. Declan Kiberd invokes the ghost of Oscar Wilde when he maintains that much of the language of the Agreement is "vague, even 'poetic.' That is because it offers a version of multiple identities, of a kind for which no legal language yet exists. The Wilde who suggested that the only way to intensify personality was to multiply it would have approved – but where is the lawyer who can offer a constitutional definition as open rather than fixed, as a process rather than a conclusion" (*Irish Classics,* 2000). It removed us from what President Michael D. Higgins calls binary tribalism.

What the agreements of 1993 and 1998 had in common was that they placed the problem on the long finger. This was some sort of anatomical progress. Irish diplomacy in the 1950s and 60s was based on the premise of "raising the sore thumb" – partition was Ireland's sore thumb and it was simply a question of raising this at the United Nations and elsewhere and the international community would fall into line by demanding that this great hurt be redressed. Reality imposed itself during the course of the conflict and the frog had to move out of its shell. In that respect the 1998 document is both tentative and sophisticated. *Tentative* in that recognized the deep psychological hurts not just of the past thirty years but of centuries of British-Irish animosity; and *sophisticated* in that it drew on the lessons of past failures and accepted best international practice.

The success of peace agreements is limited ... and for very good reason. Czeslaw Miłosz warns us that it "is possible that there is no other memory than the memory of wounds." An essential part of our political culture is our sense of victimhood. David Ervine described it neatly when he said that Northern Ireland was a place where people would travel a hundred miles to be insulted. It is the political economy of helplessness where we fail to make the distinction between victim and perpetrator. It is also the fear of the unknown. The Mitchell Commission warned that "if the focus remains on the past, the past will become the future and that is something no one can desire." In *Slowness* Milan Kundera contends " ... the source of fear is in the future, and a person freed of the future has nothing to fear." In a society in which the past carries such heavy heft the uplands of the future are not easily embraced.

It is also a question of political leadership. A scholar of peace agreements has noted that it is important "for the leaders on both sides to recognise that the game has changed, that the behaviour necessary to get to a provisional agreement is not always the behaviour appropriate for the post-agreement period." He continues " … needs and priorities change, interests must be redefined or re-visioned, and a joint learning process must be institutionalised and accelerated" (Rothstein, 1996). There is only partial evidence that our leaders have taken this on board. George Mitchell surely was correct when he said that there would have been no peace process without John Hume and no peace agreement without David Trimble. They represented what the South Africans called the "strong centre," the essential building blocks for putting the Agreement together. But they became bit players in both governments' desire to embrace the wider shores of loyalism and republicanism.

It is not that efforts have not been made since their political demise. The personal relationship between Ian Paisley and Martin McGuinness was remarkable; and that between McGuinness and Peter Robinson was professional. But there it ends. A form of infantilism has crept in. It manifests itself in the treatment of Irish – and I write as someone who is not a *Gaeilgeoir*. The withdrawal of (minor) funding for scholarships just before Christmas 2016 was an act so petty as to be beneath contempt. References to feeding crocodiles and a pathetic attempt at Hiberno-phoneticism by a senior DUP MP was a crass display of cultural insensitivity. Add to that the institutional sclerosis built into the Agreement before we even consider "cash for ash," and we are truly back in Disney World.

In the circumstances, optimism does not come easily. Long before Brexit and Trump the distinguished historian Tony Judt warned that the role of the public intellectual in the present century was not to imagine better worlds but how to prevent worse ones. Perhaps the frog has moved back into its shell.

A distinguished scholar and practitioner in international conflict resolution, Paul Arthur is a Professor of Politics, Emeritus Director of the Graduate Program in Peace and Conflict Studies, and INCORE (International Conflict Research Institute) Honorary Associate at the University of Ulster. He holds a BA and MSc from Queen's University Belfast and a D.Litt from the National University of Ireland. He is the author of five books, including Special Relationships: Britain, Ireland and the Northern Ireland Problem *(Blackstaff Press, 2000) – and approximately seventy peer-reviewed articles. In 1997-1998, he held a Senior Fellowship at the United States Institute of Peace in Washington D.C., where his research was in Track Two Diplomacy; and in 2007, he was a Fulbright scholar at Stanford University. He has extensive media experience in Ireland, Britain and the United States, including two years as an op-ed writer for* The Irish Times, *as well as contributing articles to* The Times, The New York Times, Observer, Sunday Independent *and* The Guardian.

SHOPPING FOR *BEOWULF*

―

Philip Knox

Tholing it ― with others.

He knew what they had tholed,
the long times and troubles they'd come through...

The year after the Good Friday Agreement was signed, Seamus Heaney published his translation of *Beowulf*. It is, in some ways, his great poem of the peace process. It presents a humane vision of what it might mean to be several things at once, but there is also another force at work in Heaney's imagination, something dissonant and bleak. Sometimes, these days, it looks as if this darker vision may turn out to have been the truer portent.

In 1998 I was much too young to grasp or care about the big political moment I was living through, but I think I was able to sense a change in mood. It would still be some years before I bought my copy of Heaney's *Beowulf* in the small but not parsimonious poetry section of the bookshop in the big new shopping centre in Newry ― itself a loud statement of the moment we were living through: confident, rich, a little shallow.

Heaney's *Beowulf* carries the marks of the optimism of its moment, an optimism that at times takes on the aspect of utopianism. In the Introduction he describes his student days in Queen's, when Old English lectures could suddenly open some new and strange perspective on the past. Hearing in the sounds of Old English not the orderly foundation myth of the colonial language but instead a delirious romance of mix and change, Heaney describes an intoxicating vision of the "prepolitical" and "prelapsarian": "The Irish/English duality, the Celtic/Saxon antithesis were momentarily collapsed and in the resulting etymological eddy a gleam of recognition flashed through the synapses and I glimpsed an elsewhere of potential that seemed at the same time to be a somewhere being remembered." In Heaney's *Beowulf* project, as I read it, the return to this "prelinguistic" moment can be seen appearing on the horizon in Northern Ireland after the Belfast Agreement. Heaney reads *Beowulf* as a work that takes its place in a shared, world-spanning literary history, and wants to help the reader sweep *Beowulf* "into the global village of the third millennium." There is his old, acute sense that violence and suffering repeats itself with dismaying regularity – the Geat woman who keens a lament at Beowulf's funeral "could come straight from a late twentieth-century news report, from Rwanda or Kosovo" – but it is striking also that such scenes of suffering will be beamed in from outside these islands. Ulster had had its own little End of History.

This vision captures something important about my teenage years in the post-Agreement age. My generation received the hard-won inheritance of political boredom. We had no idea how lucky we were. In my Christian Brothers school, many of the boys came from strongly nationalist households, but for most that identity was loose and dimly understood. The few young men who voiced a serious and urgent commitment to nationalist causes were, to me at least, unnerving and slightly out of place. It was hardly "prelapsarian": a name like "Knox" could still raise a few eyebrows – but this was mainly among the older generation, and several of my friends then and now were, like me, the product of "mixed marriages." Politics, when it happened, happened somewhere else. The Iraq War protests were my first encounter with the notion that there were things you might care about that stretched beyond the small compass of your daily life. Boys who wished to miss school to attend the demonstration against the invasion of Iraq needed a note from their parents. Some went without in an act of political disobedience. I stayed in class.

The hollowing-out of Northern Irish politics was perhaps the price that had to be paid for peace, but now as political bodies across Europe increasingly resemble Stormont in their antagonism, stasis, and failure to articulate a vision of a just and plural society, it seems that the old cracks might reappear in Ulster as they are reappearing elsewhere. There is where the bleakness in Heaney's *Beowulf* comes in, that other, darker force on the edges of the light. It is encapsulated for him in the dragon, which appears in the poem's third and final phase, always already there in the earth beneath Beowulf's home place, a figure of the violence and destruction that is waiting for its moment to re-emerge. Heaney sees it as "the embodiment of a knowledge deeply ingrained in the species – the knowledge, that is, of the price to be paid for physical and spiritual survival." There are now many places in the world, the North included, where that knowledge might just, unthinkably, reassert itself, as a vision of what is shared collapses back once again into the false consciousness of how we differ.

I took that copy of Heaney's *Beowulf* with me when I went to study English (in Oxford, the very cave of the dragon of philology). Reading medieval literature has now become my profession. There was something enormously enabling for me in Heaney's insight that Old English was somehow kin to Ulster English, that a line could be drawn from *þolian* to "tholing," that the past was a hospitable place. I want to keep hold of what is enabling in that vision, but I have increasingly felt the need to release the idea that we might ever return at last to that prelinguistic realm, unmarked by language. So what I look for now when I pick up my copy of Heaney's *Beowulf* is an optimism of the will but not the intellect, an encouragement to get back to the hard work of reading what is alien and finding in it something that is mine without denying it its strangeness and its power to change me. That is also the hard work of living constructively with others, and the new challenge of the past in this new present, twenty years on.

Born in 1988 in Newry, Philip Knox is a University Lecturer in Medieval English at the University of Cambridge, and a fellow of Trinity College, Cambridge. He pursued his undergraduate and graduate studies at the University of Oxford. He is one of the editors of Medieval Thought Experiments: Poetry, Hypothesis, and Experience in the European Middle Ages *(Brepols, 2018). He is also the co-curator, with Nathaniel Morris, of a music compilation,* Stand Up, People: Gypsy Pop Songs From Tito's Yugoslavia 1964-1980 *(2013). He lives in Cambridge and London.*

SLIPPERS

Jennifer Kerr

In common.

On the tenth of April, 1998 I was five. It was my dad's forty-first birthday. I think I was in Primary Three. I have trouble remembering what years go with what school years. Especially the early ones. I could have been in Primary Two. I do know that I would have been off school for the Easter holidays. Days prior to Good Friday 1998 I was probably colouring in pictures of eggs and lambs and writing around it what I thought Easter meant. My mum used to make up a wicker basket full of chocolate for me every Easter. It had those little yellow, furry chickens with the wire feet inside it. That's what Easter meant to me – a five-year-old. I am also sure that it was the year I won the Easter Bonnet competition in school – another thing my mum made for me. Chocolate was the prize.

In August 2018 I watched as he placed freshly showered feet into navy slippers. I was sitting on the floor. The carpet was soft and comfortable. That action stirred something within me. Not only did I like his feet, fresh and clean, sliding into slippers. I liked that I had myself worn them a few times – whenever there was nothing else to protect my feet. But he wanted to show me something outside. The action reminded me of something my mum and dad had told me.

Before I was born. Before I knew I would be comforted by an action such as feet sliding into slippers. Long before I knew those particular feet. My parents and my eldest brother were held in their home by the IRA. It was the early eighties and my brother was only a baby. This isn't such a novel thing for families from West Belfast. To me it is. It is incredibly surreal. They weren't hurt – physically, at least. The men knocked on their door and demanded that my dad go upstairs, and my mum was kept in the front room with my brother. They were using my parents' house as a vantage point to see over Stewartstown. I think they wanted to shoot from there. When my mum or dad talks about this moment in their lives, the thing that sticks out, and that they never fail to mention, is that my dad was wearing slippers at the time. He was embarrassed by this choice of footwear. He had to go outside to the back garden at one stage, just in his slippers. This was a big deal.

So, when I watched those *new* feet slide into the navy slippers, I could only think about how our families would have differed in those days. In those days that were only a decade before we were born. A decade before a landmark agreement was signed – promising that my family or any family weren't used in such a way ever again.

My parents haven't really talked about that incident much. Just the slippers. Just my dad's embarrassment. I think about *his* dad and whether he would have been wearing just his slippers if the IRA were to knock on their front door back then. I think about how that incident would have meant something much worse to his family. This is a thought that I find strange and confusing. It wouldn't be a funny anecdote about slippers. It would have been much more significant, and much more frightening. I think that if we would have been my parents. If we would have been sitting in the front room of our house, in our slippers, we wouldn't be telling the same story. We wouldn't have been in the same house. I wouldn't have been comforted by his feet. I wouldn't have heard his voice asking me to put on his slippers so we could walk outside in the garden. I wouldn't have been in his garden at all.

My dad owned those same slippers for many years. He likes to use things up. Like a polo-shirt that may have started as his best and then would have been slowly relegated, hole-by-hole, to a weekend t-shirt, bed shirt, painting shirt, ripped shirt my mum used to clean up with...

He and my dad have that in common. I watched myself press my hands to his chest. I smoothed them across and around his back and then I felt a small hole, just under his arm. He told me he liked that t-shirt and that it wasn't noticeable. He told me that it wasn't the only shirt he had with holes. He told me he would wear all of his shirts until he couldn't. He asked me if that was okay.

It made me pull him closer and not want to let him go.

Jennifer Kerr was born in Belfast in 1993 and educated in West Belfast. She completed a BSc in Linguistics at Ulster University, before receiving an MA in Creative Writing at Queen's University Belfast. She has been published in Incubator, *an online literary journal, and is Managing Editor of this journal. She currently lives and works on the outskirts of Belfast.*

UNSETTLING RECOLLECTIONS

Stephen Dornan

Malign shapes.

Is it too much to say that Belfast before the peace process, the Belfast of my school days, felt at times like a cityscape from a nightmare? Maybe, but I had nightmares about it. Every school day from 1990-1996 I walked from the statue of The Black Man, down past the City Hall towards the Law Courts. I walked past the soldiers, who crouched or stood in guarded, watchful boredom, dozing guns cradled in their arms, to the low corrugated shelters of the bus station at Oxford Street. In the nightmares I'd take the same journey in streets drained of colour. Gaunt, harrowed-looking souls would glide by in silent, determined evacuation. By the time I reached Chichester Street the city would be deserted, bomb-scare empty. As I walked past the mouths of alleyways, I'd notice movement: the festering darkness would be alive with fluid, indefinable, malign shapes.

It's a different Belfast these days. Much has changed and the peace process, with the Belfast Agreement as its keystone, takes the credit. So why do I feel that there's something unsettling about recollecting the Belfast Agreement?

The first unsettling thing is that I can't remember if I voted in the referendum. I was an undergraduate in Scotland in 1998. I had been in Northern Ireland on Good Friday, but it was term time by the time the referendum was held. I'm not certain, but I think I'd previously transferred my vote and either didn't qualify for, or didn't organise, a postal vote.

Of course, it was always fairly clear that my vote wouldn't swing it – the outcome wasn't in much doubt. After all, the machinery behind the "yes" campaign was formidable: most of the main political parties in Northern Ireland, including the largest Unionist and Nationalist ones, supported it. The British and Irish governments were major stakeholders and the world's greatest superpower was cheerleading. The media, in the days before digital disintegration, was supportive, with the tone ranging from enthusiastic to millennial. Even history seemed to demand its success: after all, if the Iron Curtain, the Soviet Union and the Berlin Wall could all vanish, the antagonists of our back-alley squabble could hardly resist the hand of history prodding them towards accord. Everything was slickly delivered with early Blairite panache, whilst a choreographed youthquake saw a global supergroup playing for free to teenagers in a shiny new Belfast amphitheatre that had been built where the old corrugated shelters of Oxford Street bus station once stood. It would take you to be contrary to vote against all that, and a young family holding hands in a sunset.

But of course, many of us in Northern Ireland were contrary; living in contested and violent times can make people contrary. This brings me to the second unsettling thing: if I did vote, I voted "No."

This in itself shouldn't be unsettling, though there is a certain social pressure when discussing the Belfast Agreement to be blandly effusive about it. The range of views in my circle of family and friends was probably fairly typical of Unionist communities: there were the arguments and divisions that binary questions often provoke. Some of the arguments were civil, some emotive, some visceral. Many people chose sides early and entrenched themselves in their position, as people do. But many were uncertain. They had to weigh their hope that the relative peace could hold, against their distaste, even repulsion, at aspects of the agreement. Some were enthusiastic, some bit the bullet, held their noses, and voted for it, gagging on the bitter aftertaste; others, for a range of reasons, didn't.

But maybe the most unsettling thing is how the divisions seemed to evaporate so quickly. The lasting political divisions that followed subsequent constitutional referenda I experienced (Indyref in 2014 and Brexit in 2016) didn't really feature after the Belfast Agreement referendum. It's currently fashionable to characterise the DUP as having been doggedly anti-Agreement for the last two decades, but this belies the enthusiasm with which they participated in the new mechanisms it created. So even those who opposed the Agreement, quickly realigned to embrace its structures and become firmly ensconced in the multi-party executive.

There's a third unsettling thing. I remember being out in Belfast with friends a few years after the agreement. Remarkably, it felt like things had genuinely transformed. We found ourselves in a busy glass-fronted establishment that looked out onto the City Hall, which was lavishly illuminated by colourful new Christmas lights. People seemed happy and that nightmarish cityscape I'd dreamt of seemed cleansed. Furthermore, my old friends were at Queen's and had met up with new friends they'd met there. In short, we were in "mixed company" and thought ourselves, no doubt, sophisticadoes, deftly capable of avoiding contentious topics and shibboleths. It seemed that after all, the thing had worked. Coming to terms with being wrong can be unsettling.

But twenty years on things seem less clear-cut, though just as unsettling. We can count our blessings, but we still incant our curses. We've failed to move beyond the peace process and the peculiar, and at times divisive, structures and binaries that it has perpetuated and created. We've achieved a messy political stalemate and an indefinite constitutional limbo. Sectarian headcounts are still at the core of political strategy and the middle ground remains stubbornly bereft of any genuine vision and, therefore, incapable of meaningful mobilisation. When The Belfast Agreement is mentioned these days, it is often wielded as a shillelagh in our constitutional faction fight, to bloody the pate of an antagonist. Maybe unsettling malign shapes still haunt the dark alleyways after all, writhing in the shadows, waiting again to surface?

Stephen Dornan is this journal's Contributing Editor for Ulster Scots. He was born in 1978 in Newtownards, Co Down, and educated at the Royal Belfast Academical Institution, before taking two degrees from the University of Aberdeen, where his PhD was in Irish, Scottish and Ulster Scots poetry. His work in Ulster Scots has appeared previously in Irish Pages, *and he has contributed essays and articles to a variety of academic journals and books. He is currently Head of English at Cults Academy, Aberdeen, and lives in Stonehaven, Aberdeenshire.*

AN INDETERMINATE QUIET

Stephen Elliott

Amidst intransigence more than violence.

In my first year at uni, during an early class in the autumn semester, I remember taking part in a small social experiment. Whether intended as a balm against the awkwardness in which we sat, eyeing our new course mates, or a prompt towards scholarly discussion, I'm now unsure. But, clearly in my mind, even now, I can recall the lecturer – a beret-donning middle aged woman, glasses dangling on a chain around her neck – asking us each to take up our things and relocate to a new area of the hall based on the sole criterion of our nationality. Gesturing to the left, centre, then the right sections of our seating area, she plotted out a geography in which we divided into three groups, simultaneously distinct and not so: Scottish, British and Other, respectively. The lecture hall burst into a chorale of scraping chairs and rekindled chitchat.

Some, I remember, looked uncertain, having not listened too attentively. Others, unduly pleased with themselves, remained where they sat, having somehow opted for the right spot to begin with. I was one of the latter, slap-bang in the middle: British and accordingly motionless. When all had settled into their new states, an indeterminate quiet descended once more. Between us, the aisles hardened to borders as the lecturer dallied along them. Whatever the point of this disruption had been, it seemed arbitrary – we were of a generation where nationality was, surely, secondary to identity; less consequential in conversation than music taste or which footy team you kept up with.

The Erasmus crowd that mostly occupied our Other state surely demonstrated this. The neighbouring Scottish state, however, was practically overpopulated – national spirit burned strong, there. Of course, only a year or so later, ripples of that first referendum would start to riffle the national topsoil across the country and beyond. Looking around, I began to catch on to why I felt so uncomfortable with the exercise. In the seats that immediately surrounded me sat a handful of students that had crossed the border from England. Not that I was unhappy with their company. But the moment the lecturer had incited the class to rearrange, I'd been confronted with the prickly question of my own national identity. My initial instinct, I think, had been to up and join the Other state but that, surely, would have prompted questions which, still being an unassuming fresher, I didn't really want to answer at the time. Questions about Irishness, the North, the Troubles and so on. It also wasn't lost on me that, had this scenario played out at home, sitting still might once have been considered a political act. Whether it was idleness or indecision, I stayed put, and the incident has since remained in my mind as a proof of the complexity of social and cultural experience in the North of Ireland.

Five years on, and twenty years since the Good Friday Agreement, little has changed in that cognitive landscape. Thinking specifically about the Agreement, its crucial role in the peace process is patent: demand for decommissioning, power-sharing, a timeline for progress ... but I was six years old when it was passed and am, on the whole, part of the post-Agreement/post-Troubles generation – a generation that came of age amidst intransigence more than violence. And what it feels more keenly than others, perhaps, is this particular brand of fallout; one that occurs after the trouble and beneath the indeterminate quiet. Through legislation, two polarising notions of identity were legitimised. Those notions were further ratified by a devolved government, which, bar its fitful periods of suspension and deadlock, has been primarily structured around that polarity. There is, it seems, room for little else. The result is a state of split traditions and confused inheritances, from which many of us move away for education, for work, for travel, for family. Yet, whether overseas or not, the post-Agreement generation is having to learn how to negotiate the shifted landscape, to celebrate interculturalism and to carve out a new Northern Irish Identity.

Stephen Elliott was born in 1992 and grew up in Belfast, before moving to Scotland and taking a BA in English at the University of Strathclyde. Following a stint as Editorial Assistant at Irish Pages, *he undertook a MA in Publishing at Oxford Brookes University. He currently lives and works in Oxford. This is his first significant publication.*

A NOVEMBER NIGHT

John Gray

The only game in town.

I recall one ecstatic night when everything seemed possible in our Peace Process. It was the evening of 30 November 1995. President Clinton had arrived to switch on our Christmas tree lights in front of the City Hall.

It was as though the cavalry had arrived. Could American power tip the balance? True, the paramilitary ceasefires had been achieved in 1994, but not to universal acclaim; Jim Molyneux, leader of the still dominant Ulster Unionist Party, viewed them as "destabilising" and "not an occasion for celebration, quite the opposite."

The "Framework Document" and the more recent "Twin Track Initiative" had followed but actual agreement still seemed a long way off. Had Clinton arrived because he was certain that he could drive matters forward?

His appearance earlier in the day at the symbolic venue of Mackie's Foundry heightened expectations. Once a traditional bastion of overwhelmingly Protestant working-class employment, it was now, according to Clinton, "a symbol of Northern Ireland's rebirth"; and not least because the firm was "bridging the divide, overcoming a legacy of discrimination where fair employment and integration are the watch words of the future." Now, "on this shop floor men and women of both traditions are working together."

Not for long they weren't! In what might almost have been a metaphor for the subsequent difficulties of the Peace Process, Mackies closed forever in 1999.

What Clinton said there was not explicit. But when he said that "engaging in honest dialogue is not an act of surrender" and that "you must always be willing to say to those that renounce violence and who do take their own risks for peace, that they are entitled to be full participants in the democratic process," he was surely primarily addressing Unionists – those most fearful of engagement.

Reports of the Mackies event were a spur to the enormous crowd that assembled that evening at the City Hall. As well as packing the whole area in front of the City Hall it stretched well up Royal Avenue. There were the usual parents and expectant children waiting to see the lights go on, but they were greatly outnumbered by those wishing to celebrate hopes for a better future, and an end to the agony of "The Troubles."

We in Belfast's historic Linen Hall Library had a grandstand view as the Library directly faces the City Hall. Watchers from the Library had been witnesses to many an historic occasion there. There was the signing of the Ulster Covenant by nearly half a million in 1912; and the vast "Ulster Says No" assembly in opposition to the Anglo-Irish Agreement in 1984, which sought to replicate the 1912 gathering. These occasions, although separated by most of a century, sought to re-affirm unchanging verities.

Now in 1995 here was a different crowd partly reflecting the changing demographics of the City. It was no longer "a Presbyterian citadel"; however uneasily, it was becoming a shared city, indeed Unionists were finally to lose control of the City Council only two years later. Yet it would be wrong to analyse this mass of people in sectarian terms. No, this predominately young crowd from across all social, religious and political spectrums had come to see history made, and above all because they wanted to see change, even if they were unsure what that might be.

Now the Linen Hall was in a pivotal position. Instead of closing normally at 5.30 pm, our doors remained open to all comers. Having two doors assumed a particular significance because our back door in Fountain Street lay outside the security barrier, while our front door was within the security zone. Thus the Library became a route of passage but many stayed as bottles were soon cracked open. Windows were flung open and we climbed out onto the broad window ledges directly above the seething mass below and toasted what was an unusually balmy night. Nor were we dissuaded by threats from American sharpshooters on surrounding buildings.

Van Morrison and Brian Kennedy were the most notable warm up acts, though, like President Clinton, they had to compete with the now wholly forgotten Mighty Morphin Power Rangers. I recognised Morrison's "Days Like This," a song used in an optimistic Northern Ireland Office advertising campaign that ran immediately after the ceasefires.

Inevitably, Clinton was greeted with the greatest storm of applause. Though charismatic as ever he limited himself to Christmas niceties. There was no repetition of the coded messages at Mackies, but this no longer seemed to matter — surely our politicians couldn't halt the forward march.

If anyone could, it was our Lord Mayor, Eric Smith. He set about lecturing the assembled throng on the sinfulness of man. Very few in the crowd felt sinful and Smith was rewarded with a rising crescendo of hisses. Truly no Lord Mayor in our history has been hissed by so many ...

Our party went on long after all the formalities were over. Uniformed RUC men toasted the night with Republicans and the rest of us joined in. In the morning, hangovers...

By January 1996 I was increasingly gloomy. Co-incidentally I was asked to contribute a "Letter from Ireland" for BBC Radio 4, and used it to lay out my fears rather than for some anodyne cultural travelogue.

I described how it was only with the coming of the ceasefires that I realised how exhausted we all were and not merely by violence but by years of silences (or, as Seamus Heaney quoted, "Whatever you say, say nothing") – years of trying to survive on small islands of hope, one of which was indeed the Linen Hall Library. The novelist and broadcaster, Sam Hanna Bell, had once described it as "a breathing hole in the ice cap that is closing over us." All we could do was attempt a little global warming.

Now I saw developing culture wars as a substitute for armed conflict, and dreamt with some hyperbole of "a day when a mob will assemble outside my library and demand that I separate it into its constituent parts, British, Ulster Scots and Irish, and when I point out that that these elements are inseparable in most of our books, I am handed a guillotine to cut them up page by page."

Meanwhile I described how "my incomprehension and anger had grown as I have watched the main Unionist parties... and the British government, systematically belittle what has been achieved." There was "precious little of magnanimity here. An air of disappointment, of unfinished business, of suspicion, of begrudgery."

I noted that there had been another narrative that summer – as Unionism marched into the cul-de-sac of Drumcree where soon to be Unionist Party leader "David Trimble, sash to the fore, was side by side with Paisley, arms raised in triumph ..." It was a stand-off that caused sectarian paralysis in succeeding years, reaching its nadir when three young brothers were burnt to death in their beds in far-off Ballymoney in 1998.

To my astonishment my BBC letter was subsequently published in both *The Guardian* and *The Irish News*, and to some discomfort amongst the Governors of the Linen Hall Library who felt that I had said too much.

My gloom was well-founded. The IRA ceasefire broke down a month later with the Canary Wharf bombing and was only finally restored in July

1997. It was to take until April 1998 to reach the Good Friday Agreement.

This was certainly a stupendous demonstration of the art of negotiation, and notably by Senator George Mitchell, because it was achieved in the face of continuing ill will. There was no "honest dialogue" as Clinton had urged in 1995, as until late in the day Unionists refused to meet directly with their opponents. Most ludicrously when a cross-party delegation visited South Africa, even Nelson Mandela had to address Unionists and Republicans separately.

Yet the contending parties had no option but to reach an agreement. The British could not win the war, or had lost the appetite to try. The Provisionals' "Year[s] of Victory" in their battle for a United Ireland had proved a dreadful and costly illusion. Now Sinn Féin had to settle for equality in a Northern Ireland context. Unionists could secure a guarantee of the constitutional position of Northern Ireland, but they had to swallow equality and, above all, recognise that they would never again enjoy untrammelled power.

The Agreement could hardly be an inspiring document. Necessarily, it was laden with checks and balances, and most notably it formalised the tribal nature of our politics. That was anathema to many of us but was an inevitable consequence of the realities of the situation.

———

I never again felt the spontaneous enthusiasm of that November night in 1995. The nearest equivalent was the carefully stage managed event in the Waterfront Hall during the referendum campaign on the Good Friday Agreement where 600 schoolchildren were marshaled to listen to Bono and Ash play, and to watch David Trimble and John Hume let Bono raise their hands together. They showed all the enthusiasm of a couple rushed into a forced marriage.

Although the referendum endorsed the Agreement, it was to take another year and a half before the new Executive was established. Arms decommissioning was the bugbear for Unionists who seemed to have forgotten their own history – that the 50,000 rifles smuggled into the country by the Ulster Volunteer Force in 1914 were never decommissioned.

Thus it was that David Trimble as leader of the Ulster Unionist Party took up office as First Minister in December 1999, but already armed with a potential letter of resignation which he duly wielded as early as February 2000. It was but a prelude to the chequered history of the Northern

Ireland Assembly. This became an almost two decade long blur of resignations and suspensions; indeed, it has been suspended for six and a half years of its existence and remains so. Even when sitting it failed to agree on many key issues.

Language remained telling. When David Trimble resumed office in May 2000, he declared that his first need would be to get Sinn Féin "house trained" – an old caricature here of Catholics who when first and belatedly granted houses with baths were said to have kept greyhounds or coal in them ...

Trimble had managed to lead his bitterly divided party into the Good Friday Agreement but his need to keep it on board seemed to require continued demonising of Sinn Féin, a tactic which played into the hands of Sinn Féin electorally and at the expense of the SDLP. Simultaneously Trimble's cries of betrayal practically wrote DUP anti-agreement manifestos for them, and accelerated their advance.

In this sorry history there was the extraordinary interregnum when the Democratic Unionist Party finally surpassed the Ulster Unionists, and Ian Paisley became First Minister. How was it that the lifelong architect of militant Protestant opposition to all change became the other half of "the chuckle brothers" with his Deputy First Minister, Sinn Féin's Martin McGuinness? Had Paisley simply realised all ambition by becoming First Minister or do we have to turn to St Paul's conversion on the road to Damascus? No matter, the mood lifted and there were real possibilities, though not for long. Paisley was defenestrated both by his party and his Free Presbyterian Church. Unionism has always dealt ruthlessly with internal traitors or "Lundys."

With the present DUP leader, Arlene Foster, no such danger has arisen. For her Sinn Féin, her supposed partners in government, are "crocodiles." Her reward was Sinn Féin's best ever election result in the last Assembly election, one celebrated by their supporters rigged out in crocodile costumes.

Nonetheless the DUP have an ascendancy and increasingly conduct themselves as though they have "inherited the earth," though not for the poor, as per the Bible. No, rather it has been for Ministers, MPs, MLAs, SPADs, and large chicken farmers (as the current Renewable Heat Initiative scandal is revealing).

Now, and for the first time, it is Sinn Féin that has collapsed the Executive. They have their red line issues: an Irish Language Act, same sex marriage, and a woman's right to choose, none of which are demonstrably sectarian issues. But beyond specifics lies a fundamental difficulty: a lack of respect and a failure by the DUP to recognise that they are supposed to be equal partners in government. But then the DUP opposed the Good Friday Agreement in the first place.

And how will all this pan out? The gloomiest prediction is that nothing will change as per Winston Churchill's celebrated lament about "the dreary steeples of Fermanagh and Tyrone emerging once again." Arlene Foster is certainly a doughty representative of that Fermanagh spirit ... Yet the present paralysis is unsustainable.

Do we conclude, as the disgraced former Taoiseach Charles Haughey did in 1980, that "Northern Ireland is a failed political entity?" That dictum seems increasingly credible, but if we seek an escape from ourselves we are caught between the devil and the deep blue sea – on the one hand Direct Rule from Westminster, which has failed us in the past, and on the other a United Ireland, which would still be opposed by almost all Unionists.

That remains the case despite the threat to the Northern Ireland economy, and to even such political stability as we have, which is represented by Brexit – here it should be noted that, lemming-like, the DUP remain fixedly supportive of Brexit.

On a rational basis, Irish Unity appears far more attractive than it did even twenty years ago, but not all responses to positive evidence are rational. It is incontestable that the Irish economy and standard of living have made extraordinary progress, and in contrast to the continued weakness of the Northern Ireland economy. Yet you will hear a certain class of Northern begrudgery suggesting that this is all a mirage – they'll all be back riding donkeys down there soon ...

The old complaint was about Popery and the dominance of the Catholic Church. One might have thought that the dramatic collapse of the Church's authority, and the rapid emergence of a multicultural Republic would have been attractive. Yet for the DUP multiculturalism is another threat. The party is just as opposed to same sex marriage and abortion as the Catholic bishops, and seems determined to sustain Northern Ireland as a last Irish and indeed British bastion against these satanic practices.

Pressure from Sinn Féin for a new border poll will increase, and demographics are on their side. In the 2011 census, Protestants were a bare majority of 48% to 45%. I remember that in the era of the Civil Rights Campaign, one Aidan Corrigan argued that Catholics would outbreed

Protestants and was scorned by those of us in the radical People's Democracy with the sobriquet "Count the Catholics Corrigan." Well, 50 years later there are signs that Aidan's prophecy will come true. And yet I can think of no more dismal (and exhausting) way of achieving a United Ireland.

Yet Unionists will, Canute-like, ignore this incoming tide at their peril. For the moment, they can afford to do so as the DUP hold the balance of power at Westminster, even if many English Conservatives hold their noses. The DUP should not let this accession of power lead to a rush of blood to the head. It is by its nature temporary.

There might be an alternative trajectory for Unionism – the development of a modernised and inclusive Unionism for which some Catholics might vote. Unionist leaders have periodically paid lip service to this notion, but so long as their backwoodsmen demand more visceral demonstrations of loyalty like that represented by Drumcree – and more recently in other dead-end disputes about flags and even bonfires – this is a mere chimera.

Is there any prospect of a more progressive post Good Friday Agreement settlement emerging? Perhaps: flawed though the original Agreement certainly is, it is still the only show in town. Tectonic plates do continue to shift, if almost imperceptibly. The annual Gay Pride March now rivals the traditional Twelfth of July Orange Demonstration in size. There are many growing aspects to a restless civic society, even if they do not have an obvious political dimension.

Who can predict how things may crystallise? Peel back the layers of history and you discover that there were other possibilities. I think of another demonstration at the City Hall, or rather at its predecessor, the White Linen Hall. Here in 1792, 5,000 citizens (or a quarter of Belfast's population) demonstrated in favour of the French Revolution. Their hopes were dashed. By contrast, it can be said that the objectives of those in our generation who supported the Civil Rights Campaign in 1968 have largely been fulfilled – but in the course of a conflict that we would not have wished on anyone. As Marx remarked, History doesn't repeat itself except as "farce"; but now perhaps, if our present politicians continue to fail us, a new and rising generation will demand much better.

John Gray was born in 1947 and educated at Campbell College, Belfast and Magdalen College, Oxford. He is author of City in Revolt: James Larkin and the Belfast Dock

Strike of 1907 *(Blackstaff Press, 2007)*. *He served as the Librarian of the Linen Hall Library, Belfast, from 1982 to 2008. A committee member for the new initiative "Reclaim the Enlightenment," he continues to live in Belfast, and is currently working on a book devoted to Cave Hill in all its aspects.*

WHO COULD BLAME THEM?

Noel Russell

All that hopey-changey stuff …

We were flying back from Alicante, at the end of a family holiday. We happy few were my wife, three adult (sort of) children, and I. It was her idea. "It'll be the last one before two of them go away. A moment. A milestone."

Hmmm. A milestone, or a millstone. Well, the sun had shone, two of them read their books and broiled in the sun, the third couldn't sleep in his room and bunked down half-cut in the living room. He gurned when I came in for breakfast at eight in the morning, having been awake since six. My wife had an allergic reaction to mosquito bites and spent the week laid out with her leg bandaged, like the paraplegic who never quite made it into the pool of Bethesda. Alas, I couldn't heal her. ("Sweet blood," said the sisters in the bakery where I buy my Saturday baps. "My poor mummy had it too over there. Poor woman!") The Spanish health centre did a great job. In and out in an hour – another reason for opposing Brexit, if I needed one. There was no Wi-Fi and the TV channels were mainly Austrian and I didn't get the work done I planned to. Blame the elephant, or the son, in the living room.

On the aircraft back, a baby in the seat in front cried the angry, thoughtless, selfish crying of the inconsolable. But the flight was on time, and I was glad to see the aircraft turn over Belfast and descend towards Aldergrove. The fourth green field never looked so green after the semi-desert of Spain. Then a sister of the baby, a beautiful blonde child of about four, pointed out of the port hole and shouted: "Mummy, look at the world! Look at this world!"

Blake, or Wordsworth, or Yeats. Pure joy, pure poetry. A moment alright. A vision even, one that lifted the heart and banished pettiness.

It felt good to be home. It always does. Good TV, Wi-Fi, books, a Chinese take-away for tea, lots of stuff to catch up on on the I-Player, and a lazy Sunday with the weekend papers. And the local news doesn't bother you much because your head and your body are still half away. It takes a while to reset the dials to *local*. RHI. Pathetic! Karen Bradley didn't know that nationalists wouldn't vote for unionists and vice-versa. And her the Secretary of State … *Doh*! Ian Paisley Jr. on the naughty step again. Typical!

We did the airport runs again next day, a Sunday. My daughter, ("I can't believe she's a lawyer"), was flying from the City Airport to Manchester for her first big, away-from-home job. Flat sorted, with a mate from university. A new start after six months travelling in South America. Then up to Aldergrove, (never Belfast International for our generation), with the eldest. On Monday he was starting a two-month course, something to do with Big Data, in the Big Smoke, with a very good chance of a job after it. He had packed in a post-doctoral research post at a German university and was doing a Dick Whittington. I signed an old A-Z of London for him, but he just laughed when I offered it. "We do that on our phone now, Dad. That's what they are for." *Doh.* ("But today/It is my father who keeps stumbling/Behind me, and will not go away.") The usual handshake and late, unplanned, stiff hug – he has inherited his father's physical self-consciousness – and he is into the terminal and away.

He won't be back and neither will she, we're fairly certain. Of course we'll Skype and see them at Christmas and they'll have a boozy break with their mates and we'll take them back to the airports when the trees are bare and the fields wet and the sky grey. But that's it. *They're off.*

We had taken the old Dundrod-Nutts Corner road up because of congestion on the M2. No roadblocks near the airport now, no checkpoints, nice quiet roads. On the way home, I took a turn too early and ended up on a different route. We didn't say much, and I had the "how time flies" moment. I thought a little about moments, milestones. Personal ones. I must have been close to a bar that I drove to one sunny Saturday morning in the summer of 1976. I raced up these roads in a brown Ford Escort with a bad hangover after a very late night at the Celebrity Club in Donegall Place. (How the name recalls the time!) I was 21, a few weeks into a job as a reporter on the *Belfast Telegraph,* anxious not to mess up the story. The IRA had sprayed a bar near Templepatrick, killing three people. I spoke to a relative and the police. (Those were the days when you could still get close enough to interview eyewitnesses and weren't kept away from the crime scene.) He didn't really want to talk, but I got enough to file a story, which made the page-one lead of the *Belfast Telegraph*. Next weekend the UVF sprayed a bar ten miles away, killing six people.

As I drove on towards home I found myself heading not towards Dundrod and South Belfast, but past Ligoniel and Ardoyne and down the Crumlin road. Another moment, another weekend in the summer of '76 – was it the following Friday night? – loyalists opened up on people standing at a bus stop on the Crumlin Road and hit a heavily pregnant woman. She gave birth that night in the Mater Hospital and, it seems astonishing now, I was allowed in to interview her. We got a picture too, and it was a bit of a scoop, and the nationals picked it up and it was my first page one lead by-line. (My wife tells me it is referenced in Bernard MacLaverty's latest novel, *Midwinter Break*. Wonder what he made of it.) That was the summer of '76, the summer of punk, and a heat wave, and "spray jobs" on pubs and people standing at bus stops, and miraculous births, and people coming to pub car parks in the bright sunny morning to find out what happened to their loved ones the night before. A couple of months later I left the *Telegraph* one Friday and started at Queen's the following Monday, a semi-mature student.

A week after our holiday my wife and I were talking in the kitchen and she reminded me of what my eldest son had said once, during the Flags protest: "If it wasn't for you and Dad, I wouldn't be back here." That hit me. He didn't see this place as home, apart from having family here. Of course, he had been away since he was 18, but like his sister, he assumed that he would live his life elsewhere. Just right, I thought. Who could blame them?

On our last night in Spain we were out for a meal and I was talking to the same son and daughter, about "stuff" – populism, Trump, Brexit, Northern Ireland, "all that hopey-changey stuff." Then straight out he said: "I decided some time ago not to let my happiness depend on what was going on or not going on at Stormont or on the streets." Lovely, I thought. Succinct, definitive, true. Just right. That's my boy.

On the drive home I thought also about a young woman who, many years later, had taken the Aldergrove bus from Belfast city centre. Somebody had sent her up with an explosive device to the airport and somebody else must have informed on her because she was scooped by police. I don't know how many years she got but it must have been a hefty sentence. How long did she serve? Funny how places evoke memories, of stories you covered or stories you read or heard on the news. You always know which ones you covered, though. You don't forget those.

This summer I produced a TV documentary about civil rights fifty years on. Fifty years! I was 14 when it kicked off in Belfast. Thirty years of the Troubles, twenty years since the Good Friday Agreement, and nearly two since Stormont's latest mothballing. (Soon it will be a century since "our wee country" was set up. Imagine.) It included profiles of six young or youngish campaigners, working on issues including housing, the environment, women's rights, the Irish language, and minorities. (Remember how some people used to talk about The Minority. Quaint now…) It had a slightly unreal quality. Not just because of the "fifty years on" tag. (Where did those years go? What did we do all that time? Life's what happens when somebody else is busy making other plans.) But it made me think.

The "Northern Ireland problem" has been officially "settled." The world has moved on. We've strutted and fretted our hour upon the stage and now are heard no more. The Clintons, George Mitchell, Tony Blair, Bertie, they've all upped sticks, to riches, retirement, schlepping around the Middle East or somewhere else in need of conflict resolution. We don't count any more, except as a brief footnote about the border and Brexit. We're history.

Except we're not. We should be. After all that effort, all those negotiations, all those sacrifices. *All those funerals*. We, the "decent people," we voted for the GFA, for "partnership," just as we voted for power-sharing in '74. That's 44 years ago now.

For so long, the North was the like the intersection of two sets that didn't really intersect. Now they would, we were told. We would be the pluralist part of Ireland, not the dysfunctional part, a place where two communities could get along, maybe even thrive. A light to the world, even!

We lost sight of a couple of things. Didn't we remember the bringing down of power-sharing in '74? That delirious woman holding up the *Belfast Telegraph* with the headline "The Executive Collapses?" She hasn't gone away, you know. Funny enough, the party that along with loyalist paramilitaries and a lot of other unionists, the DUP, who helped bring down the Executive, the party who voted against the GFA, they're the biggest partner in government, they're now running Northern Ireland, along with the other party, (well they weren't a real party then), Sinn Féin, who were against the power-sharing Executive too. Nearly two years ago, Sinn Féin were forced out of Stormont by the nationalist grassroots, who finally had enough of the DUP. Blame it on RHI, or "no surrender" on the Irish language act. Blame it on whoever you like.

Were we right all along, right to give it a try, or were we sold a pup? Did we have our eye wiped? Did we believe the hype and ignore the reality? Did we think thirty years of killing, nearly 4,000 funerals, would teach us that jaw-jaw was better than war-war? It didn't. Now power-sharing 2.0 looks dead, even if Frankenstein might still give the Stormont monster another shot of juice. "Fool me once, shame on you; fool me twice, shame on me."

Something has changed. We're in a *moment*, and we can't get out of it.

Maybe it's wake-up time. Hope and history don't rhyme. The leopard doesn't change its spots. Crocodiles keep coming back for more. Snouts stay in troughs. You can take them out of somewhere but you can't take the something out of them.

"Decent people" like us, what can we do? Something must be done. Will we get together and make our presence felt? Rapping doors on winter nights, standing outside polling stations, handing out leaflets? (Oh, the things that are done in the privacy of polling booths.) Will we argue on doorsteps the value of the Irish language, same-sex marriage, a legacy solution? Like hell we will. There's a good film on at the QFT or a good concert on somewhere or a good drama on BBC 1. *WTF.* Let somebody else do it.

Call me a pessimist. But try a bit of Gramsci: "Pessimism of the intellect, optimism of the will." Oooh, there's nice. I could be wrong. So I'm wrong. They're coming to me now, the clichés. Thick and fast. Here's another one: "Hope deferred makes the heart sick, but a longing fulfilled is a tree of life." Sweet.

A friend of mine has two daughters working in London. One with a big job in finance, the other a lawyer. One's got a partner, and the other's getting married, one to a Derry man, an engineer, one to a Tory councillor. My friend's an old lefty, and the Tory thing doesn't bother him. ("They're both good lads.") But he had hoped that one would come back home and settle here. It won't happen now. They're away for good.

My son and daughter probably will do the same, though there are no partners on the scene now. (My daughter calls herself and her siblings the "undateables.") They're just right. Still, now and again, I think of that beautiful child on the plane coming into Aldergrove and her calling out: "Mummy, look at the world! Look at this world!" Call me a sentimentalist, but it would be marvelous if the world outside her window was good enough to keep her. One can but hope.

Or not.

Noel Russell was born in Belfast in 1955 and educated at Queen's University Belfast and the University of Michigan. After reporting for The Belfast Telegraph *and* The Irish Times, *and serving as News Editor of* The Irish News, *he worked for BBC Northern Ireland for 24 years, first as a TV and radio current affairs producer, then as Editor of Speech Radio. He completed an M.A. in Creative Writing at Queen's University Belfast in 2015, and now works as an independent producer and writer.*

ATTEND

Tom Mac Intyre

THE RAIN

The rain, listen, pursues ...

No hiding from it, that be the hub?

Bright lad! Talk to it, drink it, wash in it.
Be sponge.

Strip, why not? So I do. It's night,
did I mention? On the slope, near
Cross Chapel, you stand, Mister,
on fabled ceremonial ground.

The rain, the rain, the rain
loves you? That be it? And
you – do you – what's your
stick? Naked, did I mention?
Would you – the rain courts you
so – could you – think of opening
your pores, your doors, your sores,
cop on, Child o' Grace, astray
in the night. It's in charge, that
be it? Now you're onto something,
open...

That was a few nights back. It won't
leave, seems. Can't, better, leave.
Have we met? Really? Late in the
day but could occur, never happen,
as kids' lingo had it in the long
ago. But. But me no buts! This,

make no mistake, is it. Say your prayer.
Stay awake. Pray. Pray again.
Your strip of ground, strip of the night,
is here, wakeful. Enquiring. And rainful.

Alive, alive, alive with the Word. Listen. Still
not too late – 85 only. Next move?
Take another walk in the bright dark.
Ask for news. Attend

A poet, dramatist and fiction-writer in both English and Irish, Tom Mac Intyre was born in Cavan in 1931. He is the author of nine collections of poetry, most recently Stories of the Wandering Moon *(The Lilliput Press, 2000),* ABC *(New Island Books, 2006),* Encountering Zoe: New and Selected Poetry *(New Island Books, 2010), and* Poppy's Leavetaking *(New Island Books, 2013). His plays for The Abbey Theatre include* The Great Hunger *(1983),* Good Evening, Mr Collins *(1997) and his version of Brian Merriman's* Cúirt an Mheán Oíche/The Midnight Court *(1999). A collection of short fiction,* The Word for Yes: New and Selected Stories, *was published by the Gallery Press in 1991. A selected retrospective of his poetry, prose and drama,* The Divil Knows What, *is forthcoming from The Irish Pages Press. He is a member of Aosdána, and lives in Lurganboy, Co Cavan.*

ON THE NOBILITY OF COMPROMISE

Moya Cannon

Ending our false currency.

Poems remind us to be open to the world, that other people, no matter how apparently "other" they may be, feel the same as us … Perhaps it is the end of poetry to aspire to this — to imagine the reality of other people's suffering. Like the other arts, poetry is an ethical space where we confront pains other than our own.

Nick Laird, *The Guardian,* 18 March 2017

An ideologue always carries inside him an assassin,
my father used say.

Joan Margarit, *"Love is a Place"*

When asked to write a short account of my reaction to the Belfast Agreement, as background to a poem, "Antrim Conversation," I hesitated because I could hear voices saying, "What would you know about it? You don't know what it was like to live there." And this is absolutely true. Nobody threw a bomb into my house or forced me to move; none of my relatives or neighbours were shot; nobody, either uniformed or masked, ever stopped me on the side of the road and hauled me out of my car at gunpoint. However, having grown up in Donegal and having close family links in Tyrone, I have been conscious from as far back as I can remember of the stresses which people living "across the border" were experiencing in trying to go about their daily lives.

I remember very vividly the announcement of the Belfast Agreement on Good Friday, 1998. For days we had been glued to the television, hoping against hope that a middle ground could be found between the representatives of the various Unionist and Nationalist political parties. I called up to my brother's house in Galway at mid-day on Friday. There was a huge sense of rejoicing that, at last, politics had broken out in the north - politics which is the opposite of war, which presupposes that although I may disagree with other members of my community, I respect them and will not do them violence. It did indeed seem a brave new world.

My sister-in-law, Kathleen Loughnane, had just finished recording a CD of harp music. The tunes on the CD, by eighteenth century Irish composers, had been dedicated both to Gaelic and to Anglo-Irish patrons. In our elation, we decided to send a copy to Tony Blair and to Mo Mowlam. I can't remember whether or not we sent one to the hero of the hour, George Mitchell. I think that we did. And made sure that John Hume and David Trimble might also get copies.

It might seem a ridiculous gesture, but music, poetry, drama and storytelling had been, for twenty years, thin spiders' webs between rocks, thin filaments bridging the gaps between communities. I think of Tommy Sands' song *There Were Roses*, which bears powerful witness to the horror of a rural farming community when tit-for-tat killings are carried out in their name; of Liz Weir's *Yarn Spinners* storytelling group in The Linen Hall Library, Belfast. Liz Weir writes herself, "When we started off, the Troubles were at their height, and somebody would get up and tell a story about an Orange Lodge dinner, and somebody else would tell a story about going to Mass. The fact was we were all listening to each other's stories, and respecting each other's stories, and I think that's very important. If you listen to someone's story, you're giving the utmost respect."

Seamus Heaney's words –

> But then, once in a lifetime
> The longed-for tidal wave
> Of justice can rise up,
> And hope and history rhyme.

– have been quoted thousands of times. The beginning of that wonderful soliloquy, from his play "The Cure at Troy," where the central protagonist sits in his tent, nursing his sores, have been quoted less often –

> Human beings suffer
> They torture one another
> They get hurt and get hard.

Seamus Heaney acknowledges the horror of "the Troubles" and yet asserts the possibility of fundamental change. As another poet, Denise Levertov, had written about the Vietnam War –

> The poets must give us
> imagination of peace, to oust the intense, familiar,
> imagination of disaster.
> Peace, not only the absence of war.

And four years before the Belfast Agreement, Michael Longley's extraordinary poem, "Ceasefire," had, with shocking honesty, told "what must be done." He partially rendered the story of Priam, King of Troy, and the Greek hero, Achilles, into northern Irish dialect as he opened with the line:

> Put in mind of his own father and moved to tears ...

On meeting the old king, the father of Hector, whom he has killed, Achilles thinks of his own father and is moved. The poem ends with a searing couplet:

> I get down on my knees and do what must be done
> And kiss Achilles' hand, the killer of my son.

This is how hard it is for at least some of the politicians on both sides of the sectarian divide. The violence was local, intimate, not international. The killer lives, not in a distant country, but in a neighbouring village or street. Revenge is instinctive, peace-making counter-intuitive. In the *Iliad*, incensed by the fact that Hector had killed Achilles' friend Patroclus, Achilles has disrespected and defiled his victim's body by dragging it by the heels behind his chariot below the walls of Troy. Priam comes to Achilles to ask him for Hector's body, so that it can be given a proper burial. Achilles, overcome with compassion, accedes to the request, has the body washed and "laid out in uniform." The two then break bread together, talk respectfully, and Achilles asks Priam how much time they will need for the funeral games and to "build the mound." (It is difficult to read this without thinking of the various prehistoric cairns and burial sites scattered on hillsides all over the Irish countryside. It is also difficult to read it without thinking of the pain of the families of "the disappeared" whose dead have not even had the dignity of a proper burial.)

There is no question but that, in his encounter with the conqueror, the hero, Achilles, it is Priam who is the greater human being. This moment in the *Iliad* might even represent a genuine leap in human consciousness.

At the time of the famous "talks about talks," preceding the Belfast Agreement, I remember talking to a friend from Belfast. Her family had been intimidated by loyalists and they had to move house at the height of the troubles. "What is not being talked about at all," she said, "is people's *hurt*." And this is, of course, what still festers – deep hurt on both sides of the sectarian divide, and consequent, deep, deep, distrust. Politics is based on trust, on seeing the opposition not as the enemy but as a fellow citizen. This involves taking enormous risks. Politics is based not on the figure of the all-conquering hero but on the much less glamorous idea of compromise. I came across an article by George Mitchell, written shortly after the signing of the Belfast Agreement, where he talked about his frustration during the negotiations when everything kept coming down to a "null sum." If one side agreed to something, the other side decided, almost on principle, that they should disagree. Nobody, he said, seemed to understand the concept of "win-win." So many of us were brought up to stand firm, "to stand by our ideals." We were not taught much about the nobility of compromise.

Growing up in Donegal, with a mother from the nationalist village of Carrickmore in Co. Tyrone, I had been aware of "the Troubles" since they had broken out in the late 1960's. As small children in the early and mid-sixties, we had often spent holidays in my aunt's house in Carrickmore and had been awed, mesmerised and terrified at the sight of a policeman patrolling the street and wearing a leather holster and with a *real* gun in it. We were also puzzled by our cousins' negative attitude to the policeman and by the fact that virtually everybody in the village was Catholic.

By contrast, our village, Dunfanaghy, in Donegal, politically in "the South" but geographically well north of Carrickmore, had a mixture of religions, with Catholic, Church of Ireland and Presbyterian communities. Our house was next door to the Presbyterian Manse and across the road from the Presbyterian church. The minister, The Reverend Anderson, and his wife had no children but two of Mrs. Anderson's nephews used often visit. They had a cricket bat and my three older brothers had hurling sticks so, between them, they devised a game that involved whacking a ball to and fro across the shared fence. In summer, particularly around the Twelfth of July, the small Presbyterian congregation was greatly augmented by "visitors" from the north and we liked to measure how far the line of cars stretched out the road. The very short tourist season, on which the village depended, peaked around the Twelfth of July and again at the August bank holiday. Although community relations were excellent, the fault lines were there – Catholics went to Catholic schools and Protestants to Protestant schools; Catholics shopped mainly in Catholic shops and Protestants mainly in Protestant shops. When the troubles in the North broke out, we worried that the dissension would tear our community apart too. Thankfully, it did not.

But visits to Tyrone became far less frequent. Two of my cousins, being the wrong age and of the wrong religion were swept up in the first wave of internment. One spent one year in prison, the other two. Although neither became involved in paramilitary activity on their release, they and their families became even more alienated from the state. My aunt's and uncle's houses were raided by soldiers on several occasions. The atmosphere was one of constant fear and bitterness.

I was reminded of that fear and bitterness in 2013, when I was in Antrim for a large gathering of my husband's extended family. On one of the afternoons we took a walk inland up along a sunny river bank, the hedgerows heavy with autumn fruit, and I was delighted to encounter, for the first time, a geology of which I had often read – Antrim chalk and flint, the flints which we associate with the rich archaeological site of Mount Sandel, which were traded far and wide in prehistoric times. I hadn't known that the flint nodules are encased in a coating of denser chalk or of how extraordinarily brittle the flints are, how cleanly they shatter if dropped. We spent a while at a chalk face examining them. As we strolled back down towards the coast, we met an elderly man who was keen to chat. The conversation meandered on pleasantly for quite a while. Recognising our southern accents, he became more confident and asked us "Do you think that there will ever be a United Ireland?" We made some vague, noncommittal answer and then the conversation took a very different turn. Eventually, he said something that we found deeply shocking.

I wrote the following poem in an attempt to register the shock and also to understand what circumstances can make an ordinary citizen, with ordinary, family concerns, condone a vicious and brutal killing. I prefaced the poem with a quote from Simone Weil. In doing so I was thinking of all those extraordinary people from the north of Ireland who have suffered dreadful loss over the past fifty years, and yet who have not passed on the pain to others, who have often taken the risk, like Priam, of crossing the lines, of trusting where trust did not appear to be warranted. There are obvious heroes but there are also the people who worked behind the scenes, often at risk to their lives, in opening dialogue between bitterly opposed political parties. And most importantly of all, there are the very many ordinary people from beleaguered inner city or rural communities whose names we do not know, will never know, who kept faith with their neighbours on the other side of the sectarian divide, who "tholed it out."

My favourite Seamus Heaney poem, since hearing him read it at the height of the Troubles, is "Keeping Going," a tribute to those who took risks, who kept channels of communication open in small courageous ways even in the aftermath of horrific sectarian killings, refusing to be associated with those killings:

> You stay on where it happens. Your big tractor
> Pulls up at the Diamond, you wave at people,
> You shout and laugh above the revs, you keep
> Old roads open by driving on the new ones.

In the autumn of 2018, Northern Irish politics are at an impasse, with no functioning Executive, with internal political complexities being compounded by external complexities relating to Brexit. We can only hope that the experience of twenty years of peace, even an uneasy peace, will be enough to give political leaders the courage to make the compromises necessary for future generations to grow up without inheriting the pain of their parents and grandparents. The past was a terrible country and few want to go back there. I am reminded here again of the words of Denise Levertov, that indefatigable worker for peace in Vietnam:

> But peace, like a poem,
> is not there ahead of itself,
> can't be imagined before it is made,
> can't be known except
> in the words of its making,
> grammar of justice,
> syntax of mutual aid …

ANTRIM CONVERSATION

Pain and suffering are a kind of false currency passed from hand to hand until they meet someone who receives them but does not pass them on.

— Simone Weil

Chalk is stained brown near the waterfall.
It crumbles
away easily
as flint nodules are prised free;
the flint itself is poised
to split into slivers,
a suggestion of blades,
a memory of trade
this sharp wealth engendered.

The small, tidy man who paused on his stick
to talk to us in the lane,
on his Sunday of rose-hips and blackberries,
had a voice soft as chalk.
He spoke first of weather and houses and sheep,
of a life working *to put wee shoes on wee feet*
and we talked on and on in September sunshine
until nodules of hurt washed out
in the stream of his words.

He spoke of being shaken awake as a child
by uniformed men with guns;
of his own young son beaten up;
of prison, of *not knuckling under,*
and then of his satisfaction on hearing
a man's head had been blown off
in a neighbouring town.

History's hard cart rattled on
as flint nodules shattered
into narrow weapons.
We wounded, dumb,
what shift of bedrock,
what metamorphosis,
might heal such wounded,
wounding ground.

What do we know of the chalk,
the flint, of others' souls
or of our own
or of what might break in us,
if history's weight
pressed heavily down?

How do we know
that we could hold the pain
and not pass on
the false and brutal coin?

Moya Cannon was born in 1956 in Dunfanaghy, Co Donegal and now lives in Dublin. She holds degrees in History and Politics and in International Relations from, respectively, University College, Dublin and Corpus Christi College, Cambridge. She is the author of five collections of poetry, most recently Keats Lives *(Carcanet, 2015). A sixth collection from Carcanet Press is forthcoming in 2019. She is a member of Aosdána.*

THE BELFAST AGREEMENT:
A NOTE AND THREE POEMS

Harry Clifton

Clouds — and a logjam of historical forces.

Twenty years ago, when the Belfast Agreement was signed, I was living in the abstract space of exile known as Paris, and had been since 1994, in the August of which the IRA ceasefire had been declared. Coming back over the years, to the flat country of mid-Ulster I had married into in 1987, I saw the gradual dismantling of crisis-management structures, the apparat of oppression — the Toome barracks reverting to corrugated rust in the wind, the passing away of the night patrols, the flashlight through the driver's window on the way to or from a drink at a lonely lakeside pub. By the time I came home in 2004, the roads were clear. Only the drone of helicopters overhead spelt out the abnormality, the anachronism of a state like a logjam of trapped historical forces, unable to move forward, belonging to the past as East Germany once had. My first poem on returning, like a bad touchdown on the ground of family, marriage, politics, borrowed its title from another unworkable entity — North Korea.

Twenty years after the Agreement, I stand in a field of the family home on the shore of Lough Neagh, looking westward. Where am I? Europe? Ireland? Northern Ireland? Ulster? The Six Counties? Or some Kansas of the mind, haulage lorries barreling east and west, day and night, presided over, like God the Father, by the benign, bearded figure of the founder of Kentucky Fried Chicken, at every roundabout his Edward Hopper oasis of light in a stateless void. Or am I simply standing in a power vacuum, ominously calm, before the next thunderclap of collapsing Empire?

Invisibly, History reverts to Time. The man in the lonely lakeside bar no longer looks up anxiously when the door opens to see what face History wears today. Instead, with Beckettian deliberation, he applies himself to the diminishing glass of Time. A while back, leafing through a book of speeches by Michael D. Higgins, I found myself quoted in one given at Queen's University Belfast, a poem, "Deep Ulster," about just that reversion to the folk-rhythms beneath the nervosities of current Northern Irish politics, but most especially, as I stand here beneath wind and passing skies, of the slowness of any kind of weather, any kind of pastness, to slide east of Ballycastle headland and be gone.

Far to the west, beyond the watery sheen of Lough Neagh, are the Sperrins, that small mysterious mountain range in the middle of Ulster – ignored in itself, its east-west valleys and subsidences passed through perpetually, on the way somewhere else. Even Robert Lloyd Praeger, on his wanderings in search of the arctic cloudberry, was hardly detained. Nor did a more local cartographer of the spirit, Seamus Heaney, find space for those uplands in his writings. There they are though, an embodiment of Praeger's east-west reading of Irish wholeness, and his hatred of north-south rupture, embodied in the border. If, Belfast Agreement or not, Ireland ever becomes one as I guess pressures not tectonic may force it towards, it will be an Ireland like the Sperrins, of geography and weather, not history, where Praeger has finally found his sacred berry, and I too can feel at home in.

———

NORTH KOREA

Can I not build you a house in North Korea,
Fry you an eel in a heavy pan,
And pollan in season, off an inland sea
When our ship comes in? O my husband, O my man

Who failed in things the rest of the world understands –
Seventy miles to the north, as the crow flies
Through the battle-zones, is a never never land
Time forgot, where he who awakens dies....

On the shakiest bed that anyone ever made love in,
Under a horsehair blanket, while we mate,
I will kick out your lights forever

And leave you asleep, through the grey and terrible years
Of No Surrender, Mongols at the Gates,
With the faintest sound of a fife and drum in your ears.

DEEP ULSTER

It was here, the elemental centre,
All the time. Eternally present, repeating itself
Like seasons, where the times and dates
For swallows and household fires are written down,

The grouse are counted, the quotas of stocked rainbows.
All that love of order, for its own sake.
Only the hill-farms, and the high sheep country
Above politics – the enormous relief

Up there, as the dialect names of skies
Return, along with their clouds, and the old knowledge
Opens the mind again. To dream, to just potter
In the yard, to fiddle with local stations

In the kitchen, where news that is no news
Finally, at last, fills up the years
With pure existence. Lit from beneath
The fields are evenings long, the tree by the house

Where Vladimir and Estragon kept vigil
With the stillness of commando and insurgent
Frightens no-one. Slow through the air
A heron, shouldering aside the weight of the world,

Is making for its colonies, coevals
In a state plantation....
                    Nowhere but here
In the high right hand of Ireland, do the weather-fronts
Give way so slowly, to such ambivalent light.

PRAEGER

Robert Lloyd Praeger, 1865-1953

Before and after the age of borders,
With the Ordovician, the Carboniferous layers
Of the Sperrins (where else could you stand

So far back from Ireland, and still be in Ireland)
Settling east to west, not north to south,
You go about searching for the edible, the medicinal,

In a single berry. Sleeping in henhouses,
Feet sticking out through the window, roosters perched
On your boots, announcing the times to come.

Huge is the shade of uprightness, through the days
Forgotten now, in the forgotten mountains
Where a Field Club spreading out, in health and innocence

Calls to itself and fades, in a wilderness of stars
Winking like space stations, dissolving like a drone
Supersonic, into silence, lintels of smashed stone,

Abandoned valleys, grass of oblivion
Grown again over everything – and that single berry
Ireland obfuscates, your great unknown.

Harry Clifton was born in Dublin in 1952 and has travelled widely in Africa, Asia and Europe. He is the author of eight collections of poems, most recently Secular Eden: Paris Notebooks 1994-2004 *(Wake Forest University Press, 2004),* The Winter Sleep of Captain Lemass *(Bloodaxe, 2012) and* Portobello Sonnets *(Bloodaxe, 2017). He was the Ireland Chair of Poetry between 2010 and 2013, and continues to live in Dublin.*

THE TWO SOLITUDES

John Wilson Foster

And a vacant middle.

In the many months since Stormont was evacuated by our devolved government, the Good Friday Agreement (GFA) of 1998 has receded from the forefront of our attention with surprising and disturbing speed. It seems almost to belong to another era: events have simplified, accelerated, transmuted, and overtaken both 1998 and even 2017. From our recent and radically altered perspective, the Agreement now seems like an extraordinary Swiss-watch-like mechanism, as though an analogue solution to what has since become a digital problem.

Perhaps the Agreement's problem arose because the ingenious intricacy of the checks-and-balance mechanism was not equal to the contra-simplification of subsequent events. It was invented by committee, as it were, with the best of intentions, and meant to cover many political eventualities and shades of opinion. Moreover, the GFA presumed a coalition of the *sincerely* willing; the Ulster Unionist Party (UUP) and the Social Democratic and Labour Party (SDLP) were the ideal partners across the political divide. But over the years the reality degenerated (especially after the death of Ian Paisley, whose caricatural personality ironically held it all together after the Democratic Unionist Party eclipsed the UUP) into a coalition of the increasingly *un*willing. By dint of amiable personality Martin McGuinness, late of the IRA, at first played his new role winningly and for a few years we thought that at last we had come into harbour, albeit in a ship whose dazzle livery distracted us from the point of that livery: the war that hadn't gone away, you know. For a few heady years it seemed as if the cooperation sponsored by the GFA might even strengthen a Northern Irish identity that would satisfy both political and cultural traditions. In any case, McGuinness for whatever reason decided to scuttle the ship, which was listing badly in any case and not wholly due to him and his party. By doing so (and to mix metaphors), McGuinness let something out of the bottle that might be hard to get back in.

Sinn Féin (who eclipsed the SDLP) and the DUP had become forcibly conjoined twins seeking their diametrically opposed ways of life and something eventually had to give. Increasingly, policies and events became pretexts for advancing the long-haul project (Sinn Féin's core objective of a united Ireland) or obstructing that project (DUP). Effective day-to-day governance assumes a constitutional status quo (the GFA as an agreed terminus for the foreseeable future) and cannot proceed when endlessly motivated by thoughts of tomorrow (the GFA as a staging-post to the unification of the island).

The evacuation of Stormont has, of course, left a terrible vacuum. There is no alternative to the GFA on the near horizon: not direct rule from Westminster, not a united Ireland (despite the giddy talk of such), not Northern Ireland independence, not the simple majority rule of the rest of the United Kingdom. It is as if we are between dispensations, but know only what the past one consisted of. We are now at sea, a Lilliputian version of the dangerous between-times that W.B. Yeats recorded in "The Second Coming" (1919), though in his customary excited reverie.

Lilliputian, but still a version. The Northern Ireland Civil Rights campaign of 1968-69 was motivated by local grievances but given impetus by the Zeitgeist, by events in Paris and on American campuses, before forcibly morphing into a continuation of the Easter rebellion's unfinished business. During the Stormont hiatus (to use an optimistic word), republicans are agitating for a border poll. Beside the prospect of a united Ireland, a return to Stormont, at least at the present moment, must seem to them small beer. The real trigger has been Brexit, of course. Yet even Brexit is both honouring as well as fuelling the Zeitgeist since it is part of a European convulsion that encompasses more than the United Kingdom's vote to leave the European Union. And the influence of a volatile Zeitgeist makes it more difficult to bring more immediate and proximate concerns into focus, distracting stakeholders with the lure of bigger game. Can the regional problem of Northern Ireland be solved in isolation when the big world beyond it is itself riven on such a large scale?

There is a restiveness in Northern Ireland, in the UK, in the United States, in Europe. And vast though the western world is, this restlessness is larger than the sum of specific discontents and grievances, which involve mass immigration, multiculturalism, the spread of Islam, the sudden seeming instability or inadequacy of democracy. There is a drunkenness of things being various. I recall a phrase from C.P. Snow's 1954 novel, *The New Men*, set during World War Two: "events too big for men." It seems an apt recall, for there is a sense of things in the West being out of control:

dispensations ending and only the ominously slouching outline of the new.

Under these influences, the two "communities" in Northern Ireland, the unionist and the nationalist, have polarised politically in an almost literal sense: each side magnetically drawn back to its pole of origin and aspiration. The UUP and SDLP are in the long grass. Against the grain of history, Irish nationalism and Irish republicanism are converging. Unmoored by the interlocking obligations of the GFA, the two sides in Ulster have drifted even farther apart, the law of the excluded middle becoming more draconian. This is not, yet, thankfully, a social polarisation among the middle classes but that could still come if the political pathology metastasises. We are in danger of becoming two solitudes, at least as political collectives, though I hope not as friends, neighbours and workmates.

Two Solitudes. Hugh MacLennan published his novel of that title in 1945, and through his main characters he tracked relations in Quebec between the majority French-Canadians on the one hand and on the other hand the English-Canadians, a ruling minority in Quebec but a ruling majority in Canada as a whole, and both founding cultures of the nation. The historical homology with Ireland, especially the north of Ireland, is for the most part striking. The problem of Two Solitudes essentially arose at roughly the same time in each country: the early 17th century. In *Two Solitudes*, MacLennan's Quebecois are Catholic, rural and agricultural, nationalistic, conservative, and determinedly French-speaking; his English-speaking Quebeckers are urban, progressive, industrialised and capitalist. The foreground denouement of the saga, with its modicum of optimism, is also familiar: what we call a mixed marriage (called that even in the novel) between the Quebecois youth (French father though Irish mother) and English-Canadian girl, though both are preceded by parents or grandparents who have in a sense courageously, and alone, crossed the sectarian divide.

Two Solitudes is set across three generations from the Great War to the onset of the Second World War. MacLennan closes his novel with the hope that the war will bring the two sides together, somehow dissolving "the two race-legends . . . remembering their ancient enmities." MacLennan imagined that the country Canada was about to know itself for the first time, becoming a "super-group" in Amy Chua's recent formulation when she talks about national entities that can claim the allegiance of opposing tribes. It didn't happen. The dreary tribal steeples of both Quebec and Fermanagh survived the war; indeed, the Second World War drove a wedge between the two Irelands and conscription was a bone of contention in both provinces, Quebec and Northern Ireland.

Yet in an historical unfolding we might do well to take note of, the Quiet Revolution of the 1960s saw a sharp decline in the power of the Roman Catholic Church in Quebec which was followed by (and perhaps in part released) a surge in Quebec nationalism. Despite the previous intimacy between Catholicism and nationalism, the latter had a clearer run when its intimate was out of the picture. The nationalist surge compelled the two border polls (sovereignty referenda) in 1980 (in which independence was rejected by 59.5% of the voters) and 1995 (rejected by 50.5%). The campaigns and the years between were divisive and disturbing. No "Quebec City Agreement" or "Bon Vendredi Accord" conjoined the two solitudes. Instead, the problem was solved by an epic of social engineering that dissolved one of the two Solitudes, freeing the remaining Solitude from fear. It was contrived by Pierre Elliott Trudeau, Quebecois-Scots father of the current Canadian prime minister.

Likewise, the decline of the Catholic Church in Ireland has not weakened nationalism, though Catholicism was long thought to be with the Gaelic language an essential girder of Irish nationalism. Once upon a time, Home Rule did indeed mean Rome Rule (the Ulster Protestants were proved absolutely correct when they asserted that and nowhere have I seen that acknowledged), but that is no longer an argument against unification. If anything, Irish republicanism has strengthened, clarified and become more assertive and sophisticated, no longer held back by what has proved to be a wounded Church; indeed, able to promote itself as a reasonable, progressive, secular force. The aim, however, remains the same: imminent unification of the island.

Trudeau's remedy to end the Two Solitudes was to impose (I believe the verb justified) multiculturalism on what is called the Rest of Canada (RoC) while permitting Quebec to opt out of the policy and impositions of multiculturalism and to retain control of its immigration. A Quebec legate told me in 1993 that Quebec would never accept multiculturalism and so it has proved. The province replaced the Canadian bilingualism legislation of 1969 with the Quebec Official Language Act of 1974, reinforcing official French unilingualism with the Charter of the French Language of 1977. Quebec sovereignty aspirations have indeed subsided as Trudeau wished, but that is because Quebec is allowed to conduct itself in several vital respects like an independent country and today is quietly de-Anglicising in a manner than would have warmed the cockles of Douglas Hyde's heart in 1892. Meanwhile, the RoC, through planned mass immigration from non-traditional cultures, is trumpeted as a pioneering and completely successful multicultural society. The aim is, in the ostensible cause of harmony across the country, to dissipate the European, and especially British, identity of Canada (the other Solitude) and *hey presto!* the Two Solitudes are no more. In fact, the Two Solitudes remain, save that one of those Solitudes is increasingly composed of a hundred solitudes. (Indeed, the jury is out, and there is an intense dispute largely on social media, on whether Canada is indeed a successful, happy and coherent multicultural society.)

Quebec proves that its nationalism does not need its historical intimate, the Catholic Church, and that language is a more important driver of its ethno-nationalism. The licence-plate on every Quebec automobile proclaims *Je me souviens*. The memory of defeat and the aspiration to independence survive secularism. They may even have survived significant multiculturalism. That anyway seems to be the lesson of the Republic of Ireland which has managed thus far, unlike Quebec, to combine a sincere desire to become a multicultural society (though chiefly a European one) with no lessening of patriotism or of the nationalist desire for completion of the republican project, a 32-county independent state, that is identical to its 1916 and 1922 selves except in so far as that state would be an EU member. (Whether in the eventuality of a 32-county republic Ireland would be as dutiful a subscriber to the EU doctrine of ever-closer union is a moot point.)

But multiculturalism (a largely improvised affair unlike the Canadian policy) is no more an answer to Irish unity as we imagine it today (unionists and nationalists reconciling in an Irish republic) than it is to Canadian unity (French and Anglo-Canadians intertwined and intertwining with other ethnicities). Northern Irish Protestants (who regard themselves as a "founding" culture) do not come in under the umbrella of Irish multiculturalism any more than the Quebecois come in under the umbrella of Canadian multiculturalism. Neither group is sincerely invited to and neither wishes to. The lesson from Quebecois nationalism for Irish nationalism is that Northern Ireland must have its identity diffused through multiculturalism and immigration; Irish as an official language in Northern Ireland would advance immeasurably the republican project, and both strategies would loosen Northern Ireland's cultural and constitutional ties with the rest of the United Kingdom just as multiculturalism has loosened

Canada's cultural ties with the UK and indeed with its own history as a senior dominion of the British Empire. Through it all, Irish like Quebec nationalism will persevere. They are not for turning.

That one can think like this is evidence of the flux at work in western societies. There is an impatience that generates scenarios and wishes to see them reach development quickly. The Good Friday Agreement by contrast was a painstakingly constructed bulwark or bridge combining enough flexibility, it seemed, to absorb vicissitudes and with an intensely local applicability. But we may be beyond the local and merely vicissitudinous now. I believe the GFA's restoration to full working order and in sincerity on the part of the main parties is an outside chance, at least in the current swirl of politics inside and outside Northern Ireland. The new tribalism that Amy Chua identifies in the United States is old tribalism here and is if anything recently refreshed. Also, it may be that a disaffection with a government structure that compels the coalition of enemies and does not provide for the genuine opposition of parliamentary politics is too great to reverse.

What is required for the GFA to be restored is not the undignified triumphalism of the demographic contest (we witness it aghast during Brexit), now played with vim by some northern nationalists, but something alas quite alien to the current political climate.

At present, that something has no voice and has not had a voice for a long time. We suffer here the tyranny of a threadbare political discourse that dominates the public sphere and drowns out other discourses. Certainly we have a fine literature, but between it and the banal discourse of our politics there is a vacant middle. We need the literary discourse of the individual: the discourse of memoir, diary, letter that interrupts the "smelly little orthodoxies" Orwell referred to at the end of his wonderful essay on Dickens. Moreover, we need not only candid conversations between acquaintances from opposite sides of the divide ("whatever you say, say nothing" can be shackling as well as prudent advice) but to have those multiple conversations eventually rise to the surface of our public and social life, to end our enactment of the Two Solitudes. E.M. Forster's "Only connect" might be a sovereign remedy applicable not only to the uneasy silences between strangers and even friends on the constitutional predicament but also to the disconnect between on the one hand individual opinions and feelings about Northern Ireland's past, present and future and on the other the tired elementary political choices they are offered. This is a version of a gulf between the private and public, and in Northern Ireland we have often been afraid to say in public what we really feel or think; it is often fear of our own tribe. This is an Irish form of political correctness whereby you cannot say publicly what you are thinking or feeling rather than saying in public what you are *not* thinking or feeling. There are Northern Irish Catholics (perhaps many) who are happy enough in the UK but cannot say so because of a tribal injunction. (Then there are all those Irish correspondents and presenters working for the BBC and living in England who have no public opinion on English-Irish relations because the tribal injunction crosses the water.) There are middle-class and professional unionists who can contemplate a united Ireland and some have said so, because the tribal injunction on their side is rather weaker. There are many more middle-class and professional unionists who cannot admit their unionism out of misplaced fear of being identified with tribal loyalists (though clearly many of them vote DUP). All in all, an unhealthy repression that aids the hegemony of political fundamentalism and sponsors the Two Solitudes.

The GFA tried in its own way to complicate in a mature way an otherwise simplistic political picture but did so through a complexity of political machinery and left untouched the moral maturity we also need. Orwell said of Dickens that in every attack he makes upon society "he is always pointing to a change of spirit rather than a change of structure"; "it is useless to change institutions without a 'change of heart'." Thinking at first that this is a conservative opinion, Orwell came to see that it carries its own revolutionary potential. The Good Friday Agreement was a radical change of structure but if there was a radical change of heart, an essential moral repositioning on the part of the chief participants, over time it reversed itself. Indeed, if anything the morality of our society, of our polity, of our interpretations of the past and actions in the present, has shriveled even more since then. A change of heart requires the exercise of empathy (feeling as well as seeing the other's experience and point of view – the source of Dickens's mastery), something in short supply where we live. In the past forty-odd years I have seen the antinomianism, as Orwell calls it, the "native decency of the common man," the "bourgeois morality" Orwell discerned and after raising an eyebrow allowed himself to admire in Dickens, stifled amidst the aridities of power politics, not only in Northern Ireland but in the UK generally, but in Northern Ireland also as the legacy of a terror campaign now retrospectively justified by its perpetrators.

The Good Friday Agreement was a remarkable machine, motivated in its planning and development by a behaviourist (and forgivably rather patronising) notion of stimulus and reward. Alas the politicians misbehaved; the adults in the room were too few. As things stand, the GFA might be reactivated but unless there is a change of heart in Orwell's Dickensian sense, it will fail again and Arthur Koestler's ghost in the machine will reassert itself. I fully believe that only when Northern Ireland is through honest effort made to work (and the innate but inadequately voiced moderateness of the majority of the Northern Irish should be the exploited motive for that) can there be an agreed avenue to possible constitutional change: and who knows, perhaps a united Ireland. The strands of the Agreement offer that avenue. Monumentally, in an act of maturity, Sinn Féin must publicly postpone their destabilising call for an imminent united Ireland in favour of minding the store in which they find themselves, the here and now. If you like, they need to declare a ceasefire in their brittle demand for the endgame which lies outside the evolutionary spirit of the GFA. Otherwise, they are extending the lifetime of the Two Solitudes and the social as well as political stuntedness they maintain.

John Wilson Foster was born in Belfast in 1942 and educated at Queen's University and the University of Oregon. His recent publications include Pilgrims of the Air: The Passing of the Passenger Pigeons *(New York Review Books, 2017),* Irish Novels, 1890-1940: New Bearings in Culture and Fiction *(Oxford University Press, 2008) and* Between Shadows: Modern Irish Writing and Culture *(Irish Academic Press, 2009). He is a Senior Research Fellow, Queen's University Belfast and Professor Emeritus, University of British Columbia. He lives in Portaferry, Co Down.*

THE BELFAST AGREEMENT
AND OTHER OXYMORONS

—

Edna Longley

Working the living stream.

As well as feeling freed up, I felt angry also. The quarter century we have lived through was a terrible black hole, and the inestimable suffering inflicted and endured by every party to the conflict has only brought the situation to a point that is politically less promising than things were in 1968.

— Seamus Heaney, "Cessation 1994"

Is it The "Good Friday" Agreement or The "Belfast" Agreement? I prefer the secular version. As with "Easter Rising," the Christian calendar can sanctify a political event and thus pre-empt necessary revision. Not that Good Friday, a step back from Easter, seems an auspicious prefix. The Agreement's great success was to move this society away from violence. But has it moved us beyond the conditions that bred violence, beyond any desire to crucify the Other? Given Brexit-induced turbulence, Anna Burns' "Troubles" novel *Milkman* is a timely warning. Burns recreates a dark "psycho-political atmosphere," receding but yet to be exorcised. We still have "peace walls." We still have punishments behind closed doors and closed mouths. And I always see as symptomatic the Executive's inability to co-write a document called "A Shared Future": a failure both of cognition and volition. Perhaps the Agreement should have been signed on All Souls Day to keep all "Lost Lives" in mind.

I retain some TV images from that tense time in 1998: Jeffrey Donaldson dithering in a car park; the hopeful faces of the Women's Coalition; the Progressive Unionists prematurely declaring that unprogressive Unionism was over. But my clearest personal memory, after the deal had been struck, is of meeting Robin Wilson in the street. Robin, former editor of *Fortnight*, compulsive political thinker and think-tanker, go-to guru as regards politics anywhere (everybody should meet him in the street), clouded my optimism by pointing to a contradiction in the

Agreement. He said that, owing to its "consociational" premise, the Agreement would freeze the binary of Orange and Green, and thus preclude the fluid politics it was meant to foster. Twelve years later Robin published his weighty study: *The Northern Ireland Experience of Conflict and Agreement: A Model for Export?* You can guess his answer.

The structures set up by the Agreement institutionalised two group-identities. As it turned out – perhaps logically – a deal built on the middle ground, on an idea that "community relations" could ultimately be transformed, came to be implemented by the extremes. Politicians who appealed across the "divide" might make modest gains, but would never be winners in a zero-sum game. Entrenching incompatible "aspirations" has also prevented agreement from turning into settlement – into pragmatic politics – although I take comfort from the increasing numbers who neutrally identify as "northern Irish;" who resist the notion that "identity" can be conceived in group-terms or singular terms. Yet, despite the Agreement's contradictions and Stormont's failings, most of us believe that contradiction is better than conflict. We have witnessed changes in policing; slow shifts in civil society (where more and more sharing occurs, even if most schools remain geared to delivering binary voters); the rebooting of Belfast for tourism and gastronomy. Even so, the "Friendly! Dynamic! Various!" city – to quote an ironical poem by Leontia Flynn – parties on a fault line. Belfast still does not agree with itself. Perhaps we have got too used to peace as formerly to war. And the Stormont dis-Agreement shows that contradiction has become ominously toxic at the political level.

The *New Princeton Dictionary of Poetry and Poetics* defines "oxymoron" as "a figure of speech that yokes together two seemingly contradictory elements, a form of condensed paradox." Examples given by the *Dictionary* include Horace's "*concordia discors rerum*," Shakespeare's "Mis-shapen chaos of well-seeming forms," and Milton's hellish "darkness visible." As for Irish poetry: more directly apt to our situation over the years is the way in which Yeats's "terrible beauty" became Heaney's "neighbourly murder." There is also MacNeice on Belfast in *Autumn Journal*: "his hope/ The other man's damnation." Outside poetry, one might add oxymorons like "peace wall," "Belfast Agreement," "Northern Ireland Executive," "Titanic Boat Tours."

Oxymoron marks a divide, a chasm, but might prompt a bridge – as between MacNeice's "incompatible" snow and roses. Oxymoron sits between *either/or* and *both/and*. Before the Agreement, there was a bustle of cultural preparation in the latter direction. "Cultural traditions," and their interpenetration, were exhaustively explored on an archipelagic as well as local basis. This body of work grows, just as admirable community-relations work continues; but with the main Stormont parties paying scant attention to either. Peace has not been a "process" that continually informs the Executive's conduct. Belfast City Council, probably because it lacks a clear majority, does a better job. One depressing aspect of the current stand-off is that the Irish language has again been "weaponised" (as has opposition to it). It's as if the progress on language-sharing, achieved by activists like the much-missed Aodán Mac Póilin, goes for nothing. And who knew that same-sex marriage was so important to Irish nationalism? During this political hiatus there is much talk of "respect." Economic gaps and power-gaps having (mostly) closed, it may seem necessary to prove that the Green/ Orange gap is actually infinite: both an empyrean of aspiration and a black hole, an oxymoronic chasm. Back in the day, I wrote that "parity of esteem" was less urgent than parity of disesteem. Of course, since 1998, culture-war has often been a surrogate field of engagement. That includes the battle over "legacy": a euphemism for rival attempts to control the narrative of "the past." This is "culture" pressed back into the political binary. To quote Derek Mahon: "The bigots shrieking for their beleaguered 'culture'."

Crucial to the Belfast Agreement was prior agreement between the governments of the UK and the Irish Republic. That, with the further backstop of the EU, has been the potential long-term solvent of our binary politics: of British/ Irish as an oxymoron. I may not be obeying the brief for this issue of *Irish Pages*. The editor (rightly) wanted personal reflection not political rant. But, *à propos* civil war and its aftermath, the personal is the political in a holistic sense. The autobiographical is the political. My own family is Irish/ Scottish/ English, South/ North, Protestant/ Catholic. Since 1998 we have all been able to relax; even if, rather than Northern Ireland becoming more like the rest of the world, the rest of the world has become more like Northern Ireland (something else I have said before). Most relevantly, the English have discovered the joys of binary politics. To quote Rafael Behr, writing in *Prospect*: "Our democratic debate is descending into shrill, angry and tribal shouting matches." Sounds familiar. Irish Anglophiles have been appalled. Irish Anglophobes have said: "I told you so." Brexit scarily threatens the hard-won relaxation of physical and metaphysical borders. It also keeps a return to Stormont on hold. The only hope is that, this time, contradiction or paradox – the Catch-22 of the Irish border – might come to the rescue.

For me, the border issue confirms what I have long thought: if the Northern Irish question is not very simple (binary), then it is very complex indeed. That's where poetry comes in. Poetry from this part of the world constantly sets its own complexity of language, image and form, its subversions of "identity," against binary structures. Witness Paul Muldoon's optimistic post-Agreement parable-poem "Whitethorns." Here "paling posts," hammered into the ground "more than thirty years ago … to keep our oats from Miller's barley," become: "maxed-out multilayered whitethorns … under which we now sit down to parley." In fact, the Agreement's intricacy has caused it to be compared to poetry. Rick Wilford, editor of *Aspects of the Belfast Agreement* (2001), refers to "the subtleties and complexities of its design." The term "creative ambiguity" recurs. But perhaps creative ambiguity has passed its sell-by date. Perhaps this is an oxymoron that now marks a chasm more than a bridge. The stark outline of the original paling posts is all too obvious within the Agreement's "multi-layered" whitethorns.

Yet – to indulge in some wishful thinking – poetry itself offers models that might take us further. Genuinely "dynamic" and "various" (Flynn), it has richer "creative" means at its disposal. Syntax and rhythm configure oxymoron with other structures of complication. In Yeats's "Easter, 1916," the "stone" of fixed opinion encounters the pulse of life, the pulse of the poem itself. This "living stream" potentially erodes the iconic oxymoronic stasis of "terrible beauty." Similarly, Michael Longley's sonnet "Ceasefire" situates the oxymoron of "kiss" and "kill" within a slow, somehow hugely burdened rhythm, which symbolises a movement of the human spirit.

Edna Longley was born in Cork in 1940, the daughter of mathematics professor T. S. Broderick and a Scottish Presbyterian mother. She attended Trinity College, Dublin, where her contemporaries included the poets Michael Longley, Derek Mahon and Eavan Boland. After her marriage to Michael Longley, she moved with him to Belfast and obtained her first teaching post at Queen's University Belfast. She is the author of six books of literary criticism and editor of many others, most recently Multiculturalism: The View from the Two Irelands *(with Declan Kiberd, Cork University Press, 2001) and* Edward Thomas: The Annotated Collected Poems *(Bloodaxe, 2008). Now Emerita Professor of English at the Seamus Heaney Centre for Poetry, she continues to live in Belfast.*

GONE SOUTH

—

Iggy McGovern

As any sinner knows.

According to *Dictionary.com*, to "go south" means to vanish or abscond, probably deriving from the mid-nineteenth century American notion of disappearing *south* to Mexico or Texas to escape pursuit or responsibility.

When I left Northern Ireland in 1978, I was no OTR nor did I feel that I owed any specific responsibility to nation or country (neither internee nor informer, as Seamus Heaney has it in his poem *Exposure*); I went south for the oldest of reasons, a permanent job.

En route I had earned the all-important BTA (Been To America), the then *sine qua non* for the aspiring science academic; but this mid-western stopover also served as a necessary 2-year quarantine, a timewarp bridging The New University of Ulster (NUU) and The College of the Holy and Undivided Trinity of Queen Elizabeth near Dublin (or Trinity for short).

This year the former (now incorporated into UU) celebrates fifty years of existence, while the latter sees that and raises it another three hundred and seventy-six. And yet, both have their roots in The Reformation: Trinity is possibly the first university to have a mission statement – to save Ireland from Popery – while the choice of Coleraine (over Derry-Londonderry) for Northern Ireland's second university joined a long list of Catholic grievance.

Trinity provided this Nordie with the safe space to reason out my feelings (what else could they be?) about my birthright. I could be confident that no member of the Arts faculty would lead a mob through the Front Gate – as had happened in NUU in 1974! And the place had a strangely-comforting whiff of tame Britishness about it (viz. the nods to "Elizabetha" and "Carolo" in the Latin grace after meat).

Through subsequent decades of filial visits north, I mumbled my own measured grace at British Army checkpoints. My southern wife took perverse pleasure in my inability to give coherent answers to the statutory "where are you from, where are you going?" I shall always remember one such early visit, sitting in a pub in Coleraine when the TV continuity interrupted with the news flash that the hunger strikes had ended; the lengthy silence that followed was finally broken by a lone barfly with his gnomic "That's that, then."

Possibly, I was thinking along similar lines when the Good Friday Agreement was announced. If I was, I kept it to myself. I have a poor record on predictions, notably my declaration to a divided Berlin that their wall would still be there long after the North was resolved.

So, like most of the South, I allowed myself to be swept along in the consensus that this Agreement was a very good thing, closing my ears to the warnings of Mary Robinson and others that it was only institutionalising sectarianism. The Reformation was writ large in this new Ten (at least) Commandments but any sinner knows that this sort of legalese is easily subverted, and indeed openly invites subversion. Two decades on it is clear that what is badly needed is a healthy dose of The Beatitudes.

A poet and physicist, Ignatius McGovern was born in Coleraine in 1948. He received a PhD in Physics from Queen's University Belfast and has taught at the Universities of Pennsylvania and Wisconsin. He has published three collections of poetry, The King of Suburbia *(Dedalus Press, 2005),* Safe House *(Dedalus Press, 2010), and* A Mystic Dream of 4 *(Quaternia Press, 2013) – the latter a sonnet sequence based on the life of the Irish mathematician William Rowan Hamilton. He is currently Professor and Fellow Emeritus in the School of Physics, Trinity College, Dublin.*

WRITERS OF BELFAST

—

Art Hughes

Proud of Belfast.

*(The following introduction and address was given at the opening of Neil Shawcross'
exhibition,* Writers of Belfast, *at the Titanic Centre, Belfast, on Tuesday 23 October
2018. See "Portfolio" for a selection of the work exhibited.)*

Lord Mayor, Ladies and Gentlemen, I extend a warm welcome, one and all,
to this, the latest in a long, impressive line of major exhibitions over the
years by our honorand this evening, the artist Neil Shawcross.

I should like to begin by mentioning some people behind the scenes, in
particular the vital part played by Michael McCann, over the last three
years, in driving this exhibition forward – *Maith thú, a Mhicheáil!,* "Well
done Michael." I also thank the City Council for their support of this
imaginative, far-sighted and momentous project, with a special word of
thanks due to Emer Henry from the Belfast City Council for all her
considerable efforts. In response to *What has the City Council ever done for me?,*
just take a look around you! This exhibition is a landmark acknowledgement
of literary Belfast. A glance around the walls here in the Belfast Titanic
Centre will tell us that *Writers of Belfast* is a world-class exhibition.

Neil Shawcross was always going to be an artist. His mother saw to it
by sending himself and his twin brother, Tony, to art school from an early
age in his native Lancashire. Neil had got to know young people from Belfast
from his student years, working in hotels in the summer season on the Isle
of Man. After graduation, Neil was offered a job in the "Art College" in
Belfast. Luckily, it was not the major form-filling exercise of today, and a
simple cover letter from Neil in the year 1960 was enough to acquire for
this city the services of one of the most accomplished artists in these islands.

As a testament to his distinguished teaching career, anytime one
mentions the name of Neil Shawcross to a past student a smile immediately
comes to their face and this, surely, speaks volumes. Many of his former
protégés have, of course, gone on to greater things as artists in their own
right under Neil's insightful tutelage and endless encouragement. In
addition to the "Art College," Neil also taught in the Lyric Theatre and in

various primary schools over many years. His long and varied career as tutor apart, Neil also continued unabated as an individual artist, potent, prolific and powerful. It must also be said that he has generously, yet quietly, donated many artworks to a number of worthy charitable causes over the years. I should point out, however, that if any art dealers are selling a painting signed "Shawcross" that contains the colour purple, then it's probably a fake.

I have been fortunate to know Neil for the best part of 20 years. I was appointed to the Belfast Campus of the University of Ulster to lecture in Gaelic Language and Literature in 1999, and on one of the first mornings in, Neil met me waiting for the lift. He asked if he could paint my portrait and also invited me for coffee. For the next ten years or so, we had coffee four mornings a week during term time in Neil's office on D Floor, where local artist, Paddy McCann, supplied the almond croissants. It would have been five mornings a week except that Neil, for many decades now, has gone swimming every Wednesday in Strangford Lough – hail, rain, snow or blow. When asked in recent years by his doctor if he ever considered having a flu jab, Neil glibly informed him that he been taking fifty a year, in the form of his weekly dip in Strangford Lough.

From his swimming and luncheons (not forgetting his tennis and scrabble sessions), it can be seen that Neil Shawcross plays hard. It must also be added, however, that he works even harder! Not a single day goes by but that Neil Shawcross is involved with his art. Indeed, one is reminded of the motto of the New York Art Students' League: *Nulla dies sine linea!* "No day without a line!" This was how Pliny the Elder, who perished in the aftermath of the eruption at Pompey in 79 AD, recalled for us the otherwise lost work of Greek painter Appeles (Ἀπελλῆς) from the Island of Kos in the fourth century BC – an artist who also knew and painted for Alexander the Great.

Neil Shawcross can be regarded as one of the few artists throughout history who have actually heeded and strictly adhered to the maxim *Nulla dies sine linea!* "No day without a line!" He is not only a gifted and remarkable artist but also a tireless worker and ceaseless practitioner. Shawcross may be said to live, breath and encapsulate art.

Leaving aside his art and sporting activities, Neil is also a very well-read and rounded man: an avid reader, an *aficionado* of music, and a film buff to name but a few of the many further strings to his well-rosined bow. It is, then, most apt that he should chose as the subject-matter for the current exhibition, paintings of book covers from the work of Belfast authors. Many of the authors on these walls, it would appear, may also have heeded the advice *Nulla dies sine linea,* "No day without a line." These three-dozen or so literary works on display here are associated with Belfast. Most are in the English language, but, and significantly, two are in Irish – an important inclusion given the Gaelic background of Belfast and many of it place-names: *Béal Feirste*, "The Mouth, or Approach, to the Sandbar," Shankill (*Seanchill,* "The Old Church"); Falls *(An Fál,* "The Hedged Enclosure"); or Stranmillis *(An Sruthán Milis,* "The Sweet Stream.")

Belfast as a city is known for the Titanic, the Yard, the Docks, the Blitz, the Troubles, Van Morrison, love, tension, desperation, hope and a lot more. All human life and experience is present here. Despite the ups and downs, I consider Belfast a great city. I was glad to be born and brought up here and I am proud of Belfast. Its warmth, humour and people make it a special place, as do, of course, its authors and performers.

Part of Neil's rationale behind this project is to donate these paintings to Belfast City for this and future generations. This magnanimous gesture, of itself, sums up the generosity and largesse of this illustrious artist and even greater humane man. The collection *Writers of Belfast* represents Neil Shawcross' unique celebration (on-seven foot high canvasses, it must be added) of a selection of works penned by some of Belfast's most renowned sons and daughters, or works of authors who have lived and worked here, such as Padraic Fiacc, or Nobel Laureate Seamus Heaney. The literary legacy of Belfast received a recent boost with the award of the 2018 Booker Prize – mentioning no names – to Ardoyne author, Anna Burns' *Milkman.* This substantial and ever-growing Belfast literary legacy needs to be highlighted and this Shawcross exhibition not only celebrates, but showcases and enshrines it in perpetuity.

A further aspiration of Neil's – and one that I can whole-heartedly endorse in the fullest terms possible – is that the entire collection should be housed in a future Museum of Belfast. We surely need a city-centre museum, where locals, visitors, schools, colleges, community groups and individuals can have access to a museum specifically devoted to the evolution of Belfast through the ages. For example, if the site of the old *Belfast Telegraph* may no longer be a centre for the production of daily news, this marvellous Shawcross collection could surely give it new stories to tell: the stuff of headlines, history and legacy.

It is a great honour for me to open this exhibition this evening and to have an opportunity to publically express to my dear friend Neil Shawcross, on behalf of my fellow citizens, just how proud and grateful we all are for all that he has done for Belfast City for over nigh on sixty years in his own inimitable, exquisite, grand-scale, unique, brilliant, caring, unstinting and modest way.

A further hope and aspiration is that this exhibition does actually find the permanent home it deserves in a soon-to-emerge Museum of Belfast City and, in finding such a home, it will help inform future generations that this was the literature and creativity that Belfast was capable of producing. Any city in the world would be proud of such an exhibition, but few can hope to produce or rival it.

Furthermore, this exhibition can also import to the viewer that among some of the finest people to ever settle here, raise a family (with the love of his life, Marge), and call Belfast their home, there was a humble lad, with a boundless talent, tireless drive and wonderful insight from Lancashire, called *Neil Shawcross!*

Art Hughes was born in the New Lodge Road area of Belfast in 1960 and was educated at St Malachy's College. He holds degrees from Queen's University Belfast and Université de Rennes. He is the author or editor of 18 books, including Rí Thoraí: The King of Tory *(Ben Madigan Press, 2018),* The Great Irish Verb Book *(Ben Madigan Press, 2008) and* Robert Shipboy MacAdam: His Life, Times and Gaelic Proverb Collection *(The Institute of Irish Studies, 1998). An occasional presenter of Irish-language documentaries on the BBC and RTÉ, he is currently Reader in Irish, Ulster University, and still lives in Belfast.*

A DAY IN DUBLIN

Gerard McCarthy

Moments of reprieve.

I drove in to Sligo Station in the early morning darkness. There were slivers of light as the train headed east. I was looking through the book that I had brought with me. It was a book of photographs of the universe. Sometimes I looked out the window. The colours in the photographs mirrored the colours outside in the brightening sky. In the carriage opposite me there was a man with a book whose title I saw: *Change Your Life in Seven Days.*

In Dublin, when the train stopped at Connolly Station, I walked quickly to Stephen's Green where a Luas train was waiting. It brought me along Harcourt Street, through Charlemont. Coming into Ranelagh, my ticket was checked by a woman from Africa. I saw her chatting afterwards on the platform with a man in a similar uniform, who looked to be Caucasian. The train carried on through Milltown, and it seemed in no time at all that we passed over the new bridge into Dundrum. The precincts of my childhood: it used to be called a village; the main street was now reduced almost to a facade with a by-pass behind it. It put me in mind of a film set. The church seemed the only thing unchanged. I carried on past it to the vast new shopping centre that has appropriated the name, Dundrum Town Centre: a consumerist cathedral where I paid my brief dues. I retreated with relief to the main street of the village. My feet drew me in to the church. Inside, I stood at the back remembering a period past that remains only in the memory of a store of people that is steadily diminishing. The church was almost empty: a few figures, who looked as if they had reached their final furlong, were sitting separately, silently praying. Laconic sounds were echoing. There was a woman spraying the flowers on the altar. Behind her the window had a picture of the crucifixion, and above it a bearded man, who did not now look old to me. He was holding a book or a tablet, with the letters Alpha and Omega. On a side altar, there was a shrine with candles. I was searching for where to put my coin when a woman came up to show me where to put it, in the security of the wall. I lit one candle, for memory. I remembered reluctant adolescent Sundays, standing just inside the side door, then increasingly going no further than the porch, barely going through the motions, before abandoning it in disaffection. A Dundrum childhood was giving way to a complex urban world where the image of the self that was growing up into it was too much constituted by the imagined estimation of others. On my way out, there was an old woman in the porch who was telling another woman of her medical complications. They made their exit. I followed them, dipping my hand in a bowl of holy water. On the way back in to the city, at Milltown the train passed over the Nine Arches. Looking down at the Dropping Well pub in the valley below, I remembered late one night a long time ago, walking along there on my way home, looking up above the dark deserted arches at the moon appearing and disappearing behind the racing clouds. A moment of youthful resolve. A glimpse of authenticity.

Back in the centre I was drawn in to Stephen's Green by the sound, then sight of a few followers of Hare Krishna, padding along with bells and chanting. Two young children with faces painted were walking beside them. The lead man was smiling and enthusiastically greeting the impassive observers on their park benches as he passed them. A group of young men and women gardeners were languidly working in a bed of blood-red flowers. As I walked down Grafton Street and into Westmoreland Street, there was a young blind man in front of me, flailing his stick widely, sometimes causing others to jump out of his way. He was giving his full energy to it, marking carefully the many obstacles with his stick. It wasn't until O'Connell Bridge that I approached him and guided him across to the beginning of the central aisle. My gladness about making a gesture of good will was tempered by a doubt about whether he fully appreciated the intrusion on his determined independence. I let him go on ahead of me and waited under the monument to Daniel O'Connell until he had disappeared. I looked up, for the first time giving the monument a proper scrutiny. The figure of O'Connell seemed lost above a circle of allegorical figures. All I could properly see was the bird perched on top of his head. The birds that make no fine distinction between the monuments of the human world.

I walked up the centre of O'Connell street. The next statue was of the nationalist, William Smith O' Brien. He was a diffident leader of the abortive rebellion that was attempted in 1848. He was convicted of treason, and was sentenced to be hanged, drawn and quartered. The sentence was commuted to exile on an island south of Australia, called after a European: Van Diemen's Land. Close by Smith O'Brien's statue was the statue of Sir John Gray, whose plinth proclaims that it was pre-eminently through his exertions that Vartry water supply was introduced to the city. Next was the statue of Jim Larkin across the road from Clery's, with his hands held aloft, and the quote beneath him: "The great appear great because we are on our knees."

The Spire was alone among the monuments on the street in not being the figure of a human with a story, dressed in antique clothes. A monument without memory: it was erected there as a replacement for the pillar that had been topped by the figure of Nelson, until it was blown up by persons unknown, in 1966, before the commemorations that were due to take place, half a century after the Easter rising of 1916. In the north of the island, the years immediately after 1966 began with civil resistance, before being subsumed in more atavistic forces, and the inauguration of a nightmare that lasted three decades, until an agreement was reached in Belfast as the Twentieth Century was drawing to a close.

Since it had been erected at the beginning of the new Millennium, the Spire had already receded into its familiarity. I saw no-one look upward from their quotidian preoccupations. It had become a place of rendezvous like the pillar before it. Unlike in the days of the pillar, the atmosphere was cosmopolitan. In the midst of predominantly foreign faces there was one native Irishwoman, no longer young, who had perhaps taken leave of her senses and was dancing alone in her own world beneath the spire, dressed like someone who might have been going out for the evening to a musical.

I passed on to the monument at the top of the street: the slightly debonair figure of Parnell. On the plinth was a quote from one of his speeches, which did not seem adequate to his political and personal complexity. It began: "No man has a right to fix the boundary to the march of a nation." From there it was a short distance to the G.P.O. I crossed the street and went back to it. Inside, its ample hall took me blurred moments before I could take it in, surrounded by the windows where customers were doing their business. The hubbub. I tried to imagine the hubbub that there must have been during the siege of Easter Week, 1916. I remembered schooldays when that history was proclaimed to us, loudly. The blood sacrifice of the leaders of the rebellion merged in the imagination with stories of the early Christian martyrs, and the child found it hard to distinguish between the political and the religious saints presented to us as moral exemplars. I wondered, if the rebels inside it in Easter Week 1916 had looked out and seen a vision of the street a century later – Nelson's Pillar replaced by the Spire, with faces from five continents gathering beneath it – what would have remained of their nationalistic conviction?

My reverie was interrupted by a man from the Near East, bearing a letter to a government department in his hand, asking in broken English into which box he should post it. I found a gladness in the small generosity of directing him. From there it was with some inevitability that my feet took me into Henry Street. There was a man standing there, holding a pole with a placard advertising a fortune teller; I heard him tell a woman at a stall close by that the fortune teller had been in a serious traffic accident, and had died twice, gaining second sight. I passed on into Moore Street. There were two Asian women in a shop there, one of them holding up two pots for the other to choose between them. I bought from a stall some bananas, for the journey home. As I walked back to the railway station, I thought of the liberation of Dublin, brought about by the presence of foreigners, unburdened by our history. I thought of those moments of reprieve when you leave the weight of your own past behind you.

It was dark on the train back. The passing lights outside were fragile terrestrial ones, and for most of the time the windows darkly reflected the carriage back into itself. I thought how, in the life of an individual and of a nation, time unfolds in a chain of unanticipated causation. What has happened inexorably happened, beyond any actor's intention. For us now, as it was a century ago, the world a century into the future is beyond anyone's imagination. I looked again through the book of photographs I had brought with me. There was one in particular, taken in 1968, that has been called Earthrise. It was taken by one of the astronauts in the Apollo 8 mission to the moon. That mission did not land there, but the three astronauts, when their capsule went around the far side of the moon, were the only humans ever to go out of sight of the mother planet. They were also the first humans to take photographs of the earth from a great distance. Then, in their capsule called after the old Greek god Apollo, they chose to read the first verses of the book of Genesis: "In the beginning God created the heaven and the earth, and the earth was without form, and void; and darkness was on the face of the deep…"

Meanwhile in the west of Ireland, the contemporary quotidian continued to hold sway. One day, I was stuck indoors all day at a seminar in Bundoran. It was led by an expert, but it seemed to me to be a case of the blind leading the blind as I looked out wistfully at the sunlight in the blue, until at last I escaped, and it was a relief to be out and down the road, through Sligo, Charlestown, Castlebar, Ballinrobe, and into Connemara. I

was headed to Rosaveal to catch the ferry to the Aran Islands where I hoped
to join a friend who was bringing a boat to Westport. I had been told the
day's last ferry was at half six; it was that by the time I reached Maam Cross,
but I headed on. Connemara was achingly beautiful on that sunlit evening.
There were still pools of light on mountains, on stone walls, on small lakes.
I took a wrong turning after Maam, or rather I went straight when I should
have turned left. It was only when I reached Patrick Pearse's cottage at
Rosmuc that my suspicion was confirmed that I had lost my way. I stopped
outside the cottage, at last accepting that the ferry would go without me. It
was closed up and deserted, a traditional cottage that served as a refuge for
Pearse, before his Fenian zeal took over. I wandered around it and
wondered: if he had been given a glimpse of his country one hundred years
later, might he have chosen a life of poetry and seclusion? Might he have
retreated to live out his life here in this small cottage in the deeps of
Connemara, surrounded by the music of Gaeilge, the daylight view out
through his window of the shifting light of the lake, and on a clear night a
glimpse into the beyond? Would he, (and we), have been better served if he
had chosen Rosmuc rather than the G.P.O.?

I retreated back through Connemara, Killary, through Westport
without stopping until I reached the tarbert at Cleggan. The sun was setting
over Achill, and an almost full moon was rising above Rosmindle as I walked
across. The low-tide had turned, and I had just enough time to reach the
shore of Collan More as the island was becoming an island once again. It was
still bright as I reached the schoolhouse. The miracle of once again returning
to it. When I came round the front of the house I disturbed a lamb in the
garden enclosure. The fence was down. The bottoms of the fuschia had been
eaten away. It seemed a small intrusion, but there was a strong smell of
sheep. Then I saw the lamb's mother, head up, caught in netting. There was
a stillness beyond sleep about her. She was dead. The lamb returned and was
sitting by her, still drawn to its dead mother. They must have been like that
all night outside as I lay inside between waking and sleeping, the image of
the morning's task of the removal of a body ahead of me. I braced myself for
the detachment required for it and set about it early. The lamb ran away as
I approached. I pulled the sheep along, still trapped in the netting. It had
become an object for me. I pulled it back through the garden, out beyond
the wall, and left it upturned there, its lifeless legs spread-eagled. The lamb
was lingering close by. I left them there and spent the rest of the morning
doing a few chores around the house to set it up for the new season. I

emptied out the rain-barrel and washed it in the sea. The tide was falling. When I went back to look again at the sheep, the lamb had left the carcass of its mother, and I couldn't distinguish it among the many sheep and lambs in the field that were seemingly nonchalantly grazing. Later, I climbed the hill. The tide had turned and was once again rising. The boundary between island and mainland was filling with water. Way out beyond the lighthouse, I could see the shape of a big boat coming in the bay. There was a strong sense of a voyage ending.

A retired social worker, Gerard McCarthy lives in Sligo. His first published essays, "Old Istanbul," "Old Jerusalem," "Home from Andalucia," "The Road to Granada," "The Silence of Seamus Heaney's Father," and "Mitlini Harbour" have all appeared in earlier issues of Irish Pages. *He is currently working on his first collection of essays.*

FOUR POEMS

Kerry Hardie

Pure enough for a future?

"PEACE IS THE ROOT OF ALL WARS"
Rumi

By day I watch the roe-deer graze,
stubby and darker-brown than last year's leaves.
They feed and look up, feed and look up,
moving over the rumple of colour,
under a fine net of branch.

The glass of the window is old, it shivers
their forms on the twig-frail slope.
There's the sound of the chink of a spoon in a bowl
and a letter from home on the bed.
This March day's still as water.

At night I go outside to stand
in starlight and the sound of owls.
I listen for peace, or the absence of war —
some stasis holding light and dark in place,
keeping them from the soft flesh of each other's throats.

Author's note: this poem was written in 2003 on the eve of the Second Iraq War at Hawthornden Castle, Scotland.

("Portfolio" is continued on page 113)

PORTFOLIO

—

Neil Shawcross

Writers of Belfast
(photographs of paintings)

One of Ireland's finest visual artists, Neil Shawcross was born in Kearsley, Lancashire, England in 1940 and has lived in Northern Ireland since 1962. He studied at Bolton College of Art from 1955 to 1958, and Lancaster College of Art from 1958 to 1960, before moving to Belfast in 1962 to take up a part-time lecturer's post at the Belfast College of Art (now Ulster University), becoming full-time in 1968. He continued to teach and lecture there until his retirement in 2004. He has also taught at Pennsylvania State University in the United States.

His work includes portraits and printmaking, but he has also designed stained glass for the Ulster Museum and St. Colman's Church, Lambeg, Co Antrim. He has exhibited nationally with one-man shows in London, Manchester, Dublin and Belfast, and internationally in Hong Kong and the United States. His celebrated work is found in many private and corporate collections. He lives in Hillsborough, Co Down.

For many years he has painted the covers of books and albums that he finds aesthetically distinctive, particularly those of writers from Belfast and Northern Ireland. In October 2018, Titanic Belfast — one of the North's major visitor attractions — hosted an exhibition of this cumulative portrait of the city's literary life over five decades. It was introduced by Art Hughes, Reader in Irish at Ulster University, whose encomium begins on page 102.

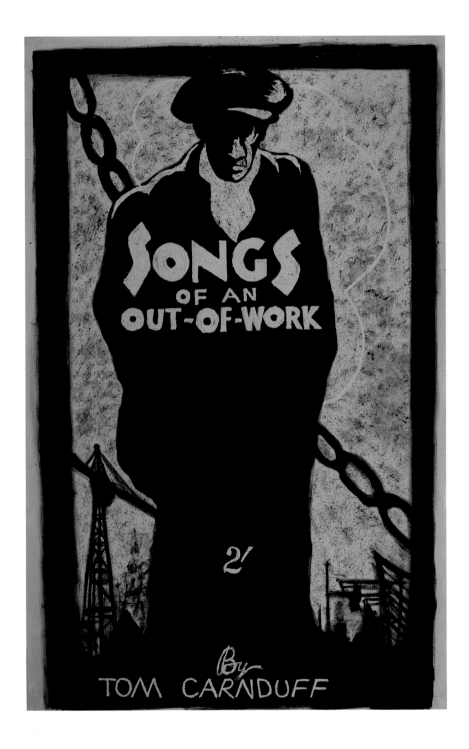

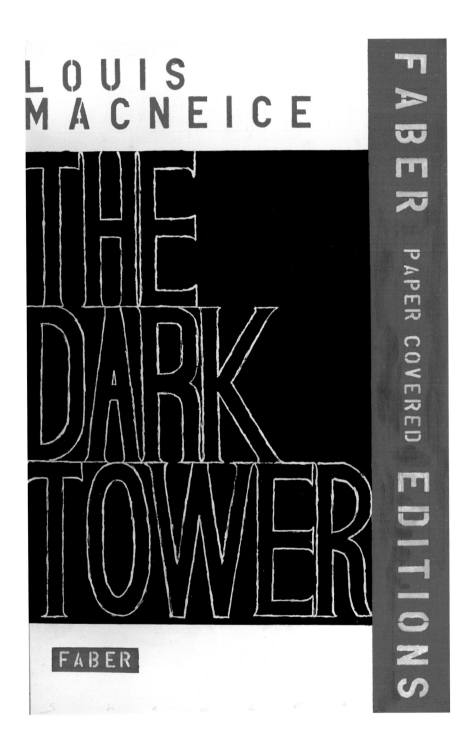

LIFE ON EARTH

Derek Mahon

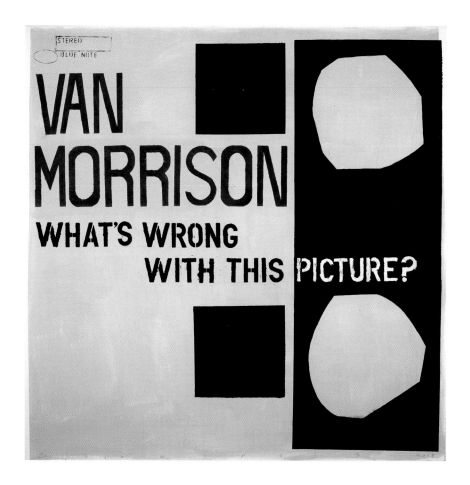

THE GREAT PROFUNDO
AND OTHER STORIES

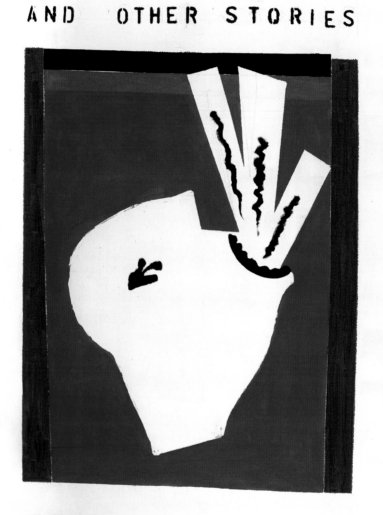

BERNARD MAC LAVERTY

BRIAN
KEENAN

AN EVIL CRADLING
THE FIVE-YEAR ORDEAL OF A HOSTAGE

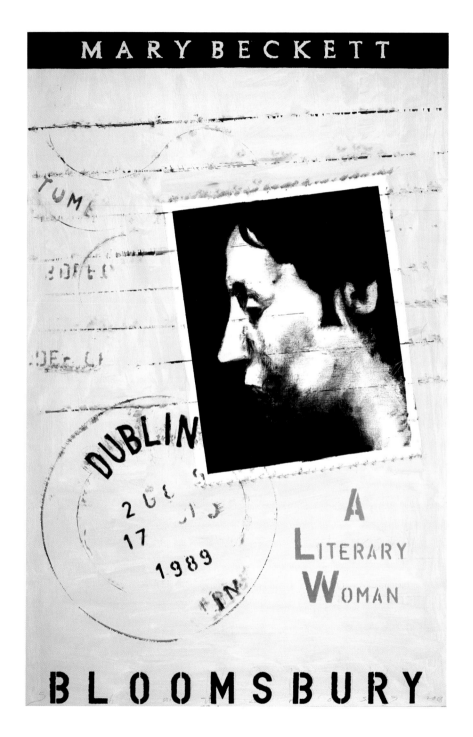

MARY BECKETT

DUBLIN
2 0 0 9
17
1989

A
LITERARY
WOMAN

BLOOMSBURY

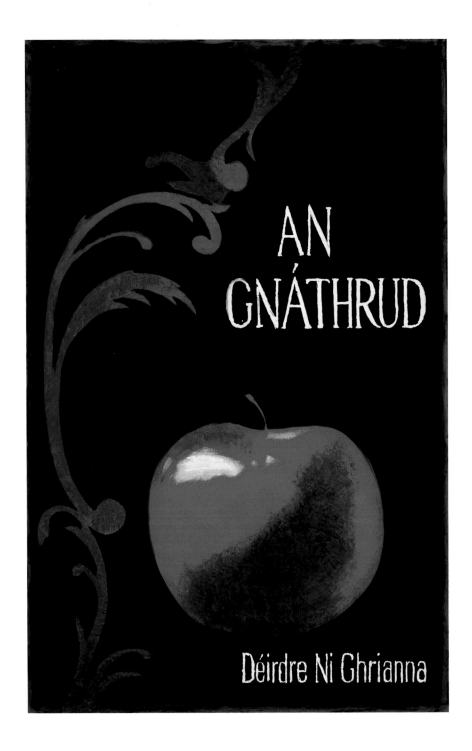

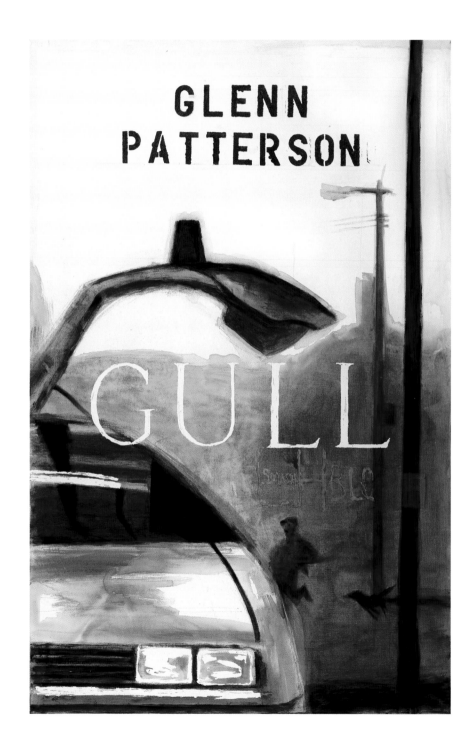

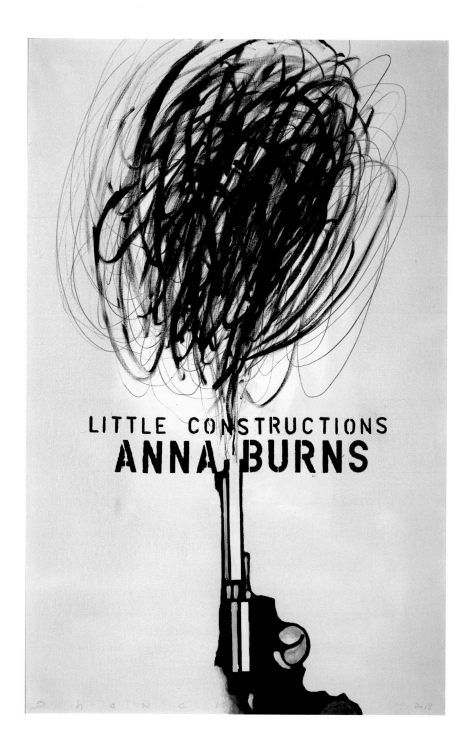

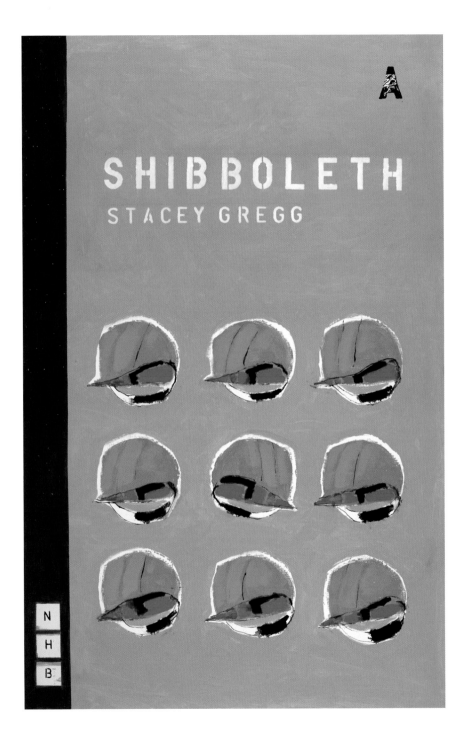

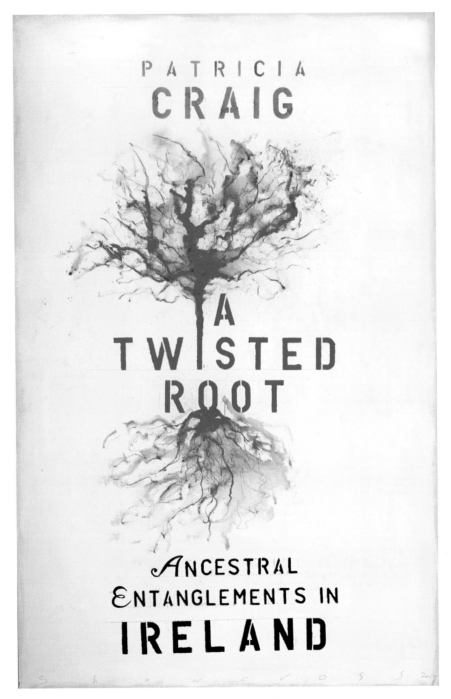

PATRICIA
CRAIG

A
TWISTED
ROOT

*A*NCESTRAL
*E*NTANGLEMENTS IN
IRELAND

PORTFOLIO

is generously supported by Nicholson & Bass Ltd, Belfast
and published courtesy of Belfast City Council

AFTER CIVIL STRIFE

When they are together now they bend to choose
the small, flat, slatey stones from the damp sand
(sometimes the round ones, smoothed by heaving seas)
then place them on their eyes and on their mouths.

There's salt on them,
salt on the wind, salt on their blood-salt lips
that lick the stones and suck them so they gleam.
This is the salve they give, one to the other.

COATS
for everyone

The moment has come to lift down the coat
that has hung on the your door all year.
The smell of the wearer has finally faded,
you can't pretend any more.

It doesn't matter, it has served its purpose,
has used up its store of residual memory
that lives inside certain objects and garments,
is ready again to be just a coat.

Time will soon pass and you'll also be dead
and that doesn't matter either, it happens—
then the spirit goes to the light,
and the flesh to the peace of the clay.

2017

CREGGAN

Walking that street the all-but-forgotten feeling
of eyes-on-my-back has come back.
I follow the dissident taunts on the walls

as those children once followed
the stones in the wood
and I find a flower shop about as likely

as a gingerbread house.
I buy a pot of tulips already in bud
and carry them home, hoping for red,

the colour of life, but they open white,
the colour of this arms-length stand-off
that passes itself as pure enough for a future.

Kerry Hardie was born in 1951 in Singapore and currently lives in Co Kilkenny. She has published eight collections with The Gallery Press, *most recently* The Zebra Stood in The Night *(Bloodaxe Books, 2017), shortlisted for the Irish Times/Poetry Now Award. She has also published two novels, and is currently revising a third. A radio play,* To Find a Heathen Place and Sound a Bell, *was broadcast by RTÉ in 2017, and another poetry collection is forthcoming. She is a member of Aosdána.*

CUCHULAIN IN THE GPO

Gerard Smyth

He is from a book of legends, a myth-maker
made him, a poet gave him
a scripted life, the flesh of divinity,
placed him on the stage in an ancient sect.

The bronze hero in his sarcophagus —
the window of the General Post Office —
faces the tourist regiments, the banners
and flags of old politics,
raised fists and effigies, schoolchildren
who cannot tell Parnell from O'Connell.

That raven on his shoulder could be emissary
of ill-omen, the end-of-battle scavenger
or just the finishing touch to this memorial.
If bronze could speak the bronze hero might ask
Is this the place where valour was wasted?
Will *the delirium of the brave* ever make a comeback?

Gerard Smyth was born in 1951 and raised in the Liberties area of Dublin. He is the author of 12 volumes of poetry, most recently A Song of Elsewhere *(The Dedalus Press, 2014). He worked for his entire professional life as a journalist at* The Irish Times, *with particular responsibility for arts coverage. He was the newspaper's poetry critic for several years and still serves as its poetry editor.*

ON "THE GOOD FRIDAY AGREEMENT"

———

David Park

Hope in the human chain.

As someone who has spent a lifetime voting in Northern Ireland elections the cumulative legacy of exercising my civic responsibility has mostly been disappointment, frustration and occasionally shame that the democratic ideal has once more been reduced to a sectarian headcount. For the last twenty-five years I have recorded my vote in a small church hall adjacent to the three-teacher country school attended by my two children. I mostly voted in the mornings when the generally empty hall echoed with the sound of my feet on the wooden floor and in which I was always reminded of the nativity plays, the prize days and the school fund raisers I had attended. The absence of children lent the experience a vaguely ghostly hue.

On the morning of the 22nd May 1998 when I went to the same location to vote on The Good Friday Agreement everything was different. For a start I found it difficult to find a parking space and the narrow country road was doing a passable impression of gridlock. People were streaming in from the farms and houses of this rural hinterland, including people who lived near me but were seldom seen as they lived down long lanes angled to our road and kept themselves austerely to themselves. As I stepped out of the car I felt something in the air, intangible but so real that it seemed to flow through me and I knew in that split second that they had come to vote *yes*. For the first time my act of voting was carried on a surge of what might be called hope and something even stronger in that it was a shared hope. We looked into each other's faces and smiled but said nothing other than a quick "good morning."

And above all what the Good Friday Agreement offered in that morning – and I like to use that title with its echo of resurrection, of spiritual and physical regeneration – was hope. Hope for an end to killing, hope for something better for our children.

Twenty years on when we look more objectively at what we voted for it becomes clear that what the Agreement created in its essence was a template for human relationships, complete with processes, protocols, codes of conduct and checks and balances that despite their supposed political sophistication don't really amount to much more than the principles we consciously, or unconsciously, try to adhere to in our daily lives. What of course could never be legislated into existence is the spirit needed to fully implement these ideals and without a practical commitment to these ideals the various frameworks are a hollow shell. So instead of power-sharing between all elected parties we eventually saw the creation of fiefdoms where power was carved up and shared only by the most powerful. The Petition of Concern designed to protect minorities became the weapon by which they might be oppressed and First Ministers saw their primary responsibility as extending not much further than the constituency from which they drew their votes. How to deal with the past became a toxic weapon with which to attack the other side.

The Good Friday Agreement promised the possibility of future reconciliation, of societal healing. That possibility has almost, if not quite, disappeared. It has been subverted by a generation of politicians too often lacking in political skill, devoid of a generosity of spirit and above all an inability, or unwillingness, to lead rather than follow their respective tribes. I can think of no worse political epitaph than to be the generation of politician who squandered the hard-earned peace and in case anyone has forgotten, where you have polarisation, the divided space that results is the best breeding ground for extremism and violence.

As we stagnate through yet another period of Assembly suspension it is easy to abandon hope, to even question the nature of what was achieved and whether it was really just – in the words of Seamus Heaney's poem, "North" – "exhaustions nominated peace." And yet there is something too in my memory of that May morning when I voted *Yes* that I can never let go, something that endures and will always do so. Nothing that happens now or in the future can ever take that away from me.

One of the finest prose artists on this island, David Park is author of 11 works of fiction (novels and short stories), most recently Travelling in a Strange Land *(2017),* Gods and Angels *(2016),* The Rye Man *(2015),* Stone Kingdoms *(2015) and* The Poets' Wives *(2015), all from Bloomsbury. He was born in Belfast in 1953, educated at Queen's University Belfast, and had a distinguished career in secondary education. He now lives near Crossgar, Co Down.*

A PERSONAL REFLECTION

Jean Bleakney

Nasty algorithms.

We moved house a few weeks ago. Thirty-two years' worth of decluttering, including a forgotten cupboard high above the cooker. There was some early artwork by our two children; annotated, dated and stashed in the enthusiasm of young motherhood. Also an accumulation of instruction manuals for small appliances I don't even remember acquiring. And there it was, our copy of *The Agreement*, resurrected on its 20th anniversary, near enough. Not sure who designed the cover, but it was a winner. Seeing it again took me back to the preceding years of pushing buggies on peace marches; to the spirit in which we voted *YES* for our children, naively imagining "Days Like This," as exhorted by Van.

Disillusionment set in fairly quickly. In particular, I was dismayed by calls to disband the RUC. I remember writing an angry admonishing letter to Seamus Mallon in early 2001. And then the decommissioning saga. Fast forward to 2018 where the sustained and deepening vilification of the RUC and UDR is an ongoing insult to unionism, something to be silently tholed. Be assured it is not a silence bred from shame, but from fear. Many of my wider family served honourably and at great personal risk. To name them was to endanger them; *is* (I still believe) to endanger them.

We now know the GFA was never fit for purpose. It institutionalised a two-tribes mentality. What was not factored in was human nature, a particularly nasty algorithm hereabouts. One of the principal failings, twenty years on, is how acceptable it has become to celebrate, elevate and keep faith with those who planned and committed terrible atrocities, murdering thousands and blighting the lives of tens of thousands through injury and loss. Even aside from the immoral marker it sets down for future generations, does nobody think this is a tad dystopian? The Assembly was stymied by self-interest and mired in blame games. Instead of looking ahead, the main parties kept looking over their shoulders. Decisions went unmade. There should have been a date, a review-by date at least.

And here we are with an incoming Brexit and a bandwagon of oh-so articulate, social media savvy, overly loud and cloyingly witty Brexitbashers, Republicans, Civic Nationalists, DUP-haters, Academics, Rights Activists, Journos, etc. An altogether shocking number of high horses saddled up with sanctimony. More than ever, somehow, everything is the fault of the Brits. Which is grist to one side's cultural dependence on victimhood, and the other side's siege mentality. Nationalism in Northern Ireland is gaining ground rapidly in terms of self-confidence and demographics. Unionism feels aggrieved, isolated and anxious. Shockingly, one can sense people retreating into their respective single-narrative echo chambers.

The principal GFA players, Blair, Ahern and Clinton, who hitched their wagon to a falling star, can but wring their hands. On the bright side, Northern Irish society is manfully and womanfully staggering on in the absence of functioning politics. But push is coming to shove – and somebody needs to get a grip before that happens.

Jean Bleakney was born in 1956 in Newry where her father was a Border Customs Officer. She studied Biochemistry at Queen's University Belfast and has worked in medical research and horticulture. Her first three collections were published by Lagan Press. Her Selected Poems *was issued by Templar Poetry in 2016 to coincide with the appearance of her work on the GCE Advanced Level syllabus in Northern Ireland. Her most recent collection is* No Remedy *(2017), also published by Templar Poetry.*

ON THE DAY

Carlo Gébler

Averting our eyes.

*Friday 22 May 1998, the day of the referendum on The Good
Friday or Belfast Agreement.*

In 1991 I went into HMP Maze (Long Kesh if you prefer) to do creative
writing with Republican and Loyalist prisoners. It was supposed to be for
six weeks but it turned into seven years of teaching, on and off.

I didn't know at the beginning what was going on behind the scenes but
talking to the prisoners, the Republicans especially, I began to put it
together. Though nobody was saying so in public, everybody knew (the
prisoners, the government, the Northern Ireland Secretary of State, the
Northern Ireland Office, Number 10 Downing Street, the politicians, civil
servants, even the prison officers), everybody knew that the way things had
been done had failed and that to go on doing things as they'd been done was
pointless. Nobody could win the war and so there would have to be a deal
which allowed everyone, all the parties, to try something different, without
loss of face.

What exactly this new dispensation would be, nobody was saying and
certainly not the prisoners, although I did learn one thing from the
Republicans: their support of whatever deal the Sinn Féin leadership
secured rested on one non-negotiable principle, and unless they got this
they were not consenting to anything. In history, they said, at the end of a
political conflict, once an agreement was struck, the prisoners always
walked; and in Northern Ireland, they were adamant, they would too. Oh
yes, they were not serving out their sentences – they were going home
although this wouldn't necessarily be bruited about much or even at all,
when the deal was being negotiated.

My informants, I must add, weren't much interested in my feelings
about their release before their sentences were finished, or whether I
thought it was a violation of natural justice, or would amplify the trauma of
the victims and their relatives. No, in their eyes this was simply what always
happened after a war. POWs went home.

They also added, in our discussions, because they could also see I was skeptical and that I found it hard to believe the British State, after decades of anti-paramilitary rhetoric, would let them go, a final caveat. "Why do you think you're here," they would say, "helping us to write?" Because the Northern Ireland Office or the Prison Service thinks it's a good thing that we should be taught to write? Because they want a productive regime? Or because they care about prisoners? No, you're here, because they know, we know, everyone knows, there is an understanding coming, we will be leaving, and when we get home, we will need skills, including the ability to use language effectively. War doesn't work, it has been shown it doesn't work: once the deal is done it'll have to be politics and you're getting us ready for that…"That's the gist of what they told me.

Thursday 21 May 1998, the day before the referendum on the Belfast or Good Friday Agreement, I was in HMP Maghaberry, where I'd just transferred from the Maze, and where I was working as writer-in-residence. My diary entry for that day is full of detail. Among other things, I tracked down a copy of Primo Levi's *If This is a Man* and *The Truce* for a prisoner in the punishment block; a prisoner I was helping with his poetry gave me a hanky with a picture on it of Timon from *The Lion King* as a thank-you present; I went over a piece about a Dublin pub shooting with a man; I spoke to a prisoner who wanted to write about the RUC's attempt to recruit him as an informer; and I talked to a prisoner who, having just had a two-day visit from his wife was "depressed, distressed, vomiting and coming down from the high induced" by the visit…

The next day, the morning of the referendum, I woke early, the bedroom full of light, and I was down at my Polling Station, the Model Primary School, at about 7 o'clock, which was when it opened. Inside the Model (which two of my children attended) there was the traditional school smell (Dettol, floor polish, baked radiator paint, dust, pencil shavings). I went to the second desk on the left of the front door: it's where I always go because that's where people whose initial is *G* are processed. I showed my polling card and my Irish passport.

"Gébler, Karl Ernest …" was announced by an election official and another official repeated the name back and scored my name off the roll. I was given my ballot paper. I went to a little booth (the same where I always vote), flattened the ballot on the wooden shelf, took the pencil attached to the shelf by a chain and made my X in the *Yes* box.

After that I popped my ballot into the ballot box, drove home, made a pot of coffee and went to my desk. I know what I did then for the rest of the day – it's in the diary: "Worked Father book" (meaning *Father and I*, my memoir). And that's the entire diary entry for that day. Now, seeing as I wrote so much about the day before, why did I write so little about the day of the historic referendum?

Answer: it was too hard, too complicated.

I voted *Yes* because I was disgusted and ashamed by all that happened in the North, by all that we had done. I wanted it sorted, I wanted it finished, and The Belfast Agreement looked like the only way that that could be made to happen.

However, when I voted I also knew absolutely what the consequences would be if *Yes* (which would get us out of the jam we were in) carried the day: the men in the Maze or Long Kesh would walk and those whose lives they'd ruined would just have to suck it up, as the saying goes.

I couldn't grapple with any of that. No way. So I reverted to the old Gébler default whenever I feel queasy or troubled: I averted my gaze from the facts and buried myself in literature. "Worked Father Book." That's what I did. "Worked Father Book." The diary says. That's what I did on Friday, 22 May 1998. "Worked Father Book."

Carlo Gébler was born in Dublin in 1954, the son of the Irish novelist Edna O'Brien. He has a BA in English Literature from the University of York and a PhD from Queen's University Belfast. He is the author of numerous books, most recently (all from New Island) The Wing Orderly's Tales *(2016, short stories),* The Projectionist *(2015, memoir) and* The Innocent of Falkland Road *(2017, novel). A member of Aosdána, he teaches at the Oscar Wilde Centre, Trinity College, Dublin, and lives in Enniskillen, Co Fermanagh.*

RESPONSIBILITY FOR THE DEAD

Anne Devlin

The kindness of attention.

I was in Paris when the news broke, in a high-rise hotel off the Champs de Mars. My view was of another glass tower, like a mirror graph, plunging skyward. It was late afternoon and I was lying down. The blue isolation outside the windows was giving me vertigo. CNN was on, when I looked from the windows to the square TV set, suddenly there were pictures of people I knew. The camera moved around a conference room in Belfast, the moment has a back stage feel, as if we are eavesdropping on a conversation. Then there was a more formal moment: Clinton's envoy George Mitchell, with his wife behind him, is smiling as he announces that an Agreement has been reached. It is Good Friday, 1998. The next day I moved to a second-floor room at a small hotel and my younger self's eternal weightlessness was stabilised. I don't think I fully grasped the nature of the Agreement, just that it meant Peace. It meant the violence would end, thirty years after it began. Or that I would return to live in Belfast, nine years after it was signed.

I am in Paris again on 2 May 2018 staying in the 18th Arrondissement, in walking distance of Gare du Nord. There is a mattress on the pavement where the Hotel is, and a temple of Ganesh. Groups of young African men wait at the corner underneath the overhead metro. I am on my way to the Sorbonne, with two academics, Paul Arthur and Chris Reynolds, to a conference: *The Imprints of 1968 Student Movements on the World.*

I have come to Paris against my better judgement, having long since distanced the political activist from the writer in me. I have written about the core year of '68 in many forms, in my early plays and stories. Enough to suggest that it is probably connected to why I write. But this is different, and very high risk. I haven't got a script. What I have are notes based on an electoral reform pamphlet, which my trade unionist father contributed to writing, as far back as 1965; published by the Executive of the Northern Ireland Labour Party, arguing predominantly for universal franchise, which was the central demand of the Civil Rights Movement in 1968. But I have a narrative in my head which I have already presented on at least four previous occasions, the most recent being at my old school – where I explained that I bunked off and went on student marches. The narrative that is guiding me is the twelve months of my involvement with street politics before I found myself out of my depth because of the violence that had been unleashed, before I made my way back to a university place to read English, and not History or Law, to my father's disappointment.

I am freezing. I am wearing a dark wool coat even though the sun is shining. While Arthur is wearing a pale linen suit and Reynolds is jacketless. Our session at the Sorbonne is called "Memories of Northern Ireland: International, National and Local Dimensions." We are here to make the case to include the NI student movement in the international picture. I must make the connection between the student protests and the bread and butter issues. The housing crisis was linked to votes and got Professor Paul Arthur his current chair of the 50th Anniversary Civil Rights Commemoration Committee. He has written a book on the People's Democracy, the student movement, of which he was a founder member. Chris Reynolds, an Associate Prof of French at Nottingham Trent University, is the facilitator of our session at the Sorbonne. The Civil Rights Movement onto the streets in '68, along with demands to end discrimination in employment, and introduce policing reform.

After the police violence in Derry on 5 October 1968 against the civil rights march, and the authorities' denunciation of it as a front for communists and republicans, the student movement was formed. The People's Democracy marched on 9 October from The Queen's University of Belfast to the City Hall in support of Civil Rights demands. Nor was this Civil Rights for Catholics. This was our generation in a show of strength. Of course, there were communists and republicans – why not? It's a democracy. The Law department was heavily represented, junior staff and students, along with other undergraduates, post Graduate students and young people. The charge against us was we were simply copycatting the scenes we saw on TV across Europe. On the bus in Paris on my way to the Sorbonne, Chris Reynolds points out some current graffiti:

On ne veut pas 68. On veut 1789. (We don't want 68. We want 1789.)

And there is the nub: in '68 we did not want the national history, the unfinished business of the civil war. We wanted to live in '68. We wanted to live in our own time. This is what gave my generation identity and direction.

I had always been happy to be a European unionist. It resolved my acute discomfort at having to choose between a British and Irish identity. Under the terms of the Good Friday Agreement (Article VI) both governments accept the birth-right of citizens of Northern Ireland to identity as Irish, British or both. This both is of major importance to me, so that when we leave the European Union my Irish passport will allow me to remain within the arc of Europe.

But there is something else of major importance, and it emerged on 2 May at the Sorbonne. The Italians are talking about punishment of the student protesters in Turin in the autumn of '69, when we arrive at the seminar in the late afternoon. Their session is before ours. To my relief the Italian paper is in English. Chris Reynolds leans over and puts it in context: there was an amnesty in France, he says, for all those arrested during the May events. A few days before coming to Paris, when speaking at my old school and it came to questions, there was a quiet rush to the table to ask not about '68, but about the Good Friday Agreement. The prisoners? How do you feel about the prisoners being let out?

And I replied: "But we have the peace. We have the peace."

And in the heat of that Sorbonne seminar room I have noted on the programme, in red ink. "The French had an amnesty." Underneath, I add, "Our Amnesty is the Good Friday Agreement." And I'm wondering if this is true. I'm wondering even now if I am prepared to accept the liabilities of that insight. Because it means I will have to accept the responsibility for the dead also.

The French students at the Sorbonne in May '68 had also been reacting to the police being called into the university. But the scale of worker strikes that accompanied the student unrest was far greater in its disruption than anything experienced in Northern Ireland. And I wouldn't see that until later in the evening when we were taken to the National Archive and shown the exhibition: *68, Les Archives du Pouvoir.*

There were the black and white photos of huge factory protests across France. There were mountains of cobblestones, where they pulled up the streets to make barricades in Paris in May. By August '69 we had barricades, across Leeson Street in West Belfast; they were dismantled by the Parish Priest to let the schools return in September.

Marguerite Duras is in the archive as a young woman, the writer of *Hiroshima Mon Amour*, and there's an orgy at Nanterre on film archive in black and white. It's shot like the orgy in *Zabriskie Point*. It reminds me that when my grandmother took me to see South Pacific as a child, she covered my eyes at the kisses, and let me watch the explosions. What I had emphasised at the Sorbonne in my talk was the impact of image, and how a press photograph of myself from that time, at the centre of a Pieta, revealed that I hadn't in fact escaped the hard wiring of Catholic martyrology after all.

The other French connection was the schoolgirls' movement. Ronald Fraser in his oral history of *1968* quotes a French schoolgirl Lilly Metreaux: "I wasn't fighting the police, I was fighting the nuns." I shared her anti-authoritarian stance. It was the music that delivered my generation, the protest songs of Dylan and Baez for the anti-war movement, the black civil rights anthems, *We Shall Overcome* for racial equality. Race had more of an impact than class; we identified as black and perceived Protestant workers as white and privileged. This drew condemnation of us from the English student Left; particularly after the four-day march from Belfast to Derry, modelled on the Selma to Montgomery march, was ambushed at Burntollet Bridge. They believed we were asserting our right to march through Protestant areas. The Easter march in 1969, from Belfast to Dublin, was to prove our non-sectarian nature, to protest the lack of civil rights for Protestants in the Republic: no contraception, no divorce, and banned novels on the Catholic index. We carried copies of Edna O'Brien's first novel, and *The Ginger Man*. I remember discussions about the need for the Government of the Republic to drop articles 2 and 3 of the Irish Constitution, which claimed sovereignty over the North. We thought the English students were mad: the Republic was never going to do that. And then came a day in the run-up to the Agreement in 1998 when I sat in the BBC lobby in West London and watched as Bertie Ahern signed up to removing Articles 2 and 3 from the Irish Constitution.

In the months after the Good Friday agreement, and the Referendum that followed, I was working on a film with Roger Michell. It was an adaptation of the novel *Titanic Town* about a peace campaigner in the seventies. I wrote the screenplay and a speech for Julie Walter's character Bernie. It became my contribution to the campaign to accept the Good Friday Agreement:

> "Every time a soldier is shot we keep quiet. Every time
> a civilian is shot we condemn the security forces. We're
> so predictable. I'd like to see a real change: I'd like to see

us have the humanity to criticise the shooting of a soldier. I'd like to see the Army show real regret over the shooting of civilians. You have a chance to make the first move. On your way out of here today you can either stop and sign the peace petition – or pass by and fail another generation."

In *68, Les Archives du Pouvoir* the pictures show the re-militarisation of French society after the May events. The older generation marching with De Gaulle were the victors of '68.

At the end of my session I am asked was the influence more American than European? It may have been much older. Flying from Belfast in May 2018, I was accompanied by a class of North Antrim school children several of whom were of mixed race; it reminded me that I stayed in Bastille when I worked on *The Venus De Milo Instead*, my 1988 screenplay for Danny Boyle, about a Catholic teacher in a Protestant school, a hymn to Paris as a place to tackle sectarianism by taking the kids away to. But it is the first glimpse of the Venus de Milo in the Louvre that affects a transformation, when a schoolgirl dreams she is embraced by a goddess. In other words, this is not the monotheism she has grown up with. It gifts her a powerful sense of enlargement.

Edith Hall reminds us that "When the Oresteia was first performed in 458 BC, Athens was recovering from devastating violence in a primal class struggle caused by the opening up of rights to the lowest class of citizens … " The Greeks wrote their great plays after their wars were over. But supposing we have no choice, supposing we have lived and written in the time of (civil) war. And in the Peace it is time to re-configure, both the subject and the audience.

In December 2013, we failed to take up the Haass Report's recommendations for the establishment of an Archive to allow us to contend with the injuries of the past. The combatants don't know how to live, and the civilians and survivors don't know how to grieve. The younger generation don't know. And without the commitment to a level playing field in terms of social mobility, via housing, employment, health and educational opportunity appropriate to our potential at whatever age, we will continue to see ourselves as victims. And we will have lost the opportunity to enlarge our capacity for compassion.

I have been very critical of the Good Friday Agreement, because I have insisted our identities have been much larger than the political equation we currently inhabit. Our votes don't reflect what we are capable of. The disappearance of the Shankill Labour Party in Paris Street, and the Falls Branch from Albert Street is the unintended consequence of our youthful struggle against conformity. Meanwhile, the reigning silence of the aftermath has felt like a refusal or enforced restriction because no one is going to break the Peace by telling tales from the war. The Good Friday Agreement has given us a blueprint, it just needs to be formalised in the direction of an amnesty attached to the establishment of an archive. We need to listen to the testimonies of the others. The idea is not to rush to judgement, the idea is to bring our best selves to the encounter. The danger of not proceeding in this public way is that our future stability is vulnerable to the dead hand of un-collaborated testimonies and leaks from various archives around the world. At present the desire to speak is there; so is the kindness of attention.

A playwright, short-story writer and screenwriter, Anne Devlin was born in 1951 in Belfast, the daughter of the politician Paddy Devlin. Her plays include Ourselves Alone *(1985)* and After Easter *(1994); her screenplays were written for the film* Titanic Town *and the BBC serial* The Rainbow. *Her radio play,* The Forgotten, *was broadcast on BBC Radio in early 2009.*

HUMAN RIGHTS IN NORTHERN IRELAND

Brice Dickson

The Holy Grail.

Apart from power-sharing, the release of prisoners and the decommissioning of weapons, the idea which most animated the Belfast (Good Friday) Agreement (the GFA) in 1998 was that better compliance with human rights standards would help maintain the peace in Northern Ireland. Within the section headed *Rights, Safeguards and Equality of Opportunity* the GFA devoted 13 paragraphs to the topic.

The British government promised to complete incorporation of the European Convention on Human Rights (the ECHR) into domestic law. A Bill to achieve this for the whole of the UK was already going through Parliament at the time and received Royal Assent in November, just ten days before the Northern Ireland Act turned many other provisions of the GFA into binding law. One of these imposed duties on public authorities to carry out their functions with "due regard to the need to promote equality of opportunity" and "regard to the desirability of promoting good relations between persons of different religious belief, political opinion or racial group." Another created a new Human Rights Commission and an Equality Commission, each replacing existing bodies but with enhanced powers. One of the duties given to the Human Rights Commission was to advise the British government on the scope for adding rights to those in the ECHR so as to form a Bill of Rights. The additional rights were to be drawn from international precedents and to reflect the particular circumstances of Northern Ireland.

The Irish government said it would bring forward measures to ensure at least an equivalent level of human rights protection as that pertaining in the North. It too promised to create a Human Rights Commission, with the same mandate as that of the Northern body but without a duty to advise the government on a Bill of Rights. It also said it would "further examine" the incorporation of the ECHR into Irish law. A joint committee of the two Human Rights Commissions was to consider the establishment of a charter of rights for the whole island, endorsing agreed measures to protect the fundamental rights of everyone living there.

Twenty years on, nearly all of these governmental commitments have been met. The promised legislation and institutions have been put in place. The Human Rights Commissions have been energetic and productive, despite being hit in recent years by significant budget cuts. In each jurisdiction the level of human rights protection is noticeably higher than it was in 1998, even if it is not yet the same: on some issues human rights are better protected in the North, on others they are better protected in the South. There is not yet an agreed all-Ireland charter of rights.

So if human rights have been a success story in the North, why have rights issues featured so prominently in inter-party talks aimed at restoring the power-sharing Executive there, inoperative since January 2017? There are two main reasons. The first is that claims which were not human rights issues back in 1998 have since become so – the use of Irish in official discourse, the demand for same-sex marriage and the right to truth for those who suffered in the troubles. The second is that the idea that Northern Ireland needs a Bill of Rights has not gone away. It still inspires many human rights activists who think such a document would solve a host of problems.

Human Rights and Politics

Experience in human rights work over the last 40 years has convinced me that, while protecting human rights is fundamental to any society's well-being, human rights are, ultimately, social constructs. They are not handed down in tablets of stone, they are not deducible from any theology, they are not the bleeding obvious. Reasonable people can reasonably degree over whether a claim is a human right and to what extent it can be limited. We might all accept that there should be rights to free speech and a fair trial, but do we agree that a child should have the right not to be smacked, a 17-year-old the right to vote and adult men the right to pay for sex? Sometimes our disagreements depend on local history or culture. In Germany there is no right to deny the Holocaust, whereas in Ireland there is; in France a criminal's previous convictions can be taken into account when a court is deciding if he or she is guilty of a further offence, while in Ireland that would be anathema.

Human rights, then, are fashioned. They are political compromises. The fashioning is achieved by elected politicians, aided by judges and civil society. But it behoves all such players to examine competing claims around human rights in the same way. I cannot see why groups of nationalists and unionists sometimes seek to anchor their conception of human rights in their self-identification as Irish or British, especially when such an approach almost inevitably leads to double-standards. Those who want families of people killed in the troubles to be told the truth about what happened to their loved ones, for example, are not always clear that paramilitary organisations as well as the State should be under a duty to provide that truth. And those who ostensibly support equality are not always willing to do so if preserving the unequal status quo is more to their political advantage.

Human rights advocates must also be prepared to move with the times. As more categories of injustice are highlighted – the systematic mistreatment of women, for example – more needs to be done to address them. There is nothing magical about the label we put on an injustice: whether it is designated a human rights abuse or not, our focus should be on remedying the suffering. We must admit, too, that injustice itself is a social construct. At present we do not see it as unjust that people with higher IQs tend to be more successful in life than others, or that women tend to live longer than men, but in years to come perhaps we will.

Close to 15 years ago I would not have seen a human rights abuse in the fact that while gay people could enter into civil partnerships, which carried much the same legal status as marriages, they could not marry. I changed my mind when I became aware of the depth of hurt gay people were experiencing due to the fact that society accorded less recognition to their love than it did to the love expressed by heterosexual people. In addition, allowing gay people to marry hurts no one, and to argue that it undermines the concept of marriage is perverse, since it actually enhances it.

How the Law Can Best Protect Human Rights

Just as difficult as knowing what the parameters of a human right should be is the problem of how best to protect it through law. When a new State or sub-State is created it is often endowed with a Constitution setting out basic rights which people living in that entity will enjoy. The 1791 US Bill of Rights (comprising the first 10 amendments to the 1776 Constitution) is a good example, as is France's Declaration of the Rights of Man and of the Citizen, which originated in 1798 and remains part of the Fifth French Republic's 1958 Constitution. Those documents have had chequered histories, but few would doubt their huge importance over time.

Prior to Northern Ireland's recent spate of troubles there were several calls for a Bill of Rights to be enacted. An English document with that title dates from 1688, but it is not a modern document like its successors in the US and France a century later, and there is doubt over whether it was ever extended to Ireland. Shelagh Murnaghan tried to get her fellow Stormont MPs to adopt a Bill of Rights in the 1960s, but without success. Her Bill was really an anti-discrimination statute, understandably focusing on religious prejudice. It was nothing like the catalogues of rights in the 1948 Universal Declaration or the 1950 ECHR.

After the Sunningdale Conference a Standing Advisory Commission on Human Rights was created for Northern Ireland in 1973. In 1977 it reported on whether a Bill of Rights would be a good idea, initially concluding that it would, but only if it extended throughout the whole of the UK. Later the Commission conceded that the Bill would be valuable even if it applied only in Northern Ireland. No legislation ensued, but SACHR still played a significant role in ensuring that innovative anti-discrimination legislation was enacted in the '70s, '80s and '90s. Meanwhile a number of civil society organisations, ranging from the Ulster Political Research Group to the Committee on the Administration of Justice, prepared their own draft Bills of Rights. The latter's appeared in 1990. It was against this background that the GFA kept the idea of a Bill of Rights alive.

The draft Bill of Rights produced by the Human Rights Commission in 2001 was one of the most detailed of its type but it was received with considerable negativity. A special issue of the *Northern Ireland Legal Quarterly* at the time is testament to that. The UK government and many unionist politicians were opposed to it because it dealt with a lot more than "the particular circumstances of Northern Ireland." Unionists may have been in favour of guaranteeing some of these non-particular rights but could not see why they needed to be protected in just one part of the UK, thereby driving a wedge between Northern Ireland and Great Britain. Just as nationalists were glad to see the GFA requiring the Irish government to provide equivalent protection to rights protected in Northern Ireland, so unionists wanted to see equivalence between rights in Northern Ireland and those in Great Britain.

Nationalists and human rights organisations were dissatisfied with the Commission's draft because in their eyes it was not as comprehensive a Bill as it should have been. Some even interpreted the draft as undermining existing equality legislation because it recognised that people in the majority community deserved to have their rights protected just as much as people in the minority community.

Looking back I see the Bill of Rights process that ran from 2000 to 2005 as a missed opportunity. At the time I sincerely believed that a Bill of Rights would help to consolidate what was then a fragile peace process. It would have been an important symbol and a welcome reassurance. Unfortunately, as so often in Northern Ireland, the perfect was allowed to be the enemy of the good. As a result no change occurred at all.

The successor Commission, led by Monica McWilliams, took up the baton and, after taking into account almost a year's worth of debates in a Bill of Rights Forum chaired by a human rights expert from Australia, delivered its final advice to the British government at the end of 2008. That Bill was even longer and broader than the 2001 draft. It pleased human rights organisations but not unionists, whose two representatives on the Commission expressly dissented. The British government, predictably but discreditably, treated the document with disdain.

The Way Forward

In the 10 years that have elapsed since the Commission submitted its advice, strenuous efforts have continued to be made by the Human Rights Consortium and others (largely funded by Atlantic Philanthropies) to keep the Bill of Rights idea on the table. In the talks between the DUP and Sinn Féin, which failed in February 2018, the leaked "draft agreement" refers to an ad hoc Assembly Committee being set up "to consider the creation of a Bill of Rights that is faithful to the stated intention of the 1998 Agreement."

Maybe I am getting too long in the tooth, but to me the continuing pursuit of a Bill of Rights is now as fruitless as a search for the Holy Grail. I accept that such a view is difficult to swallow for those who have spent so much valuable time and effort on the campaign to date. Their minds may be locked into the infallibility of their cause. However they should not despair. For three reasons the protection of human rights can still be substantially enhanced in Northern Ireland even if a Bill of Rights were de-prioritised.

For a start, focusing on a single Bill of Rights can be a wasteful distraction. It's the human rights equivalent to the political mantra which holds that "nothing's agreed until everything's agreed" – a recipe for foot-dragging and stasis. Moreover, imposing a Bill of Rights when there is no cross-community support for it could be very destabilising to the still precarious peace process and is sure to lead to the Bill's failure. A more disparate approach, one that ticks off the items on the human rights agenda in a more targeted manner, is likely to reap greater consensus and real change.

Secondly, in a democracy where politics is not working well, civil society can play a greater role. Bringing civil society together over specific human rights issues can produce quick and effective results. This is how same-sex marriage was achieved in the Republic. It may be how changes to UK law on the use of plastic packaging are achieved in the near future. Even in the US the power of civil society looks to be leading to some alteration to the gun laws. There are many other rights issues that deserve society's collective focus at this time, particularly in the socio-economic sphere.

The third reason for downplaying the campaign for a full-scale Bill of Rights is that a "list approach" to rights is not always wise, especially if the list is made difficult to change. Americans lived with slavery for over 70 years despite their 1791 Bill of Rights, and they are still living with the consequences of the right to bear arms in Article 2 of that Bill. The ECHR, and the Canadian and South African Bills of Rights, have been more successful, but they too are already a little dated and have to rely on (unelected) activist judges to preserve their relevance. Lists, moreover, tend to acquire an iconic status that devalues rights that do not happen to be included and they tempt judges to adopt an "originalist" interpretative approach.

At a British Academy event in Queen's University in February 2018, the philosopher Baroness O'Neill made an excellent case for prioritising "giving" over "receiving," duties over rights. As Bentham reminded us in the 1840s, a list of rights is, by itself, nonsense. What really matters is the way each of us, and all organisations, treat one another. Rather than seeking to compose a single document purporting to lay out exhaustive rules for how such treatment should occur – a modern day Ten Commandments, only many times longer – we should put our efforts into locating where specific wrongs are being suffered and how they should be addressed and prevented.

Emeritus Professor of International Law at Queen's University Belfast, Brice Dickinson has published books on the Northern Irish legal system, French law, judicial activism, the European Convention on Human Rights, and the Irish Supreme Court. He was born in Belfast in 1953 and attended Wadham College, Oxford. He is the former Chief Commissioner of the Northern Ireland Human Rights Commission, and a current member of the Northern Ireland Policing Board. He continues to live in Belfast.

ON THE GOVERNMENT OF IRELAND ACT (1920)

Anonymous Citizen

This about says it — in a citizen's italics.

*House of Commons Debate
29 March 1920
(Vol 127, cc 925-1036 925)*

Captain Craig:

"I come now to the third and the most distressing of the problems we had to face, and I refer to that of the area. As Hon. Members know, the area over which the North of Ireland Parliament is to have jurisdiction is the six counties of Antrim, Down, Armagh, Londonderry, Tyrone and Fermanagh. The three Ulster counties of Monaghan, Cavan and Donegal are to be handed over to the South of Ireland Parliament. How the position of affairs in a Parliament of nine counties and in a Parliament of six counties would be is shortly this. *If we had a nine counties' Parliament, with 64 Members, the Unionist majority would be about three or four, but in a six counties' Parliament, with 52 Members, the Unionist majority would be about 10. The three excluded counties contain some 70,000 Unionists and 260,000 Sinn Feiners and Nationalists, and the addition of that large block of Sinn Feiners and Nationalists would reduce our majority to such a level that no sane man would undertake to carry on a Parliament with it.* That is the position with which we were faced when we had to take the decision a few days ago as to whether we should call upon the Government to include the nine counties in the Bill or be satisfied with the six. *It will be seen that the majority of Unionists in the nine counties' Parliament is very small indeed. A couple of Members sick, or two or three Members absent for some accidental reason, might in one evening hand over the entire Ulster Parliament and the entire Ulster position, for which we have fought so hard and so long, to the Hon. Member and his friends, and that, of course, is a dreadful thing to contemplate.* Nothing — and I say this with all sincerity, and I am sure everybody will believe me — nothing was more heartbreaking to us than to take the decision

135

which we felt we had to take a few days ago in Belfast when we decreed more or less that our Unionist fellow countrymen in the three counties of Monaghan, Cavan and Donegal should remain outside the Ulster Parliament; but in judging our action we must ask Hon. Members to try and place themselves in our position. They must remember that we are charged with the defence of the Ulster position, and surely that carries with it the duty of undertaking the government and the defence of as much of Ulster as we can hold. We quite frankly admit that we cannot hold the nine counties. *I have given the respective figures of the Unionist and the Sinn Fein and Nationalist inhabitants in those three counties, and from them it is quite clear that as soon as the Ulster Parliament was set up, the first task which the Sinn Feiners would set themselves, in those three counties at any rate, would be to make government there absolutely impossible for us. They have made it impossible for the English Government in practically the whole of the South and West of Ireland, and we recognise facts sufficiently clearly to know that they could make it impossible for us to govern those three counties. Therefore, we have decided that, in the interests of the greater part of Ulster, it is better that we should give up those three counties rather than take on a bigger task than we are able to carry out.*

I knew that the accusation would come sooner or later that we had broken the Covenant which we signed in 1912, when we bound ourselves – all the Unionists in all the counties of Ulster – to stand by one another in the crisis which then threatened. There has been a great deal said on this question of the breach of the Covenant by those of us who voted in favour of the six counties of Ulster, and I am quite prepared to admit a technical breach of that Covenant. But I say to those who charge me with that, that if I kept the Covenant in the letter as regards the excluded counties, I should be breaking it in the spirit, and true meaning, to the six counties. I see an Hon. Member opposite shake his head. I would like to ask him what was the first object of the Covenant? It was to prevent a Dublin Parliament being imposed upon Ulster, and I would like to ask him how we could carry out the intention of that Covenant by assuming the government of such a large area in Ulster that we could not hold it, and in the course of a month or two, or possibly a few years, that area had to be handed over to the Dublin Parliament? Obviously, when we set ourselves to safeguard Ulster and to prevent Home Rule from being imposed upon us, the best way to carry that pledge into effect was to save as much as Ulster as we knew we could hold. To try to hold more than we could hold would seem an act of gross folly on our part, and in the difficult circumstances, I have no hesitation in saying we took the only commonsense business decision we could possibly take. On that matter I leave those who come after us to judge whether we took a right or a wrong decision.

This citizen works in the media and lives in Belfast.

ON EDUCATING MEMORY

Robert McDowell

Doing good.

What is peace? It is not resolution of all disputes. It is avoiding armed struggle. It is non-violent politics.

What does it mean, *a generation of peace*, twenty years since our daily politics was marked by shootings and bombs? One fact: over half those alive today in our Province have had no direct experience of the worst of The Troubles. Only memories of what they have been told; or can read about, or see in pictures, or imagine in symbols of flags, parades, and territorial murals; or sense in the bitterness that still lingers; or can deduce from continuing echoes of sectarian tension and stress.

The same could be said of the generation after Vietnam, or more recently of those after the conflicts in South Africa and The Balkans. A generation has still to pass before the same will be said of the Arab region and other parts, assuming they get a lasting peace sometime soon. If that can be achieved, will Northern Ireland's example have had any useful lessons to impart?

How nice if we could confidently say that, in our experience, time alone does heal the historical wounds. If we are some way healed, what or who else did that healing? – or was it us? Is peace our own accomplishment, or simply thanks to external agencies? Is our peaceable construction also American, Canadian, British – and/or due too to our homegrown Irish siblings in the South?

Internecine strife and intercommunal warring are not unusual, but commonplace. Elsewhere in the world, where dispute has triggered war, some leaders have looked to the example of Northern Ireland's peace process to learn how to get there. But, do we ourselves truly believe in it?

I am reminded of French philosopher and moderating influence in the seventeenth-century Wars of Religion, Michel de Montaigne. He, in a manner inspiring to Strabane's famous son, the writer Brian O'Nolan – who for modesty's sake used various pen-names, notably Flann O'Brien and Myles na gCopaleen – told of a man who by force of his (English) imagination so studied the essence and emotion of folly as to unsettle his initial opinions of everything permanently... I fear the arrival of a similarly disappointed cynicism in Ireland.

O'Nolan said there was abroad in his day an all-pervasive *blague*. He was bemoaning those in possession of a distinction often encountered among politicians, students, clerics and the better-off: they enter the wider world with an *educated memory*, but lack any experience to account for it.

Only people of my age, pensioners, can recall what the peace was before the Ulster Troubles. We can speculate what life might have been like, had we not had our thirty-year war. Invited to address a Beirut human rights conference during the Arab Spring, I at first thanked the Lebanese from the bottom of my heart – by remarking that it was precisely thanks to seeing how ghastly their civil war was, that might have helped check our paramilitaries going so far. The wars in the Balkans in the early 1990s were, perhaps, another similar warning.

Ireland's foremost contribution to the history of world peace is *the boycott*. It derives from the Irish Land League's struggle in the 1880s in Balinrobe, Achill Island, Co Mayo. The word was, in fact, coined by the London *Times*. As a name for non-violent protest, it was so necessary that it entered into every major language. It was singularly inspiring to both Leo Tolstoy and Mahatma Gandhi.

The Ulster Troubles of 1969-1998 were arguably the longest period of continuous conflict in Irish history. The concept it ended with was "parity of esteem." This resonates less through the world than "boycott." A diplomat's idea, "parity of esteem" means, essentially, the withering away of the centrality of nationalism. Different from national self-determination and other freedoms, it derives from the 1990s, from the fall of the Berlin Wall and from how war was ended in the Balkans.

From the 1970s, my father helped found *and* finance Northern Ireland's Alliance Party. It was to speak for the squeezed and excluded middle – for non-sectarianism, for "moderates" so-called – but above all for non-violence and for reconciliation. Its share of the popular vote was passionate, but rarely attained 10%. It may have been damaging in one respect: by attracting too many moderates out of other parties. Perhaps it should, in time, have merged with the NILP and the SDLP, or maybe even a moderate UUP. But it did help to keep alive intelligent peaceful "civil society."

In all the years of the Troubles, relatively normal daily life persisted. Even though everyone's life was variously touched, often dramatically and tragically, "the silent majority" for peace had little or no public voice. It was, relatively speaking, ignored in media coverage. This was a fixed rule of war-reporting, adhered to by broadcasters and others. They could only address themselves to incidents of violence by talking mainly to those directly involved – but no one else.

Did Alliance, the Women's Peace Movement and New Ireland Forum help bring peace? We have to believe so. But there is little in official history to sustain directly that idea. The official account tells us peace only came about in secret talks between paramilitary leaders and inspired foreign politicians and their highly intelligent civil servants, including the personal involvement of North American and Dublin interlocutors.

I like to think a basis for peace was always present in our Province, in Ireland, in the views and actions of countless uncelebrated heroes working variously, however they could, for peace.

If war is about winning or losing, the aftermath is really about how peace is won or lost and about how sustainable that peace proves to be. I met or knew a score of unsung heroic individuals who risked, even lost, their lives for peace. They were a few of the hundreds and thousands who were sufficiently concerned to do good, and did so – and who were also good enough to care about not only their neighbours but also their enemies and who took Christian morals seriously. To my shame, I cannot today recall all of their names.

Christian ethics were not absent in all that was going on at any time. If our peace is to be sustained and to have long-lasting meaning, it needs to be understood as the outcome so many in our civil society struggled for right from the beginning – and not only the result of who said what to whom in this or that back-room, and then again in front of the world's cameras at the close.

Robert McDowell was born and raised in Belfast, and educated at the Royal Belfast Academical Institution. He studied at the Belfast, Slade and Hamburg Art Schools, before attending Cambridge University. In 1970, in Belfast, he founded the interdisciplinary "Troubled Image Group" of artists, the forerunner of the city's Art & Research Exchange, before taking up a career in international banking. He is the founder and director of Edinburgh's Summerhall, now one of the largest arts centres in Europe.

THE SECRET OF 64 MYRTLEFIELD PARK

Manfred McDowell

A prescription without prior diagnosis.

11 May 1974: *banner headline,* Evening Standard.

And there it was: a large-spread picture of our family home in what, for the London reader, was described as "Belfast's stockbroker belt." Pushing "Nixon Calls Ford to Crisis Talks" from the front page (the House Judiciary Committee had opened its formal impeachment hearings) was a breathless report of the security chiefs' "elation" on uncovering "the Belfast HQ of the Provisional IRA."

13 May 1974, *Burn Belfast. PM reveals IRA Scorched-Earth Plot*

In an "unprecedented statement" to the Commons, Harold Wilson announced that the stakes in the security operation could not have been higher. In addition to our tenant, Belfast Brigade (and "Bloody Friday") OC Brendan Hughes, and to arms, ammunition and bomb making equipment, the army had netted in a cache of documents plans for an all-out IRA offensive.

The Provisionals would combine a *reprise* of Dublin 1916, the seizure of key buildings across the city, with incendiary incursions into Protestant districts, car bombings and, "not ruled out," false-flag attacks upon their own areas. Intended to "manipulate emotions" and present Republican forces as "protectors of the Roman Catholic population," it was, the Prime Minister proposed, "a deliberate and calculated plan to plunge Northern Ireland into civil war."

I did not contact my father – walk a pocket of change down North End Road to the Tube station and call. If he were to talk, I had perhaps the sense then to realise that it would be in his own time. Yet looking back, I am struck by how so little curious I seemed to be. I am not sure, now, that I followed the reporting much beyond the shock headlines.

It is true that, if only the year before, I had crossed the water and, in London squats, was already contending with revelations for which

Myrtlefield Park had not prepared me. But I think it is also that, in leaving Belfast, I had carried with me a weary disregard for the cover story.

14 May 1974: *Blitz Plan on Belfast Genuine, say IRA.*

Sources within the Provisionals were conceding that the British Government had got their hands on important documents and that the Prime Minister's statement had been "a tremendous publicity coup." But at issue were possible IRA responses to a civil outbreak ("we'd, of course, defend the Catholic districts with everything we have"), not a plan to provoke one (that "would never be our intention") and that these had been formulated "some time ago." The "Myrtlefield papers" had been "doomsday" planning.

His Unionist partners on the new "power-sharing" Northern Ireland Executive were under enough pressure for conceding a role for Dublin without Wilson frightening "everybody out of their wits." My father's friend, Paddy Devlin, saw this Blitz Plan "nonsense" (for "hit-and-run merchants" like the Provos it had to be "cloud-cuckoo land material") playing "into the hands of hardline loyalists."

18 May 1974: *Our Own Bloody Friday.*

In the silence after stepping away from Dunnes Stores, Marian Kennan remembers only the people who approached her: "the old Dublin lady who wrote down the number of my local shop to let my Mum know" and "the young boy from Guiney's who helped me onto the bus and laid my legs carefully on one seat and the rest of my body on the other." It had been a Friday evening: three hundred injured, thirty-three killed.

Coming just one week after Hughes was told his game, as a "toys salesman," was up, the Dublin and Monaghan bombings must have been in the planning. But reports from Portadown did suggest that a "close study" of Wilson's statement had steeled senior UVF resolve to employ IRA tactics "industrially" south of the border.

In the North it was day two of the Ulster Workers' Strike. By the end of week two of the Loyalist stoppage, London has resumed direct rule and the brief ministerial careers of Paddy and his colleagues were over.

What had been knowledge on the street I first learned only years later, and from my father. Behind Wilson's bombshell had been an acute intelligence embarrassment. Brendan Hughes and his fellow "businessman"

Denis Loughlin had for months a direct tap on Army HQ communications. Recorded tapes were found coiled around the winding drum of our grandfather clock.

During my infrequent visits from the United States the need for a story seemed to be getting the better part of my father's discretion. With my mother he had actually left Belfast before I had. For my last school months, I and a brother were alone in the newly-partitioned house. The urgency, as we understood it, had been Loyalist threats. But now my father was placing himself on the edge of the action, (in a story of a roll-away grapefruit), as a tenant in the flat above Hugh's (from where "the wires were dropped"), and then as the returned and outraged landlord.

After making great show with the workmen of being indignant at the damage caused by the British Army, my father searching up through the attic for an incendiary, thought, for an instant, they had been caught in a blast. A car sent up the park had broken down under the weight of explosives, demolishing the house of a librarian.

20 February 2017: *Michelle O'Neill:*
I have a Right to Remember IRA Dead.

"There is no single narrative to any conflict anywhere in the world or at any time in history." Michelle O'Neill, having only just assumed the Northern leadership of Sinn Féin, was responding to criticism of her commemoration of the Coalisland Martyrs.

Addressing a candle-light vigil in her home village of Clonoe, O'Neill had spoken of "four ordinary young men" (she had known the "lads" personally) who had "responded to the defence of their community and also of their country." Patrick Vincent, Sean O'Farrell, Peter Clancy and Barry O'Donnell had "never gone looking for war." War had come to them. (War came to the four East Tyrone volunteers for the last time in February 1992. Minutes after they had disengaged from a heavy-machine gun attack on Coalisland RUC station, they were gunned down in a local churchyard by a Special Air Services unit).

O'Neill had demonstrated a "lack of respect for the victims of IRA terrorism," belying her pledge to work for reconciliation. Unionists brought forward the son of Leslie Dallas who, with two of his customers, was shot dead at his service garage in March 1989 by the same East Tyrone brigade. Noting that Michelle O'Neill's cousin, Tony Doris (21), was shot (by the

SAS in June 1991) a few hundred yards from where Leslie Dallas was murdered, Allan Dallas believed that there was "a strong possibility he was one of the ones involved." By honouring Doris's comrades, O'Neill had shown "her true colours."

But for O'Neill, it was enough to observe that under the Good Friday Agreement there could be no "hierarchy of victims." "Republicans understand and accept" that "we all have a different narrative and we'll *always* have a different narrative."

In all its 11,000 words Eamonn McCann finds not so much as a hint in the 1998 Agreement as to "how or why the conflict which the Agreement was designed to end had arisen in the first place." No narrative, it is "a prescription written without benefit of prior diagnosis." But was that not the magic: a ceasefire from which everyone would walk with – "parity of esteem" – their own cover story?

11 July 1921. *Black Sunday. Outbreak of Sniping. Pitiful Tragedies Enacted. Armoured Cars in Action.*

"The politics of situation" were never my father's theme. There were no *isms* in his recollection, only, as from the very beginning, the witness of Hugh McDowell.

Not yet four, he is coming home up the Grosvenor Road on the tram with his father. They would get off on the left, Distillery Street. The others, they would get off on the right, Cullingtree Road and St Peters. But people are running.

His father pulls him into the doorway of the corner pub, but not through to the shelter of the bar (my grandfather was Temperance Union, total abstinence). So, standing in the doorway, they see the Whippet Car come up the road, the turret turn, and the fire rake the rooftop. As the man comes down with the chimney, my father remembers feeling "sorry."

There did remain something almost childlike in recollections of fifty-sixty years later. Eighty-ninety years later the stills and rushes which, at the last, seemed to spin on a reel, were never spliced into any order we could recognise. For some episodes, it seemed, nothing could be lost in the retelling. And then there was his favourite wardrobe prop: a broad-rim hat, "like Augustus John," under which my father always seemed to be one step, or one bend in the road, ahead of the gunmen.

Careening, lights out, over the border around Jonesborough: he had

"had to" slap the face of the policewoman behind the wheel. In one replay, this connects to the disappearance of Captain Nairac. Seconded to the SAS, the Guardsman had had his improbable cover as a Stickie from Ardoyne fatally blown in The Three Steps pub in Dromintee in May 1977.

The consternation he caused Margery, friend and confidential informant: left to come looking for him, she is greeted by his suit leeching blood in the bathtub. Years later I was to bathe our children in the flat above (our Hugh was born in the kitchen), just across from St Brigid's Malone.

A burst of fire brings my father down and across. This would have been 16 January, 1983. Judge William Doyle is slumped at the wheel of his car. The midday Mass-goers tell my father that the two gunmen were Protestant – it was the cut of the hair.

Back to what must have been the winter of 1969: my father, unwell, has to come away from a funeral on the Falls: the solicitude of people as they help my mother steer the car down through the crowd towards him. But then on the Grosvenor Road, as he waits unsteady on his feet, from a six-wheeled Saracen – the "peacekeepers" only just deployed – he is showered with "Fenian bastard" abuse.

9 April 1984: *Magistrate and his Daughter Gunned Down at Point Blank Range.*

I never debriefed my father. There was not a story that I wanted from him. There were only the stories he wanted to tell. Now, with virtually all the other principals gone, I only have the public record with which to compare my recollections of his recollections.

In my father's telling, the police recovered the guns in Doyle's murder when, on the Lisburn Road, a young woman was unable to explain why she had pushed her baby all the way from Andersonstown. But record has it that the two handguns were not recovered for another fifteen months and found, not in the well of a pram, but strapped to the thighs of Mary Ann McArdle.

McArdle was stopped outside The Botanic just minutes from St Brigid's where the guns had been used once again against "a prominent member of the North's Orange judiciary" and "token Catholic." Mary Travers, 22, leaving Mass to go marshal her school pupils for first confession, was cut down by a single bullet. Her father Tom took six and survived.

Like my father's young mother, McArdle, just 19, refused to talk. She served 14 years before being released early under the terms of the Belfast Agreement.

Was this a trick of memory or, being a little too inventive, a storyteller unwilling to let facts, or his inability to recall them, stand in the way? As my mother faded away, my father increasingly was alone with his imagination. Did I know that he had met Nelson Mandela? Yet always this injunction: when it all became just a little too exhausting he would look at me kindly and say, "you know, some of the lies I tell are true."

What could you say? We chose our lies. The lie I am keeping for my children has their grandmother Marlies, in one of her rare appearances, atop the stairs some frighted night: "I have a gun, and I don't care who I kill. I'm German!"

10 April 2018: *The Long Good Friday. The Belfast Agreement 20 Years On.*

To have to live with free-walking narratives, some esteemed with more "parity" than others, in which the loss of a father, a daughter, a cousin or a set of legs is collateral, somebody else's story, "always" somebody else's story, may be beyond bearing. David Ervine understood this: "Don't call what we did war!" Yet Ervine, comrade to the Dublin and Monaghan bombers, to the last remained true to that good Friday.

Together he and I were leaving some presentation at the Equality Commission. This after the bloom was off, the Trimble-Mallon power-sharing Executive had broken up and the first Assembly had been suspended (October 2002). Whatever it was I said to Ervine, he understood the invitation to decry the absence of leadership, the political obduracy, the tribalism – the usual lunchtime Talk-Back whingeing. But Ervine was having none of it.

The Agreement had worked. It was working: the parties would return to the institutions, things could only move forward … But he was turning from me, hastening his departure from someone who clearly had been, and was, somewhere else, someone who didn't know the difference between a good Friday and a bloody one.

Reflecting on the outworkings of yet another Glorious Revolution in England – *Brexit: A Cry from the Irish Border* – Clare Dwyer Hogg proposes that, even as we continue to feel "trapped in other people's boundaries," there has been "magic." It is "nothing outward . . . just a gentleness in the mondality, daily travel across political lines, work, school, grocery shops,

back again." "Magic," she writes, "is the absence sometimes."
    Maybe so. But where in absence is the story?

Manfred McDowell was born in 1955 in Belfast and took degrees from the London School of Economics and Boston University. He taught political science for 20 years at a number of American universities, including Dartmouth and the University of Massachusetts, before returning to Germany in 1996 and Northern Ireland in 2001. He now lives in Drumbeg, Co Down.

MISSION IMPOSSIBLE

Matt Kirkham

Pinky stuff.

Luton, summer 1989

"Don't tell your mother."
— My father, on my telling him that I was considering taking a job in Belfast.

~

Belfast, early August 2018

W (aged 8): What are we going to record?

Me: Just gonna record our conversation.

W: Why?

Me: There's a magazine. A magazine of writing and poetry, stories and ideas. It's called Irish Pages.

W: Irish Pages?

Me: Irish Pages. And what they have asked me to do is write something about what's called the Good Friday Agreement, right? Cos remember that I told you that way back there was lots of trouble going on in Northern Ireland, right, and lots of violence, and bombs, and bullets, and shootings, and killings, and soldiers on the street. Do you remember that police car we saw today? It was like a Land rover, and it was, it's a very tough kinda looking police car. You don't often see police cars like that, do you? If you go back twenty years every police car looked like that because they had to deal with riots on the streets quite a lot.

W: What are riots? I've heard of people saying like riots, like guns and riot shields and stuff.

Me: Uh-huh. But like you guys, all your lives have been you know... E's ten years old, right. The Good Friday Agreement was the agreement that put a stop to a lot of that. It happened twenty years ago so like E's you know kinda half as old as the Good Friday Agreement, OK? So all your lives have been without that kind of thing going on, without much of that kind of thing going on in Northern Ireland.

W: Uh-huh.

Me: So you've grown up, you're really in the generation that's grown up in peace, unlike if you think about, erm...

E: You?

Me: Well cos I grew up in England. Right. It didn't really affect me directly. There were bombs in England, to do with the Troubles and things like that.

F: Where was I born though?

Me: You were born five years ago mate.

F: No, *where*?

Me: Where?

W: Ulster Hospital.

Me: The Ulster Hospital. In Dundonald, yeah? But you remember A-M, A-M said about there being soldiers on the streets where she grew up, I think there were even soldiers in her house once...

F: No, what country?

Me: Northern Ireland...

F: Dad!

Me: Yes mate?

F: Erm... When there was wars, people would've lived in holes in the ground.

Me: Yeah mate, to get away from it you mean? Why would people have lived in holes in the ground?

F: Well, I saw that in a book. In the library at school.

Me: Do you mean like bomb shelters?

F: Yeah.

Me: Yeah, cos Nanna and Grandad would have been in bomb shelters in the...

E: Anderson shelters?

Me: Anderson shelters, that's right, in the Second World War.

F: Oh.

Me: But it wasn't, it wasn't really like that in Northern Ireland, cos you had you know lots of people, lots of people still going about their business.

E: There's one in Ballyhalbert.

Me: An Anderson shelter?

E: Yeah.

Me: There's an airfield near Ballyhalbert that was used in the Second World War too, as well, wasn't there?

E: It's still there, it's just got a lot of grass growing on it.

Me: This particular conflict that we're talking about, it lasted for thirty years. That's a long long time.

W: Wow.

Me: Yeah, it lasted thirty years. And like when we see pictures of Syria or Yemen, it didn't get you know sort of whole towns permanently destroyed and all the people having to run away though you did get some people had to move out of some streets and some streets were pretty much destroyed.

W: (making a fanfare-type noise): Dun-dun-DUN!

F: In World Wars, people should have been crying a lot.

Me: This is different to World War Two though mate.

W: What is it?

Me: It's what we're talking about, it's what you call the Northern Ireland Troubles, that was what you call the thirty years of bombs and bullets and riots.

W: I don't know much about riots.

Me: You don't know much about it?

W: I only hear the word like and don't know what it means.

Me: What about you, E? What do you know about it apart from what I told you?

E: Nothing.

Me: You know nothing about it at all? How important do you think it is to know about it?

F: Well, I know about some of the people but not *it*.

Me: Yep? Do you think it's important to know about it, and do you think it should be...

(*E* nods.)

Me: Why do you think that?

E: Cos it's good.

Me: Why is it good to know?

E: So you know you're not going to get shot.

Me: So thinking... I mean do you think it's good to know about what happened in the past?

E: Yep.

Me: And why do you think that?

E: It just is.

W: It might happen again.

Me: How do you think people can make sure it doesn't happen again?

W: They could make it against the law.

Me: It is against the law. It was against the law then. Lots of people were put in prison over this.

W: They should put them in prison for really long.

Me: Well, what happened with the Good Friday Agreement was that they agreed to let them out of prison, right, they agreed to let them out of prison but they said that part of the reason why they let them out of prison was that the groups that they belonged to were gonna stop fighting. OK. So the groups said, the groups that were fighting said, let the people out of prison and we'll stop fighting. And the government said OK we'll do that, we'll do a deal, and you guys are gonna stop fighting, and we'll let the people out of prison. Yeah?

F: How do you know about all this stuff, Dad?

Me: How do I know about this stuff? Cos I was alive when it happened, and when I first came to Northern Ireland I was working for a group that was trying to get people from different sides to talk with each other.

F: Oh.

W: Dad?

Me: Yeah mate.

W: Wasn't you talking with us earlier about soldiers being in our garden?

Me: Soldiers being in our garden?

W: At Mum's house.

Me: At Mum's house? I don't know that there were any soldiers in our garden at Mum's house.

F: Dad? I still remember the days when you still used to go to my house and stay a lot before like we went to your house.

Me: Yeah. What about those days mate?

F: I remember all those days when you read me half of a story and C read me the other half or something like that.

Me: Right? You musta been very very tiny, mate.

F: No, I was about three? Or two?

W: You were about two inches tall.

Me: You might even have been about one, mate, I think at that stage. So, erm, yeah…

~

W: …yeah, probably disappeared in a puff of smoke…

Me: OK. So, Good Friday Agreement tried to erm, tried to make sure that people were not fighting each other, like we said, and it meant that whatever you felt about the direction Northern Ireland should take there would still be a place for you in the government if you wanted it, that kind of thing, you know it meant nobody could be excluded from being in the government of Northern Ireland…

W: I could be in the government?

Me: You could be in the government if you want. Get enough votes, you could be in the government. You have to, you know, get in to politics and all that…

E: What's politics?

Me: Do you think it's a good thing that people can get into the government?

W: What's politics?

Me: Politics is where you go and you say what your opinion is about things, and you go and try and get votes and you get into… You know Stormont? Right? There isn't a government there at the moment, but there's meant to be a government for Northern Ireland up at Stormont. So you could get elected up there if you get enough votes.

E (spookily): There's nobody there…

Me: They're not there at the moment, no? Do you know why they're not there at the moment?

E: Because of the Irish flag.

Me: The Irish flag?

E: The writing.

Me: The Irish writing. Tell me about the Irish writing, E

E: You know on the signposts in Northern Ireland. They want more Irish writing.

Me: More Irish writing on the signposts and things like that.

F: No but maybe when the government was sleeping the guy in the world someone could want to destroy, could take over the world and while the government was sleeping he could change over the computers like.

Me: Mmm. I think we'd have to watch out for things like that.

W: Like a spy.

Me: Like a spy and things like that.

(*W* hums Mission Impossible.)

Me: So, erm, you know, the idea is so whether you want, you know, whatever you want, whether people call themselves Irish or Northern Irish or British or whatever, they can still have a role in the government...

W (in a nasal, accented, sing-song voice): I'm Northern Irish.

Me: ...and they can still have a part in the government and that's kinda guaranteed as part of the Good Friday Agreement.

E: Even Donald Trump?

Me: Donald Trump not being Northern Irish I think we can safely say...

W: My name's Donald Trump. He has blond hair and he's Donald Trump.

Me: You have much better hair than Donald Trump.

W: His is too messy and too short and I don't like, I don't like Donald Trump's hair.

F: I hate Donald Trump. Every single bit of him.

Me: Why is that?

F: He's a *idiot*!

Me: What's he do that's idiotic then?

W: What would he do if you said up close to him "You're an idiot" to his face?

Me: I don't know what he'd do. He'd probably get into a bit of a fit and start shouting at you and call you names and that sort of thing. He seems to be that kind of guy doesn't he?

W: Is he able to arrest you if you do that?

Me: I don't think he's able to arrest you himself because he's not a policeman, he's a president.

W: No, is he able to call the police and say, arrest him?

Me: Well, is it against the law? Is it against the law to insult the President? In some countries it is against the law to insult the President and you would end up getting arrested...

W: It's against the law to insult a policeman.

F: Dad, no, W, remember when you were very young and you didn't know about Donald Trump and you wanted to live in the country?

W: Which country?

F: The country where Donald Trump...

W: America.

F: Yeah. Yeah.

Me: Anyhow, getting back to the Good Friday Agreement.

(*E* laughs.)

Me: What do you think the difference… I mean I can see the difference it's made to your lives compared to the people who have gone before. But you don't know much, you don't know much about it… What about… It's difficult to kind of put isn't it? It's difficult to kind of describe. What do you think it means to be from Northern Ireland? To be a young person coming from Northern Ireland?

W: It means I'm from the country, since I'm from Northern Ireland. And maybe other people from their country are very different.

Me: Tell me about that. In what way.

W: They could have a different language, like from England and have a different voice, stuff like that.

Me. Uh-huh. E, what do you think?

E: It means you're Northern Irish.

Me: What is Northern Irish? I mean, I'm English aren't I? Let's say… are things different when you go to Donegal?

W: No.

E: Everything's in Irish for a start.

Me: So what's the same? What's similar when you go to Donegal?

W: There are a lot of beaches everywhere.

E: Just seems the same.

W: It's more fun. It has lots of different stuff.

Me: It's more fun because you're on your holidays and stuff? And the people there, are they Northern Irish people?

W: Some are. I have my friends there.

Me: So what was different when you went over to England for a holiday? What was different about that?

W: Wait, we are English.

E: We're not English.

W: We have an English accent. Half of our family is from England.

E: Still doesn't mean we're English.

W: Wales was different.

Me: In what way was Wales different?

W: Lots of people speaked a different language. And there was more mountains and rivers.

Me: Uh-huh.

W: Like pretty much like Donegal but a different language.

Me: Like they speak Irish in Donegal, don't they? Do you ever hear people speaking Irish in Donegal?

W: But they don't speak Welsh in Donegal.

Me: It's true.

E: When I went to France it was different.

Me: How was it different there?

E: You couldn't read any signs cos it was all in France-ish.

W: French.

E: French. So everyone spoke French and they had a different accent and they had different hair and they wore very stripy clothes.

Me: Very stripy clothes?

E: Yep.

Me: So what you're saying is Northern Irish, it's like being from Donegal, it's like being from England…

W: It's like being from Dad's pinky finger.

Me: It's like being from my pinky finger? OK, that's fair enough.

Coda

When I was asked what the Good Friday Agreement meant to me, twenty years on, my first thought was that it meant my kids growing up in peace. It was an agreement born of impossible conversations. A man with English roots and Irish shoots, it is difficult for me to comment on troubles that, unlike my friends here, I didn't grow up with. As is talking with my kids about the legacy of the past they don't as yet know. All impossible conversations, yet conversations we need to have.

Of course, in time I want them to question the past. I want them to question the narratives. Milan Kundera, writing in *The Book of Laughter and Forgetting* about a different time and place, said "The only reason people want to be masters of the future is to change the past. They are fighting for access to the laboratories where photographs are retouched and biographies and histories rewritten." Does that have to be true? We can look back twenty years and see how far we have shaped a future by having those impossible conversations. With all our contradictions, may we keep on having them.

Matt Kirkham was in born in 1966, lives in Belfast, and works as a teacher. His two poetry collections are The Lost Museums *(Lagan Press, 2006) and* The Dumbo Octopus *(Templar, 2016). He was raised in Luton, England; attended Cambridge University; came to Ireland in his twenties; and has now lived in the North for most of his life.*

INTRACTABLE ACTIVISTS

Ed Moloney

The grim political reality.

The Good Friday Agreement – the Peace Process if you prefer – is in trouble not because of Brexit but because of something more fundamentally flawed with its internal engineering: it was constructed from the top down, mostly in secret and largely behind the backs of the activists in the main competing parties or against their wishes, and that has set a natural limit to its wellbeing.

What do I mean I mean by "from the top down"?

One way I can explain that to you is to take you back to the day that the IRA ceasefire was announced – 31 August 1994 – when Sinn Féin held a celebration rally outside their party headquarters on the Andersonstown Road in West Belfast.

All the party's luminaries were there. Gerry Adams, holding a fresh bouquet of flowers; Martin McGuinness; the people who were key figures on the so-called Think Tank, Morrison, Gibney, Howell and so on.

Behind them were the rows of minor Sinn Féin figures, the councillors, the gofers, the people who worked in the advice centres and who churned out the press releases, often in the name of activists who first read what had been told to the world in their names in the columns of the next day's *Irish News*.

Smiles decorated every face, backs were slapped. It was a time for celebration.

But if you moved your gaze away from the pavement, to the crowded street where the rank and file republicans had gathered – the so-called "grassroots" – it was a different picture, quite literally.

Those faces that were not glum wore a puzzled, subdued look, an expression that hovered between disbelief and suspicion or sought a re-assurance that it would not last, that maybe this was just a bad dream.

As I looked over that scene, my mind went back to a few days earlier when I had attended a select press briefing hosted by a senior Sinn Féin figure at which we were told that yes, the ceasefire would be announced very soon, this week in fact. The speculation was correct but as a condition of being made privy to all this, we were to embargo the news. We agreed.

Afterwards I made my way to a bar on the edge of West Belfast and the city centre, which was popular with the Provos' foot soldiers, former or current IRA members, SF activists and ordinary Provo supporters. It was also not a bad place for lunch.

For weeks I had been writing that a ceasefire was imminent and each week I was ridiculed and mocked by the bar's patrons; once or twice, when enough drink had been taken, the sneers threatened to turn nasty.

It wasn't quite as bad that lunchtime but it wasn't long before a snide remark came my way: "So when's this fucking ceasefire, then?" followed by laughter.

The truth about the IRA ceasefire and Sinn Féin's participation in the peace process is that it was a conspiracy successfully contrived by one or two handfuls of senior activists in both organisations. While they were busy orchestrating this, they were also re-assuring their rank and file that the ceasefire, and all that it implied, would never happen. But it did.

I was not in Ireland when the DUP's day of equivalence happened, 26 March, 2007, when DUP supporters switched on their television sets to see Ian Paisley seated, albeit at an awkward angle, beside Gerry Adams to announce their devolution deal; but from accounts I was able to piece together later, the disbelieving mood in the grassroots of the DUP that day matched that of the SF grassroots thirteen years earlier.

The DUP-Sinn Féin deal had been agreed in broad principle at a conference convened by the British and Irish governments at the Fairmont Hotel in St Andrew's on the Scottish east coast in October 2006.

By all accounts Ian Paisley had to be restrained by colleagues from giving the shop away, so keen was he on getting into government – encouraged by his wife Eileen it was said – but it was soon evident that selling the deal to a party grassroots nurtured on decades of "No Surrender" was going to be the big problem.

Throughout the early years of the peace process, the DUP had been where it was always to be found when change was in the air: outside the gates protesting. So successful had their protests been against attempts by the Official Unionist leader, David Trimble, to put together a deal with Nationalists in the wake of the IRA ceasefire and the Good Friday Agreement, that Paisley's party had whittled away at his electorate, so that by the mid-2000s, the DUP had become the largest Unionist bloc.

Power and office were within the grasp of Paisley and his colleagues, some of the most ambitious of whom knew that the ailing Paisley would soon have to be replaced as leader.

The problem was the DUP's grassroots. Nurtured on decades of "No Surrender" politics and convinced that Paisley would never sell them out, much of the rank and file opposed the St Andrews' deal at internal party gatherings that were held that autumn and winter.

If the decision was to be left to the DUP grassroots, St Andrews might have been a dead duck.

So what did the DUP hierarchy do? They prepared a four page pamphlet explaining what the St Andrews' deal amounted to and paid *The Belfast Telegraph,* NI's widest read daily, to insert it in the paper; the insert included a detachable coupon on which the reader could tick a *yes* or *no* box and return it to DUP headquarters.

A similar exercise was repeated on the DUP's website.

Both of these exercises were designed to bypass the DUP grassroots. *The Belfast Telegraph* was NI's only non-sectarian newspaper; it was widely read by Nationalists as well as by Unionists. Those returning the detachable coupon could as easily be Sinn Féin supporters as they were DUP. The DUP's website, similarly, was accessible by anyone.

Had the DUP wished to canvass just Unionist opinion, the coupons should have been inserted in *The News Letter*; but they weren't; and only DUP members should have been permitted to vote on the website, but they weren't.

Predictably, when the coupons and computer votes were counted and the results of party meetings assessed, the DUP hierarchy announced that 90 per cent had voted in favour of St Andrews. The leadership had got their way.

So, to summarise, Northern Ireland secured a decade of shared government because the Provo leadership had lied to their members about their intentions and the DUP had tricked and sidelined theirs. But it could not last.

Both sets of leaders could not trust their followers enough to be truthful to them and that, I would argue, reflected, and continues to reflect a weakness at the heart of the peace process that has proved to be insuperable and which predates and surpasses Brexit. It set a limit to co-operation and eventually led to the collapse of Stormont over corruption; but if not that it would have been something else.

This grim political reality has put a brake on the two leaderships' freedom of movement and their ability to move further than their grassroots would otherwise permit.

The peace process, in other words, was ahead of the political activists of Northern Ireland; not necessarily the people, but those who made and make politics work on a daily basis.

Ed Moloney is a journalist and author best-known for his coverage of the Northern Irish Troubles and the activities of the Provisional IRA. He worked for the Hibernia *and* Magill *magazines before serving as the Northern Ireland Editor for* The Irish Times *and subsequently for the* Sunday Tribune. *His first book was* Paisley, a biography of Ian Paisley, *co-authored by Andy Pollak (Poolbeg, 1986); his second was the bestselling* A Secret History of the IRA *(Norton, 2004). Subsequently, he published* Voices from the Grave *(Faber, 2010), which featured interviews with Brendan Hughes and David Ervine, compiled by researchers from Boston College. In October 2010, RTÉ aired an 83-minute television documentary co-produced by Moloney based on* Voices from the Grave, *which won the best television documentary prize at the annual Irish Film and Television Awards in 2011.*

BORDER CONCERNS

Peter Geoghegan

Back to the future?

It is inconceivable that a vote for Brexit would not have a negative impact on the [Irish] Border, bringing cost and disruption to trade and to people's lives.

Theresa May, June 2016

Nobody wants to return to the borders of the past.

Theresa May, July 2016

Around three hundred roads bisect the circuitous three-hundred-and-ten-mile border that separates the six counties of Northern Ireland from the twenty-six of the Irish Republic. Some are barely paved country lanes that snake over and back from one jurisdiction to another multiple times in a matter of miles. Others – like the motorway that connects Dublin and Belfast – are major arteries, as seamlessly asphalted as any German autobahn. The only way you can tell which side of the border you are on – as British television reporters have become so fond of telling viewers back home on "the mainland" – is whether the speed signs are in miles or kilometres, or the names in Irish as well as English.

I grew up about forty miles into the southern side of the borderline. For an over-eager child in a monochrome 1980s Irish home, Northern Ireland was strikingly exotic, simultaneously always present and continually absent. Each night it seems the news was filled with macabre tales from Belfast, less than a hundred miles away. But we seldom ventured north. When I was about seven years old my mother took us shopping in Enniskillen, the closest large town across the border, in Fermanagh. We must have passed barbed wire and concrete lookouts manned by acne-scarred teenagers from Derby or Newcastle touting automatic weapons, but I have no recollection of any of these. My only memories are remarking to my mother about how smooth the northern roads were – I was a serious boy – and how colourful was the window display in Enniskillen's Woolworths. Northern Ireland seemed so much more modern. There were no Woolworths in county Longford.

By the time I went to university in Dublin, in 1998, the border that had been erected in the early 1920s had started to disappear. The customs posts had already been dismantled. Most of the green wooden border huts were gone. Those that remained rotted slowly in the countryside. The signing of the Good Friday Agreement effectively brought an end to the Troubles. The IRA's war was over. So was the British state's. The imposing watchtowers that hugged the hillsides of the southern reaches of Down and Armagh were dismantled. The squaddies went home, or eventually ended up in Afghanistan or Iraq. Roads that had been closed during the violent years – or simply bombed into uselessness – were opened. In the early 2000s, by which time I was living in Belfast, I often travelled on a rickety country bus back to Longford to visit my mother. I would occasionally pass the time by trying to figure out if we had crossed the invisible line based on when my mobile phone switched providers. I was seldom certain.

Politically, the border started to fade, too. As southern politicians no longer had an immediate need to worry about the insoluble "national question," attention turned towards getting filthy rich. The Celtic Tiger roared. Property prices doubled, then tripled. Semi-detached houses in Longford sold for €400,000. Now it was Dublin that was modern, all wine bars and hundred-grand sports cars. I often headed south from Belfast at the weekends, escaping a half empty ghost city where people were still fearful of venturing after dark. By the time the boom turned to bust – from 2008 – most Irish voters had forgotten about the "black north." Even Sinn Féin, the party of the IRA, campaigned on working-class demands for higher wages and social security, not the need for "Brits Out."

I was the only person I knew from my school who spent any time living in Northern Ireland. Over Christmas pints in the local pub nobody asked about life in Belfast. In the south, Northern Ireland had become an embarrassment. A place famous around the world for bombs and bitterness. A Lacanian "Other" that can never be assimilated, nor totally disavowed. Better to ignore and move on least the atavism proves contagious.

The border has not withered away but it is far less noticeable. There are still the fireworks stores on the northern side, and the incongruous petrol stations. Occasionally police from both jurisdictions team up to bust illegal fuel rackets. But, for most, the border has ceased to matter a great deal. People in Donegal give birth in hospitals over the border in Derry. When my brother needed to get his driving licence at short notice he took the test in Enniskillen, where waiting times are far shorter.

In March 2016, I was in Dublin for the centenary commemorations of the Easter Rising, a rebellion that led to the war of independence and then to partition. The fiftieth anniversary of the Rising – a story of blood sacrifice still told in gruesome detail when I was a school child – had been celebrated with high nationalist pomp. The rebels of Easter 1916 were the heroes. The villains were the British. Everybody else – the vast majority of the population who had little interest in insurrection – was ignored. The IRA even got in on the act, blowing up Nelson's Column on Dublin's main thoroughfare, O'Connell Street, in March 1966. Out of practice, the republicans misjudged the amount of explosives needed, leaving behind a stone stump that the Irish Army was left to dispose of. The tone in Dublin a half-century later could scarcely have been more different, or more ecumenical. There were solemn silences and visiting dignitaries from well beyond the republican family. There had even been rumours of an invitation being extended to the Queen. There was little talk of Irish unification, or the border.

———

A few weeks before the European Union referendum I went on a reporting trip to Belfast. Elections to the devolved assembly in Stormont had taken place a fortnight earlier. Round-faced middle-aged men still smiled down from placards on lampposts. The Democratic Unionists and Sinn Féin once more topped the polls. Barely half the electorate had voted. There seemed even less enthusiasm for the EU referendum.

"We're not allowed to vote in that. It's only England," Sean Morgan told me inside his souvenir shop on the Falls Road in republican West Belfast. I thought better of correcting him. His shop was called Fenians after the 19th century Irish republicans committed to a United Ireland. Replica guns and copies of the proclamation of Ireland adorned the walls. There were rolls of red, white and blue union flag toilet paper at £2.50 a pop. "You'll never believe how many of those we sell," Morgan laughed.

None of the pro-EU parties spent more than £10,000 on their campaigns. A few weeks before the vote, the DUP received a £435,000 donation for Brexit but spent almost all of this in Great Britain, mostly on a wraparound advert in the Metro newspaper. The freesheet is not distributed in Northern Ireland. (Because of donor secrecy laws influenced by the Troubles, the source of probably the biggest donation in Northern Irish history remains a mystery.)

In Belfast I counted a single Leave poster, on the Shankill Road, on the opposite side of the 15-foot-hight corrugated iron "peace wall" that has cut off Catholics from Protestants in west Belfast for more than four decades. In the interests of balance – or so I told myself – I called into Ulster Souvenirs, halfway up the Shankill Road. Across the street, faded images of hooded loyalist gunmen looked down from a gable end mural. Inside the narrow shop, a portrait of a serious-looking Edward Carson, Stormont's Dublin-born founding father, hung over the till. How will you be voting, I asked the shop's owner. "Oh aye, out!" He smiled. "People are fed up with the way the country is run, with being in the European Union." His customers were voting leave, too. "You can't say too much or you're a racist, but immigration is the big thing," one told me.

Two decades after the Good Friday Agreement, Northern Ireland remains one of the most ethnically homogenous places in the UK. Non-white faces are still something of a rarity in Belfast. But the squat capital has changed since I left for Scotland in 2009. The city centre is no longer a dead zone after dark. The rebirth of Belfast as a "cool" destination has been celebrated by journalists from around the world. Where once even a cup of coffee on a Sunday afternoon was hard to find now there is a plethora of cafes in the modish fashion, all exposed brick and customers with fixed gear bicycles.

When Britain first voted on Europe, in 1975, Northern Ireland was the most Eurosceptic of the "home nations." Where two-thirds of English backed the then European Economic Community, just 52 per cent of Northern Irish voters supported membership. In 2016, positions were reversed. Where English opposition to the European Union swung the Brexit vote, in Northern Ireland fifty-six per voted to stay in the EU. In the border counties, the Remain vote rose to 65 per cent.

My mother rang the day after the Brexit vote. It must have been the afternoon because she asked about Scottish independence. (In the morning, Nicola Sturgeon had said that a second referendum was "highly likely.") But she was mainly interested in the border. "What will it mean for Northern Ireland?" she asked. "Will I need to bring a passport to go to Belfast?" I said that I did not know but was sure it would not come to border controls. I was only half honest. I wasn't sure it wouldn't come to that.

That nobody on the BBC's rolling referendum coverage was talking about what Brexit might mean for the Irish border was hardly surprising. Northern Ireland rarely features in news headlines anymore, in Britain or in Ireland. There was little said about Northern Ireland – or the border – during the campaign. The Democratic Unionists supported a Leave vote, without providing any discernible rationale, while almost every other local political party opposed Brexit, mainly on the basis that anything that might unsettle the notoriously fragile political and economic ecosystem could hardly be a good thing. Such caution seemed particularly justified when, a few weeks before the referendum, then home secretary Theresa May warned that a leave vote could create border chaos, "bringing cost and disruption to trade and to people's lives." In 2015, Northern Irish farmers received 87 per cent of their income direct from European Union grants. Polls suggest many famers subsequently voted Leave.

Under the terms of the Good Friday Agreement, Northern Ireland is governed by a "consociational" system. This approach – in which ethnic blocs are given vetoes and balances – was initially devised in the Netherlands, to deal with regionalist demands. Since the 1990s it has become the solution of choice for post-conflict societies: Bosnia, Lebanon, Iraq. Under the Northern Irish iteration, the largest unionist and nationalist parties must share power. But in government the DUP and Sinn Féin, always uncomfortable bedfellows, have drifted further apart, not closer together. The DUP has consistently blocked Sinn Féin legislation, including a law to permit gay marriage.

Since the Brexit vote, Northern Irish politics has collapsed. Divided on the most significant issue since the peace process, relations between DUP first minister Arlene Foster and her then deputy, the late Martin McGuinness, quickly deteriorated. When a botched green energy scheme was revealed to have massively overspent – apparently largely on grants to DUP-supporting farmers – Sinn Féin pulled the plug on Stormont. Few expect power sharing to return any time soon.

Brexit has put the border back into Irish politics, in ways that would have seemed impossible only a couple of years ago. In Belfast, senior people from Alliance – an avowedly "cross-community" party borne of a split in the Ulster Unionists in the Troubles' early days – talk of the need to make plans for Irish unification. The Fine Gael government in Dublin held up as a major victory the Brussels' confirmation that a post-unification Northern Ireland would seamlessly rejoin the EU. Having emerged from the pro-Treaty side after the civil war, Fine Gael has long been the most fiercely anti-republican force in Irish politics.

Along the border, life goes on, in its own quiet way. After Ulster Gaelic football championship games, queues of traffic still snake out from Clones, in County Monaghan, over the border into Northern Ireland. The questions of who did what to whom during the three-decades-long dirty war remain, waiting for answers. Peace, however, has not given way to prosperity. The border remains one of the poorest parts of the country. The large houses dotted across the drumlins belie a general shift from the rural to the urban – from the towns to Dublin and Belfast – that has characterized Irish life in recent decades. Where there has been sustained – and sustainable – investment in the border counties it has often come with a large sign bearing the European Union's starry standard.

My first proper job, at the University of Ulster, was funded by the European Union. It was 2008, just before the financial crash. We were not so starry-eyed as to imagine that our attempts to reconcile Catholics and Protestants on either side of a peace wall in Derry would bring the barriers down overnight, but there were minor moments of success. A film night on Derry's walls. A talk on social enterprise well-attended by both sides. Small steps. Nobody expects that London – or Dublin – will replace the £500m that Northern Ireland receives from the EU each year, especially for the slow, difficult work of rebuilding communities after conflict.

Last spring I was back home for a wedding. The reception was in a stunning colonial castle nestled by a lake in rural county Leitrim, barely fifteen miles from Northern Ireland. The road signs were peppered with destinations on both sides of the border. The following day, I visited my mother. She was planning to get her teeth fixed, in Enniskillen. She had the name of a dentist there who charged only a fraction of the price on the southern side of the border. "The NHS is great," she told me. "We should have it here, too."

An Irish journalist and writer living in Glasgow, Peter Geoghegan is Investigations Editor at OpenDemocracy, *and author of* The People's Referendum: Why Scotland Will Never Be the Same Again *(Luath Press, 2015), nominated for the Saltire Society First Book Prize. He is also co-founder and Director of* The Ferret, *an investigative platform launched in 2015, as well as Editor of* Political Insight, *published by the Political Studies Association.*

BODY POLITIC

Natasha Cuddington

Mutualities of the footpath.

My eldest son was two or three the original time I felt *place* had deposed a *liberty*. We ambled the short distance through gated entries and terraced streets to a nursery in the protection of a blind alley. It was after eight and before nine in the full glare of morning. As I rounded a windowless elevation of red brick, I happened into a raid on a small domestic dwelling.

In the proximity of this narrow street, any number of police flanked the terrace's entry, stoppered the paths and played witness to this fugitive moment, a street's inactivity. In these intimacies, what these men disclosed was not the concealed pistol of a police known to me in my country, or even the long arm of a hunter. There were assault rifles – possibly a Heckler and Koch MP5 or some variant of submachine – readied to hand and at my son's sight-lines.

One gun was adjacent to his person in a style that drew alarm from me. It was an alarm that transmuted to pique through the lens of his eyes, their spatial relation, susceptibility. My son will not remember this, but I made no attempt to veer from the footpath. I held a course of closeness with these men, who were members of a state police. Police that in my country I had not learned to fear, or shy from. Police whom I could be expected – perhaps naively – to experience as employees of my tax return, coeval citizens, and a function of any territory or city.

In this glare of morning, I could feel a burning in the slim volume of air between us. Our closeness, my female body – the body of my child – who might have been identified as anyone in another city. Anybody making a way to school or otherwise in the busynesses of a street. Yet this was a cul-de-sac, a blind entry. It was also in Belfast. Here I was explicitly staying a course with my son to a Gaelscoil in the west of the city.

Perhaps time has deformed these happenings, and the only danger was the possibility of a discharged gun. Yet I had confronted guns on the ranches and farms of my family, tolerated their latent contiguity in adulthood in a variety of locales with American boyfriends or in the company of a Canadian motorcycle gang. This particular situation of daring had been shaped by another kind of malice. Its danger had elided with a promise of continued civic impediment. Such stoppering, to be experienced by anybody, was to express itself both within and between West Belfast's allegedly ethnic discreteness of community. A series of enclosures, its streets and footpaths were, and continue to be, obstructed from themselves and from their city.

It was a stoppering of the fluency and tolerances inherent in the "fine-grained mixtures of street" that Jane Jacobs had descried in her treatise on town planning, *The Death and Life of Great American Cities* (1961). As per Jacob, it is this admixture of activity and motile bodies that guarantees civic safety. It is both an expression of and central to the success of any conurbation. In a chapter entitled "The Uses of Sidewalks: Contact," Jacob disparages planning reformers who seek, through misapprehension, to disrupt the incidental, accidental and fleeting loiterings of the busy urban footpath. By way of analogy, Jacob also conjures the fellowship of the old-time testimonial banquet as it may have been enacted in the very public theatre of the hotel. Here, she is keen to distinguish its participations from those enacted at any site shaped by familiarity – say, a prayer meeting or social party in a domestic dwelling:

> The point of both the testimonial banquet and the social life of city sidewalks is precisely that they are public. They bring together people who do not know each other in an intimate, private social fashion and in most cases they do not care to know each other in that fashion.

Although we may not care to know each other across the tracery of the stoppered – and often effaced – thoroughfares of West Belfast, it is the footpath that may proffer some kind of communication between bodies. Here, it is the participation's voluntary style that chances accident and experiment in what might be a transformative sociality. According to Jacobs, while "ostensibly utterly trivial" the "sum of such casual public contact at a local level – most of it fortuitous ... all of it metered by the person concerned and not thrust upon him by anyone – is a feeling for the public identity of people, a web of public respect and trust."

Keen to distinguish village or town from metropolis – and here one might tender Belfast or West Belfast as a collection of its villages – Jacobs details three areas of function in any "city street equipped to handle strangers, and to make a safety asset, in itself, out of the presence of strangers, as the streets of a successful city always do." These include a "clear demarcation between what is public space and what is private" and that "there must be eyes upon the street, eyes belonging to those who we might call the natural proprietors ... They cannot turn their backs or blank sides on it and leave it blind." Lastly, Jacobs presses that the "sidewalk must have users on it fairly continuously."

Having been reared somewhat nearby, my husband has suggested that in this, my own particular situation of civic daring, I had been fortunate not to receive a rifle butt in the back or side to move my body, along the footpath or at least in tandem to a sound heckling. His expectation speaks to the imaginative slippage in a civic territory that was, contemporaneous to my memory in what was likely 2003, well into its brokered peace.

My memory understands it to have been a scene of silent communications between myself and these men in their role as a police. The air of its filmic repeat is thick with the fallacy of signifiers. It has been designed with blind gable ends, blocked or barred windows, and certainly drawn laces or profusions of curtains. There are corrugated expanses laminated with confusions of paint and graffiti's injunctions and further confusions of paint. There is razor wire or barb wire and shards of coloured domestic glass embedded in each horizon, on any interface. A palpability of disengagement or obfuscation had come from some style of rebuke or intimidation. There was certainly a fatigue.

That the air was thick in this inner film speaks not only of impasse as experienced by anybody but is also due to its scene being dressed with at least two imaginative realities. If for the sake of its peace, a city or territory must include itself in the legislation of a civic contrariety like that which has been articulated in this "Belfast Treaty," there can be no civic mutuality. Far from being an expression of confluent activities – Jacob's "fine-grained mixtures of street" – Northern Ireland has what Brendan O'Leary has called a "bi-national" civic imagination ("The Nature of the British-Irish Agreement," *New Left Review*, 1999). This unreality is, at best, a voluntary travelling across stoppered paths with little access to junctions. It may also be experienced as an enforced conceptual impasse, or collateral blind alleys.

Acted out on any body – female, child or otherwise – this unreality is also danger when we abandon windows or footpaths and look to the police to enforce what a police commissioner describes as "the right of every person to walk any part of the city in safety and with impunity as a basic right" in one of Jacob's chapters ("The Uses of Sidewalk: Safety"). Within this ambiguity, any body cannot be expected to rely on their participation in relation to strangers. In West Belfast, we walk a confusion of apparent peace and the injunctions of others' countries:

> The first thing to understand is that the public peace – the sidewalk and street peace – is not kept primarily by the police ... It is kept primarily by an intricate, almost unconscious network of voluntary control and standard among the people themselves and enforced by people themselves. No amount of police can enforce civilization if it has broken down.

As a freelance writer without academic affiliation, Jane Jacobs walked the footpaths of New York and later Toronto radically, as mothers do, of necessity. Like me, her eyes were on her children through windows as they played at tolerance on the street. I have walked the footpaths of West Belfast as a stranger both within and across its discretenesses of community for almost twenty years. It is a civic participation that has shaped my body's relation to other bodies for more years now than any other territory. Most often, I move in the busyness of thought, having learned to demur to the implications of the street. I am alert to the patternings of helicopters over domestic dwellings and the fleeting presences of armed police. I also hear the speech of neighbours who have failed to cross out of the confines and tracery of incomplete thoroughfares or footpaths, to chance this proximity.

In an essay fragment entitled "Transport" (*Nilling: Prose Essays*, 2012), Lisa Robertson – by way of *flâneur* and photographer Eugène Atget – walks in a Paris of activity and bodies. Here, she has recorded a soundscape to the silent movie of my Irish memory in that fluent, successful city. Each additional fragment that builds the grid of the essay "Disquiet" is, according to Robertson, a near 30-second burst designed as homage to the original exposures of Atget's photography. Through their sonic prosody, we are somehow privy not only to Atget's images of Paris, but to Jacob's unobstructed footpath, busy with strangers in a mutuality. These fragments instruct chance and experiment in the sociality of the urban street. Here, there is noise. They turn a corner that becomes a crossing – you being *other* for a while. They speak of any body's possibility: "I find the site, take my stance, press record, begin to count to 30 and replace myself with the intricate density of the city's noise. I become a plenum, no longer individual." They are fellowship – and so a participation that is voluntary.

Natasha Cuddington was born in Regina, Saskatchewan in 1974. She holds a BA in Creative Writing from Concordia University, Montreal and an MA in Irish Studies from Queen's University Belfast. Together with Ruth Carr, she organizes the "Of Mouth" reading series at Linen Hall Library, Belfast. Her debut poetry collection, Each of us (our chronic alphabets), *was published by Arlen House in 2018. She currently lives in Belfast.*

FASTING

Frances Byrne

Not myth, flag, dotted line, currency — but geologies of place.

My body is a land made of two peoples.

In April 1998, I was 33 — the same age Jesus was when he died. The previous year my insides had eaten themselves out. I'd been persuaded that my advancing cancer (its blood and its agony) was imaginary. After several way-out months, it was diagnosed on St George's Day, Shakespeare's birthday, April 1997: *Stage 4*. On the Good Friday of the Agreement, I was one year on from being told I was dying; still in shock to be dying and in shock to be alive.

That day, I'd bumped into my former psychiatrist at the Passion and she invited me to her house for a cup of tea. That's where we heard it on the BBC and I felt elated to have lived to hear it and be hopeful. But hope is awful. I remained suspended in hopey horror that I might, just might live to hear more, despite my prognosis. I didn't feel that 33 years were long enough for me to have been myself, unlike Jesus. Not in the same way, a year later, Princess Di's death would make me feel that 30-something is a good span. I'm not being flippant.

Princess Diana! Perhaps it's being from more than one place that makes me associative. In one country I long for the other. In the thick of a British city, Ireland's purply mountains haunt me; at a stiff funeral here of someone mourners hardly mention, I long for an Irish wake. When Irish cousins twitter and detail like birds, I think of my taciturn, dry England. Responsible England. *To blame England.* It's restlessness; there's no peace in it. I have to come to an accommodation of my mixed-ness, or I'll eat myself up.

I'd already nearly died of my split self in my teens. It began in the summer of the Royal Wedding. Dad had been laid off. He drove us from Northern England to his homeland, in the school holidays. "Brits Out" was painted on the harbour walls when we landed at Dun Laoghaire. I'd never had this from my Irish side. It was shocking. "Why do they hate us, Dad?" I mean, me; hate me. He said *Ah now, that's a long story* and drove South and West. We'd obviously done something wrong. *To us. My English to my Irish.* I was petrified of being found out and wouldn't speak in public.

Bobby Sands, newly dead, was depicted on gable ends. I was already not eating but this added an enabling romantic narrative: and to protest at my English side, for letting him die; to protest at my Irish side, for using him in dying. But that's not why I'd stopped food. I shared a sense of powerlessness, a problem with anger and was overwhelmed by the times: Dad's lost job, strikes, women bashing dustbin lids on pavements, a visceral hatred of Mrs. Thatcher for humiliating our fathers, punk, the National Front.

I hate Nationalism. Probably because I'm from more than one country. I'd resolved all this distress by living on one egg and half a grapefruit a day, and four cups of black coffee. And two crispbreads spread with yellow gunk called *Outline*. I was into this sorry solution, and outrage does land on sorry solutions – *c.f.* Brexit – as we drove in the summer of 1981 towards my Irish side's cakes and fries.

But when we entered the farm of my grandfather, great-grandfather, the land of my great-great grandfather, my father's summers "at the hay" until he was orphaned younger than I am in this story and he came to England for rough work – there, on that land, I felt so at home, in the mountain, that bracken, that sandstone, the Atlantic – that I felt calm and drank tea and even ate tomatoes. I said, "Dad, how could you ever leave here for England?" It was beyond beautiful. "You can't eat the view darling." Why eat? I would rather be there not eating, than in our poor, de-industrialising city in England, eating bowls of ash, flavoured with red sauce.

I think our bodies recognise homelands. Our DNA zings with our geologies. And we're hybrid, and we have more than one. Our bones swill the mix of local matter, more than we know of. A new landscape shifts in us; in me, somehow, the lilac sandstone of there, the millstone grit sandstone of here; heather moorlands and Skellig sea, iron ore and green road, ancient wood and gone forest, arc furnace and cow byre. These materials mean more to me than myth, flag, dotted line, currency. I like our distinctive cultures; how there, words conjure up worlds whereas here, words pin down worlds – and I don't find either superior. I like independence and I like working together. Different musics, different relationships with time, different manners, all at play in us, those of us from two places, brought together by our parents' love and by economics. And nobody owns poverty. The bandy-legged rickets and the cholera here; the TB of there; the TB of here, the forge dust-lungs; the hunger of there. The hunger and thirst of both countries.

However appalling British industrial diseases and poverty, people in England are still, though, imperialists, almost fantastically ignorant of their/our culpabilities elsewhere. Mum (daughter of a British Army soldier, RSM, ex-India, ex-Africa) referred to Dad's family as "the Irish" and she had all sorts of attitudes, opinions oddly split off from her fondness for him and for them in person. When it was discovered, through my primary school BCG, that I'd had TB, my mother made my father take me to the hospital for my lung x-rays. She wouldn't be seen near that illness; it must be on "the Irish" side. As an example of TB's shame, when she was a teenager, her friend's mother had sighed with relief when she heard that her daughter had bone cancer and not TB, even though the girl had been treated in a TB sanatorium in the open air for a year, isolated, for the wrong illness, and her paralysis could have been cured, if diagnosed correctly earlier: "Thank god," said the mother on hearing it was cancer, "I knew my house wasn't dirty." Such was the shame on this side, Dad had to own the TB as from his side (after all, one of his sisters had just died of it in Kilburn). He put on his one suit and faced the English hospital with his half and half girl and her scarred lungs. The Consultant, I remember, said to Dad that I at least looked well-fed and to keep up with the nourishment.

Ten years later, that summer of '81, Dad stayed on with his sisters in Ireland as he was unemployed in England. I flew into Manchester alone, yea thinner. Was my parents' love secondary to work? Was their being together dependent on him having a job? Mum's and Dad's natures were at war in me. At Cork airport my cousins, most of whom I'd no idea who they were, had crammed a plastic bag with chocolates and sweets on me at the barriers. I said to the duty-free shop girl as I waited for my plane, "Would you like this bag of sweets?" When she looked circumspect, I added, in earnest, "It isn't a bomb."

It was blue and green, the day of the Royal Wedding. I sat under the apple tree I still love, whilst – inside – mum gave cups of tea to people she'd met at the bus stop, of all nations. They *oohed* at the TV, and disapproved of Di's frock. Back in Ireland, some cousins were molten with excitement about the whole Royal shebang, to Dad's horror. We're all more than one thing. Even Mum: perhaps she didn't know that her great-grandmother, a Murphy, had fled the famine to settle in Yorkshire on the land of a recusant aristocrat, the Catholic Duke of Norfolk, whose own English tenants had themselves been emancipated by an Irishman, Daniel O'Connell? Our histories crisscross; they plait in my stomach, my ravenous peoples.

I carried on not eating until I met someone who could help me get better. That's my psychiatrist, the one I chanced on, at The Passion on the Good Friday of the Agreement. She was a rule breaker and her remedy was honesty.

In the short decade between not eating and being eaten by my own blood cells, possibly related, I had thrived. One of the things I did in those years, my early twenties, was work in Derry. And in my freefall associations, this is what stays in my mind, in the light of now: in 1989 Mrs. Thatcher censored free speech with her Broadcasting Ban. And one shock is – not only was it 20 years ago there was the Belfast Agreement, but only nine years before it had been possible to silence people like that.

I'm not a metaphor for England and for Ireland. I simply, here, describe my experience. I don't interpret, because I'm not clever enough to extrapolate significance from my own small *mixedness*, half Irish, half English, if there even is any. I do think it's worth noting from my own experience, that hope is terrible, it's an appalling feeling and needs courage. And that it's possible to be healed. But I don't relate my own near-death diseases to our history. I just now, here, relay the inklings that came to me, when you said you would be commissioning thinkers; I thought – what about our bodies? My body contains my parents' joint landscape – their conflicts and their love. I love my ancestors, my father land, my mother land, they're in me – but I hate nationalism, since I contain more than one place.

Frances Byrne is a freelance radio producer and writer. She has made documentaries and written dramas for BBC Radio 3 and 4, and the BBC World Service. She has a particular interest in working with dancers and was shortlisted for a Best New Director BAFTA for The Pavlov Ballet. *She grew up in Sheffield, England.*

IRELAND AND THE ENGLISH PROBLEM

Mathew O'Toole

Sheer bovine indifference.

Everything is dislocated in my flat at the minute. Cookery books are on the floor, next to plastic toys. Phones are stuffed down the back of the sofa. A large proportion of the loose objects in what we indulgently call our living space are not where they are supposed to be, where everything is ordered neatly. They have been dislocated. But that dislocation and disorder is in a way normal: I have a 16-month old son.

He was not yet born when a different dislocation happened: that of Northern Ireland, after the vote. That vote. It hasn't moved physically, it's still there in the northeast corner of Ireland – stretching further west than you remember, reaching to within a few miles of the Atlantic at Bundoran. This is clearer when you see a map of Ireland without the border drawn in.

Northern Ireland is also remarkably close to Scotland. A closeness that can be missed when you look at Ireland as a single unit removed from the island to the east. These are geological facts, but also physical intimacies. They hint at that notorious psychology of wanting to be in two places at once. Or more accurately wanting one place to be two different things, and the associated worry that it may not truly be either.

Explaining it to others is at once boring and flattering. For most of my younger adulthood after leaving, studying in Scotland then working in London – with a few months overseas here and there – there was mild shame at the durability and parochialism of the northern quarrel. But there was also mild pride at what was, in the 1990s and 2000s, a badge of authenticity: knowledge of real-life conflict in a period defined by its absence. It may be uncomfortable to admit, but it marked you out, and not entirely in a bad way.

I was not the only Northern Irish student who came of age around the time of the Good Friday Agreement who, having left Northern Ireland, traded off its problems. I often did this in mildly patronising conversations with English acquaintances asking innocently ignorant questions. I was usually the one doing the patronising.

Yes, I'd seen many army checkpoints. What I feel personally? I felt Irish, but I respected those who felt British, or Northern Irish, or both… dude. Sometimes the interlocutors in these conversations would pass comment on the distinctiveness of the Ulster accent, or our tendency to be decisively "from" a place, with a remembered ancestral claim – real or imagined – over said locale. At university, and subsequently, I rarely met people from the English Home Counties who felt "from" Bracknell or St Albans in the way that I, inevitably and perpetually, am from Downpatrick. The same people would also invariably claim not to possess an accent.

Somehow I assumed Bracknell, or St Albans or Hitchin, were less intensely located in the minds of its sons and daughters than Downpatrick was in my mind. Or that may be me being patronising again. Bracknell is certainly more securely located in another sense. It is English and British, but these have not (yet) been in conflict. My hometown is permanently dislocated because it is in Northern Ireland, a disorderliness that has never applied to the commuter belt in Berkshire.

Bracknell voted leave in the referendum. At 54 per to 46 per cent, the margin was slightly higher than in the UK has a whole: but not much. It was lower than the proportion of voters in Northern Ireland who voted remain, and it is to be assumed that the peculiar predicament of that place was not at the front of the minds of Bracknell's voters.

It was however at the front of mine. When the referendum happened I was in a strange place: *10 Downing Street*, where I had been working as a press spokesman for nearly a year. Stranger still, I was spokesperson on Europe, which meant arguing for the UK remaining in the EU. It is often said that Northern Ireland, or indeed the entire island of Ireland, was little discussed in the referendum campaign.

This infuriated me at the time and has struck many people as an injustice. But it should not be a surprise. Irish affairs do not intrude upon the collective political consciousness of the UK. Or more specifically they do not intrude upon the consciousness of England. This was a truth revealed to me over many years working in Westminster, and indeed long before. It is understood by practically everyone in Northern Ireland: including those who have an interest in thinking otherwise. Neither loyalism's imagined umbilical cord nor Republicanism's treasured image of a colonial overlord is borne out by the sheer bovine indifference of most English people to Irish politics.

Should we be angry about this? In the context of the referendum's outcome, we – meaning those with a connection to the island of Ireland –

are at least entitled to be disgruntled. That disgruntlement should be qualified by an acknowledgement that broad English indifference helped birth the peace process. The compromises required to end Northern Ireland's squalid conflict involved no real domestic political risk to British Prime Ministers, even Conservative ones. There might be critical leader columns in right-wing papers, and the obligatory protest from unionist politicians, but the blind spot among British voters for the island immediately to the west meant no votes were lost when concessions were made in the name of a muddy peace.

Margaret Thatcher, a year after nearly being murdered by the IRA, signed the Anglo-Irish Agreement establishing a formal say for the Irish Government in Northern Ireland. However much it pained her personally, it will have cost her nothing electorally. The only votes ever provably cast because of the Anglo-Irish Agreement were by Northern Irish electors forced into January weather to vote in by-elections prompted by the mass protest resignation of all Northern Ireland's unionist MPs. The gesture did not go entirely to plan: they returned to Westminster with one fewer MP, having lost a seat in the process.

Britain's electors, those to whom its politicians are ultimately forced to listen, will have been deaf and blind to these protests, despite their intensity. Just as they were deaf-blind to the concerns of Civil Rights protestors two decades before and to the scattered, muted words of warning about the complications posed by Brexit two decades later. Northern Ireland is insecurely located in their mental map of where they are from. For all the accusations of imperial delusion made against Brexit voters, at least as prevalent is the opposite of imperialism: retrenchment, security, boundaries.

So it is in the case of Northern Ireland, a truly baffling entity. "Why don't we just give it back?" asked a baffled Brexit voter in a recent vox-pop interview on the border question. "Northern Ireland isn't actually part of Great Britain," said Dec, of Ant & Dec fame, on their programme *Saturday Night Takeaway* in March 2018. Some Ulster loyalists were affronted at this factually accurate statement because it disrupted their sense of Britishness (an equivalent phenomenon occurs among some republicans when RTÉ show maps of the Irish state with Northern Ireland cut out).

This place, so insecurely placed in the minds of British voters, played no part in either referendum campaign nor the critical six months that followed the vote, when Theresa May and a couple of now-discredited advisors devised a Brexit strategy from which she is now trying inelegantly to resile. I was still there, in the same role as I had been before the referendum, but with less involvement and less purpose. The desiccated May premiership had little use for civil service opinions, at least prior to last year's calamitous general election. Though I am certainly not a Tory, the Cameron regime was relatively catholic in seeking and tolerating the help even of middling officials. This may itself have been a symptom of the terminal over-confidence that led to both the calling and administering of the vote in a most cavalier fashion.

During that miserable campaign I droned on about Northern Ireland and its vulnerability to a Leave vote to the extent that I became apologetic about it. I still have the email I sent to senior people on the campaign calling for more focus on Irish issues, going so far as to invoke the recently deceased Terry Wogan. But in truth even then I knew that from a hard-nosed campaign perspective – meaning from the perspective of actually persuading British people to vote remain – Northern Ireland, and the Irish dimension in general, were not saleable produce. A significant number of English voters had a shaky grasp of what the European Union was, and a sizeable proportion of the same cohort had a limited grasp of which piece of Ireland was in the United Kingdom – and why. Attempting to "land" (to use the language of political communications) a connection between the two in the minds of voters was near-impossible.

More damning is how little policy development went on in relation to Northern Ireland in the months after the vote and before Article 50 was triggered in March 2017. For a shamefully long time, the official script used by both ministers and spokespeople stated only that there would be "no return to the borders of the past." I know because I was one of the people responsible for ensuring that the rest of Whitehall stuck to the script.

Of course barely anyone asked. Back then, Northern Ireland still had MPs other than the Democratic Unionists (begging the pardon of the estimable but solitary Sylvia Hermon) to ask serious questions of Brexit strategy. But other than these few politicians, no one at Westminster was challenging Government Brexit policy on the basis of consequences on the island of Ireland. Northern Ireland rarely occurred to people, either in Parliament or in the media, except as either another bloody Brexit headache, or – if you were a Brexit supporter – a piece of marginalia with which to dispatch along with what to do with office space vacated by British officials in Brussels.

But there was no space for Northern Ireland in these plans. The "Global Britain" that Theresa May began expounding as soon as she announced her intention to replace David Cameron excluded Northern Ireland in the most literal sense. As Ant and Dec attempted to explain to their viewers, Northern Ireland is not in Britain; even if it is British.

I never felt British, even when I worked there. Nor did I feel foreign. Distinct, but then people from Northern Ireland stand out wherever we go. And, perhaps, some of us were starting to enjoy to that contradiction too much, while Bracknell, and places like it, had had enough contradiction.

So back we go, doomed once again to our distinctiveness, dislocated from our latest dislocation.

Mathew O'Toole was the Prime Minister's Downing Street Brexit Spokesman between 2015 and 2017, when he resigned. He was born in 1983 in Belfast and grew up in Downpatrick, before attending St Andrew's University. Along with television appearances, he writes articles and opinion pieces for The Irish Times, The Guardian, The Evening Standard, New Statesman *and* Politico. *He currently works for the communications firm Powercourt and lives in London.*

TOXIC TORY BOX

Jason Gathorne-Hardy

Endgame time.

The principal driver for the United Kingdom's EU Referendum seems to have been the internal divisions within one political party. It happened also to be a party that was in government and rapidly losing ground to more right-wing anti-migration and anti-Europe political campaigns. Rather than facing these down, it took another route.

It offered a referendum with a simple binary in-or-out question:

Should the United Kingdom remain a member of the European Union or leave the European Union?

This may have been a useful question to put before a divided and fractious group of MPs from one political party – safe within the protective walls of Westminster. And it would certainly have been constructive to place it before Parliament as a whole. The framing of the question invites debate: a discussion to better understand the question itself, and its implications.

What is the UK? What are the historic and current legal ties that unite its diverse and varied parts? What is its relationship to the EU, in terms of trade, the movement of people, the passing of laws; and environmental and social protection? Does immigration enhance and enrich the United Kingdom of Great Britain and Northern Ireland, or weaken it? And where do people moving into the UK come from – and where are UK subjects going, when they leave the country?

And if, as the question asks, the UK were to choose to be "in" or "out" of the European Union, what are the legal, social, economic and environmental implications of this question? And what might the UK's aspirations be, in seeking to do this? To be a pioneering, innovative and principled world leader, drawing upon a unique cultural heritage that brings together the European Union, the United States, the Commonwealth Realms and broader Commonwealth of Nations, with additional historic links to the Middle East and Russia? Or to be a deregulated lower common denominator in the global marketplace – a territory in which hitherto world-leading social, economic, environmental and judicial policies are further discarded?

The fact that few if any of these underlying issues were addressed by the party in question through internal or Cabinet debate, or put before Parliament prior to the Referendum, reinforces the view that the principal driver was narrow and blinkered. It was internal party politics, rather than the national interest.

The decision to make the result of this advisory plebiscite *de facto* binding was clearly another step in this direction. It was done for political rather than parliamentary reasons. And so was certainly not in the national interest, for reasons expanded upon below.

All of this — the Referendum question, its framing, and the decision to bind the government (but not Parliament) to its result — would have been good material for a party to put to before its MPs and members for open debate. And it would make constitutional sense to then place the entire subject before Parliament to debate more fully, in order to decide if a Referendum was in the best national interest; and, if so, how the question should be framed.

But this did not happen. None of these issues were addressed. A commitment to hold a referendum was placed in an election manifesto; and a single binary Remain-Leave option was placed before the electorate of the United Kingdom of Great Britain and Northern Ireland.

To go over these points may seem pedantic — or fussing over spilt milk. But there is more to it than that. The United Kingdom as a whole — England and Wales, Scotland, Northern Ireland and many other dependent parts — has been forcefully pulled into the complex internal machinations of one political party. A party that has been irrevocably split over the issue of EU membership for decades; and which has allowed austerity and endless, seemingly ad-hoc privatisation to become the overriding policies of government for all major Departments of State. This is not firm ground for a referendum vote.

Moreover, the implications and consequences of the referendum do not seem to have been planned for. A fire-fighting approach has engulfed most government departments; and proponents of leaving the EU have shown a pattern of departing from positions of responsibility. These strange realities have all combined to place immense strain on civil servants and the normal functioning of government.

In effect, the Conservative Party seems to have pulled the whole nation

– complex, deep-rooted and multi-stemmed as it is – into a zero-sum game with itself and its minority government, in which one or other of the following seems likely to collapse: either the Conservative party and its minority government, or the UK and its component parts.

The place in which this endgame must – and can only – take place is within the Westminster Parliament. Which way the balance tips will depend upon MPs. Regardless of their own politics and which party they may belong to, MPs have a duty to uphold the sovereignty and absolute authority of Parliament over both government and party politics.

This is not to question the Referendum itself, nor the result. But it is to challenge the way it was launched, with little apparent planning for the consequences; and the way in which it has been handled.

By parliamentary convention, if not strictly constitutionally, previous UK referendums have been always been treated as advisory, rather than mandatory. In 1978, the Labour government under Harold Wilson drafted, debated and passed the Scotland Act and Wales Act to prepare for the Scottish and Welsh Devolution referendums. For various reasons, both referendums failed to deliver the expected results – and both Acts had to be repealed.

However, the proposals made within the preliminary Acts and the implications of the referendum votes were fully debated within Parliament. The contents of the Acts and the full consequences of the referendums were well-understood both by Parliament and the respective electorates.

In 1997, a Labour government led by Tony Blair adopted a different strategy. Two referendums were debated and then placed with the voters; but this time, the referendums were conducted before the relevant Acts of Parliament for devolution of power were debated. The results of the two votes were favourable and this helped to prepare the ground for the Government of Wales Act 1998 and the Scotland Act 1998.

In comparison to these, the EU Referendum looks rushed. It seems to have been relatively lacking in full Parliamentary debate, both before and immediately after the event. In many ways, this reflects that it was largely a party political affair. But surely this should never be the case for a topic that is of such significant long-term national interest?

Another mistake – or tragedy – was to treat the EU Referendum as a battleground. Such an approach may be suited to internal party politics, but it is not the way to manage a nation and its future, whatever the chosen path may be. The binary nature of the single question, and lack of full inter-party parliamentary debate prior to the vote, have both favoured division. More recently, serious concerns have been raised about the way in which certain Referendum campaigns were financed and orchestrated – which has begun to undermine the legitimacy of the vote.

Brexit means Brexit has been an oft-repeated phrase. But what does it mean? The United Kingdom of Great Britain and Northern Ireland is a complex and delicate entity. In its present fullness, it encompasses at its heart England and Wales (joined since the Gruffyd treaty of 1056), united with Scotland to form Great Britain (through the Acts of Union in 1706 and 1707). These were joined by Gibraltar in 1713 through the Treaty of Utrecht. The relationship of Northern Ireland to Great Britain is now ultimately governed by the Good Friday Agreement of 1998 and, directly consequential to this, the Northern Ireland Act of 1998. This allows for dual nationality and self-determination through a plebiscite. If and when this might be called, the result will be binding under UK law. The important and vital implications of this reality do not seem to be fully understood in Westminster. And a great arrogance seems to have been shown to the Referendum result in Scotland, which places further strain upon the Union.

And this is not the end of it. Arranged around the United Kingdom of Great Britain and Northern Ireland are constellations of dependent and independent territories: the Crown Dependencies of the Isle of Man, the Bailiwick of Guernsey and Bailiwick of Jersey; the British Overseas Territories of Anguilla, Bermuda, British Antarctic Territory, British Indian Ocean Territory, British Virgin Islands, Cayman Islands, Falkland Islands, Gibraltar, the Pitcairn Islands, St Helena and Dependencies and the Sovereign Base Territories of Cyprus.

While only the voters of Gibraltar and the Sovereign Areas of Cyprus were able to take part in the EU Referendum, all of these Dependencies and Overseas Territories rely upon the United Kingdom for defence and for the supervision of their international relations.

Consequently the UK and its government – and above all its sovereign Parliament – have a duty of care to all of these Territories and Dependencies. And by implication, all of UK voters do as well, regardless of our personal differences. For ultimately, we are all one of another: we have a common interest in seeking the best for each other and all component parts of our nation.

Beyond the Crown Dependencies and British Overseas Territories are the remaining Commonwealth Realms: fifteen nations that are deeply independent, but which retain the British monarch, Her Majesty Queen Elizabeth II, as their Head of State. And finally the Commonwealth of Nations, of which the UK is now one of 53 member states. Although neither the Commonwealth Realms or Commonwealth nations have any direct connections through government to the UK, they may, one hopes, retain an interest in the future path of the UK and its international relations.

So where does all this lead? To a mess? To a showdown with a minority Conservative government in Parliament? Or Parliament itself finally re-asserting its authority?

And is that what Brexit *really* means? An acknowledgment that we never really lost control of our borders, our laws and our sovereignty; that many voters in England and Wales were disillusioned by Europe and years of neglect – perhaps by central UK government more than anything else; that other territories joined to Great Britain by treaties and acts of union (and also many cities within Great Britain) voted differently and preferred to remain within the EU; and that subjects in many Dependencies and Overseas Territories are looking on with confusion and concern, hoping for clear leadership from the centre?

As a whole, the United Kingdom of Great Britain and Northern Ireland seems strong. It sits within web of Dependent and Overseas Territories which rely on continued strength, resilience and good governance at the centre. The threads that bind all these entities are also robust and vibrant – but they are delicate, too.

The sensitivities, hopes and expectations of all the component parts of the United Kingdom are at present still holding together. But variations in EU Referendum voting results and outlooks for the future of the UK in its different component parts need to be respected – including the politically difficult reality that the only territories which voted by a majority to Leave were England and Wales, still joined, but with a revived Welsh Assembly. This all needs to be treated with care and understanding.

In short: the confusion arising from the EU Referendum result is ultimately the consequence of one party's internal politics being forced on a nation, without effective parliamentary debate; followed by a political decision, rather than a parliamentary one, to make the referendum result binding on the government.

This decision seems to break with recent convention on referendums – as well as the spirit of the older principle of sovereignty, that one parliament cannot bind another, or even itself at a later date. This decision is owned by one political party alone – and not by Parliament itself.

And maybe for the nation of the UK as a whole there is a greater truth: the EU Referendum was never something to be won or lost. It was something first to debate in Parliament and, thereby, the means by which to reach a prior cross-party consensus. Whoever framed it as a battle and sought to bind the functioning of Parliament to previous political promises should be held to account. And only Parliament can do that – so it is time for her to re-assert her authority over government and uphold our Constitution, unwritten as it is.

That will require MPs to stand up across party boundaries, to debate and then vote *for Parliament and for the integrity of the UK*: out of the national, not party, interest. The treasured Sovereignty of Parliament remains intact, but must be upheld.

It has not been lost … yet.

Pitres, La Taha, Spain

A graduate of Oxford University, Jason Gathorne-Hardy was born in 1968 and is the Founder and Director of the Alde Valley Spring Festival, in Suffolk, England. His father, Lord Cranbrook, of Great Glemham House, near Saxmundham, has been a global leader in the fields of mammalogy, ornithology and zooarchaeology for more than 50 years, and was responsible for the legislation protecting bats in the United Kingdom. The Gathorne-Hardy family has long-standing personal and political connections to Ireland. Gathorne Hardy, 1st Earl of Cranbrook (1814–1906), was a prominent moderate British Conservative politician who, as Home Secretary, was forced to deal with the Fenian Rising of 1867.

THE HUBERT BUTLER ESSAY PRIZE

INTRODUCTION

Roy Foster

Crashingly into reverse.

Hubert Butler wrote essays all his long life, though he gained wide recognition only when they were published in a series of volumes from The Lilliput Press in Dublin, beginning with *Escape from the Anthill* when he was eighty-five years old. His reinvention of the essay form received mounting acclaim, from writers such as Joseph Brodsky, Neal Ascherson, Fintan O'Toole and John Banville, who contributed introductions to subsequent volumes. Into a short compass, often no more than half a dozen pages, Butler compressed multitudes; moving easily from memory and observation to reflection in a style which was subtly inflected, sometimes laceratingly vivid, and utterly his own. His analytical cut-and-thrust was scintillating, shewering double-think or sloppy reasoning with one swift metaphor. And he was unnervingly prescient about questions of religion, national identity and the fractured histories of Central and Eastern Europe, no less than Ireland.

Though widely travelled, and resident in Yugoslavia, Austria and Russia for prolonged periods, Butler was firmly established in his family's house above the River Nore in County Kilkenny, viewing the outside world with a kind of serene dissidence. As the roll-call of his admirers might indicate, his sensibility was passionately European; like John Stuart Mill, he situated Ireland squarely in the main current of European history, whereas England occupied a kind of eccentric backwater of its own making. (The vote for Brexit would not have surprised him.) From early on, he took a sharply sceptical line on the mounting flood of synthesized Anglo-American culture; before the words "dumbing-down" and "globalization" were coined, he forecast exactly what these inelegant terms entailed. Moreover, in the 1930s he had seen totalitarianism up close, and with his extra-sensory ability to catch history on the move, he was sharply alert to the insidious ways in which it took effect.

Along with his steady commitment to small communities, minority nationalities, and the humane traditions of cosmopolitanism in its widest sense, Butler sustained a lifelong interest in the way states are made – particularly in the drastic reordering of national boundaries after the First World War. Time and again, his questing intelligence probed the question of borders, and what they signified. As a southern Irish Protestant who disliked partition, the border between Northern Ireland and the Republic held particular interest for him. In the early 1950s he wrote a draft editorial for a projected new Irish literary journal which never transpired. In this piece, called "Crossing the Border," he denounced the kind of passive intellectual stagnation that prevents creative discussion of our differences. "We have been hypnotised into thinking that there is a real barrier there, and, like those neurotic hens which can be kept from straying by drawing a chalk ring round them, we do not venture across." Later in the same essay, he forecast that, if Ulster's unique kind of Irishness were generously recognised, "the border will cease to become a menace and an anxiety. Either it will become meaningless and will drop off painlessly like a strip of sticking-plaster from a wound that has healed, or else it will survive in some modified form as a definition which distinguishes but does not divide" (*Grandmother and Wolfe Tone,* 1990, pp. 64, 68).

After the Good Friday Agreement of 1998, this benign scenario edged a little nearer; but the Brexit referendum of 2016 threw the gears crashingly into reverse. At the same time, the migration crisis across Europe brought questions of boundaries and borders to centre stage once more, while the idea of easy transition between countries, which inspired the Schengen Agreement, was negated at a stroke. For these and other reasons, it seemed to the judges of the first Hubert Butler Essay prize that the topic of borders within Europe was of pressing relevance, and also carried an appropriately Butlerian resonance. Nearly all of the thirty-odd entries bore this out, many of them combining reflections on the Irish Border with a broader consideration of frontiers within Europe at this uneasy moment of the EU's history.

This is true of the winning entry, by Nigel Lewis. Opening beguilingly with Saint Benedict in Umbria during the late Roman Empire, his essay fans out to consider the era of Adenauer, Schuman and Monnet, and the competing ideas of "Europe" as a common cultural heritage, or a new Holy Roman Empire in the making. While judicious about the retention of national "sovereignties," and what this means, the author recognizes (unlike many English commentators) the important point that "the EU, like the

EEC before it, has been defusing Europe like an unexploded bomb left over from World War II." But he also recognises the brush-fires sparked by separatist nationalisms and alt-right identity politics within European borders, and the dangers inherent in over-expansion and unprecedented migration: ending with the sobering reflection that we may be witnessing "a desperately sad, modern version of something that empires fear, barbarian invasion." The conclusion of Nigel Lewis's essay returns to Saint Benedict's city of Norcia, this time in terms of its location in an earthquake zone, where an ancient pattern of seismic convulsions potentially awaits reactivation. In its structural development from personal experience to general reflection, its easy and imaginative range of historical reference, and its clear-eyed confrontation of unwelcome truths, this essay invokes the kind of approach and values that Hubert Butler represented, and is a worthy winner of the first Hubert Butler Essay Prize.

One of Ireland's most celebrated scholars and essayists, Roy Foster was Carroll Professor of Irish History from 1991 to 2016 at Hertford College, Oxford. His most recent of many books are Words Alone: Yeats and His Inheritances *(Oxford University Press, 2011) and* Vivid Faces: The Revolutionary Generation in Ireland, 1890 – 1923 *(Norton, 2015). He is a Fellow of the British Academy and Fellow of the Royal Society of Literature.*

EUROPE'S TECTONIC PLATES

Nigel Lewis

In an earthquake zone, a room with a view.

In these troubled times for the European Union, one might do worse than pray for guidance to the patron saint of Europe, Saint Benedict. In Italy this summer, I was in Umbria, in the central Apennines, and happened to visit the ancient town of Norcia, where Benedict was born. I didn't go there to pray, but since the referendum of June, 2016, when the British voted to leave the EU, there hasn't been a day when I haven't worried about Brexit, and Norcia did prompt a prayer of sorts, a meditation on the past, present, and future of the EU.

Benedict lived in the final days of the Roman empire, more than a millennium and a half ago. The monastic order he founded, the Benedictines, carried the Christian message to the far corners of a Europe whose main dividing lines were rivers, lakes, seas, and mountains. In Umbria one picks up echoes of this primordial Europe. A travel article urged me to cross the Apennines into the neighbouring province of Le Marche, the forbiddingly named "borderlands." "You can almost taste the pioneering spirit," it said, "You may feel you have crossed a new frontier." A frontier isn't only a line drawn on a map – it also means something like the edge of the known, civilised world.

An EU brochure on the Schengen Area says that "removing borders, ensuring safety, and building trust took many years after two devastating world wars." The Area is a showcase for the EU – it realises the old dream of a "United States of Europe." However, a much older dream is regaining its hold on the European mind – the dream of living among one's own people within secure, defended frontiers.

Few remember that Saint Benedict was one of the original inspirations of European union. In Norcia's Piazza san Benedetto is a statue of him. The inscriptions on its plinth take us back to the years soon after World War II, when Europe and Germany were divided by the Iron Curtain, and much of it was in ruins. They draw discreet parallels between Benedict's mission in late antiquity and the European Economic Community (EEC) set up in the Rome Treaty of 1957.

Benedict is called *Pacis Nuntius*, messenger of peace, and *Unitatis Effector*, the "realiser" of unity. Among the *effectors* of the EEC were devout Catholic politicians consciously inspired by Benedict's example. The German chancellor, Konrad Adenauer, was one of them. Another, the French Foreign Minister, Robert Schuman, spoke in 1958 of a European unity "deeply rooted in basic Christian values," which in the wider, Cold War context of the time, were also denominated as "western" or "democratic" values. A democratic system of government remains a pre-condition of EU membership, but a union of democracies no longer commands the passionate belief and popular support that it did before the collapse of the Soviet empire.

For Schuman, Europe was a "community of peoples" sharing a common homeland and drawing upon similar cultural sources. The 1990s saw a doctrinal shift from Schuman's ideas to those of the EU's other leading theoretician, the French economist Jean Monnet. It is evident in the Maastricht Treaty of 1992, and in the name-change from European *Community* to European *Union*. For Monnet, the "ever closer union" of the Rome Treaty wasn't a post-war reconstruction of European "community" but a brand-new construction project from the ground up. "Europe," Monnet once said, "has never existed. One must genuinely create Europe."

The French political scientist and former member of the European Parliament, Jean-Louis Bourlanges, describes the EU as divided over whether it is "the political expression of a common cultural heritage" or "the organised affirmation of an interdependence of chosen values." It was, said Bourlanges, "essential" to choose between them, but the choice "has never been made." If the EU cannot or will not define "Europe," it should come as no surprise that EU member states have differing ideas about what Europe is and should be; or that some prefer their received values to the EU's chosen ones; or that millions of European citizens, any number of political groupings, and some governments, are now "pushing back" against the EU.

In Benedict's time, the schisms that would tear Christianity apart, and Europe with it, lay many centuries in the future. So did the Treaty of Westphalia and the advent of the modern nation state. Ever since, the driving ethic of European history has been the territorialism of competing states, whose frontiers have been frequent flashpoints of war. The EU originated in a profound mistrust of the nation state, yet it is an organisation of nation states, not quite a confederation, but with federal ambitions to be the "single European State" of Monnet's vision. It is sometimes compared to the Holy

Roman Empire, and in its enormous "territorial" expansion since 1957 it is indeed a kind of empire. There is also an analogy with the League of Nations. Like the League, it is a sort of permanent peace conference, whose core mission, inherited from the EEC, was to reduce the frictions generated by nationalism and prevent the frontiers from bursting into flame again.

Without sovereign powers of its own, it has had to tread carefully around the sovereignty of its member states. It accepts the *status quo ante* of their frontiers when they join, and as far as I know it has never taken sides in a border dispute (Gibraltar, for example). It doesn't remove frontiers as such – they remain in international law; but it pulls their teeth by negotiating the removal of their provocative apparatus – fences, border-posts, checkpoints, and so on – so that they no longer matter as much, or at all. The EU, like the EEC before it, has been defusing Europe like an unexploded bomb left over from World War II.

The Schengen Area enjoys the "de facto solidarity" that Robert Schuman outlined in his Declaration of 1950 - nations co-operating in a common market, and so enjoying greater prosperity, would understand one another better and settle their differences amicably. In 1952, this policy of enlightened self-interest was pioneered by the European Coal and Steel Community, with the aim of pacifying Germany's borders with France and the Benelux countries. Almost seventy years later, it seems to have eradicated a recurrent black spot in Europe's history, a contributory cause of both World Wars – the German and French dispute over Alsace-Lorraine. Recently, however, Hungary has rekindled a border dispute with Rumania dating back to the Treaty of Trianon of 1920, and Brexit threatens the return of another black spot. The relaxation of the northern Irish border since the Good Friday Agreement of 1998 would have been inconceivable without Irish and British membership of the EU. No new border, not even the softest, could replace one that has been magicked away, psychologically and practically.

Elsewhere, the relaxation of tension *between* nations has had the effect of inflaming tensions *within* them. All over Europe, the long-lasting peace under the aegis of the EU has emboldened separatist movements in countries whose origins are themselves federal. When issues of internal sovereignty arise, the EU expects its members to fend for themselves, on condition, however, that they abide by EU rules and do not settle these conflicts by force, as they were usually settled in the past, and as Spain has come within an ace of doing, and may yet do, in Catalonia. One shouldn't underestimate the fissiparous effect of separatism. The rise of Scottish nationalism was a potent factor in the UK referendum – some voted for Brexit to spite the Scots, others because they feared the break-up of the United Kingdom.

Some see the Schengen Area as the crowning achievement of the EU; to others, it is an ideological step too far towards the "fusing" of nations that Monnet anticipated. Though I think of myself as "a European," I don't feel any more of one in the Schengen Area. Convenient for trade and tourism, but also for drug-smuggling, people-trafficking, and terrorism, it reminds me of the "drive-through" states of the USA. When the EU urges me to "hop in a car and visit your neighbours," something in me even murmurs that "good fences make good neighbours."

The Schengen Area shows that the core mission of "defusing" Europe has been accomplished. In a way, however, the EU is a victim of its success. As memories of conflict recede into the past, it is harder to demonstrate the historical necessity of a "Europe without frontiers." In the 1950s, it wasn't difficult to define what Europe was. It was in crisis, but it wasn't an identity crisis. The Europe that didn't yet exist was what the geopolitics of the day prevented it from being. Nations to the east were cut off behind the hardest of frontiers, the Iron Curtain. Over the Pyrenees, Catholic Spain and Portugal were ineligible for EEC membership because they were dictatorships. Once the Iron Curtain came down, the western democracies had no nearby tyranny to define themselves against. Since then, and since its massive fifth expansion of 2004, it has been harder for the EU to say what it "stands for."

It is a secular body that no longer subscribes to Christian or western values, but to "common values" – including religious freedom – held to be those of humanity as a whole. These values, however, are of no help in defining Europe in terms of anything specific to it – its culture, or history, or geography. Some countries of the 2004 intake – notably, Poland – claim that the EU actively promotes secularism and has an "ideological" bias against Christianity. The EU has been unable so far to reconcile the eastern European experience of the 20th century with western Europe's. Poland's Christian belief and sense of nationhood were its immune-defences against Nazi occupation and Soviet domination. It was, I suggest, always unrealistic to expect countries that had just escaped the clutches of the Soviet Union to cede too much of their sovereignty, too soon, to another union, even one that they had signed up to.

It seems self-evident that EU member states must be European, but that only became an explicit condition of membership in the Copenhagen criteria of 1993. By then, existential unease had been sown over the years by the EU's ambivalent responses to Turkey's applications to join. The EU seems to see Turkey – European or not – as a tempting prize. In 2017, its most recent application was turned down on the grounds, *inter alia*, that Turkey isn't a stable democracy, not that its population is Muslim, or that Europe and the Ottoman empire were at war for centuries, or that Europe traditionally ends at the Hellespont.

The background to Brexit and the other reactionary movements is the same disillusion with "big" government and western democracy itself that is felt also in the United States – we are seeing the breakdown of the post-war "West." One of the things that they react against is the sheer size of the EU. It aspires like Christianity to be an empire of the spirit without frontiers, disseminating belief in democracy and other chosen values. But it is also an "empire" of this world, which has probably reached the limits of its expansion – in the present decade, Croatia has been its only new member. Its twenty-eight member states, as against the EEC's original six, cover an area of four million square kilometres, with a population of more than half a billion.

For obvious reasons, a "Europe without frontiers" can never be without external frontiers – the EU's stretch to more than 17,000 kilometres. In its foreign policy, set out in Article J of the Maastricht Treaty, the EU has nothing to say about these frontiers. To the east, hopes of Ukrainian membership are thwarted by Russian willingness to use force, Poland frets about the security of the EU's eastern boundary along the River Bug, and relations between Greece and Turkey are at a new low. To the south, uncontrolled mass migration over the porous Mediterranean frontier has made nonsense of the EU's system for processing refugees and asylum-seekers, the Dublin Protocol of 1990.

The salient point about this difficult and emotive issue is the "breakaway" effect on the EU and on the wide-open Schengen Area – the effect, magnified on the nightly TV news, of a desperately sad, modern version of something that empires fear, barbarian invasion. Uncontrolled migration has crystallised a crisis in European identity that has been brewing for a generation. The knowledge that it is a humanitarian catastrophe does not mitigate the feeling that the EU is fiddling while Rome burns, or the fear that people are in danger of losing "their" Europe – the corner of it that they know and love. Against this backdrop, "identity politics" rejects the EU's pursuit of a single European State and asserts the idea of Europe as a "community of peoples."

The Italian movement led by Matteo Salvini grew out of the separatist Lega Nord and calls itself, significantly, "Noi Con Salvini," usually translated as "Us With Salvini." The "de facto solidarity" of nations has moved closer to home. A new frontier has sprung up in Europe, between people like "us" and an alien, threatening "them." Communities are welcoming up to a point – then they can turn nasty. In embracing the "us" who belong to them, they necessarily exclude a "them" who don't. The European Community was both inclusive and exclusive (of Franco's Spain, for example). It affirmed an identity - the EU has no clear identity. The EEC curbed nationalism – the EU provokes it.

On the day in August, 2015, when Chancellor Merkel made her "we can do this" speech opening Germany up to almost a million migrants, a young German woman told me she had never felt so proud of her country. I asked her about the effect on the German right. She stared at me – "What German right?"

The EU has neglected its external frontiers. The member states whose outer edges are contiguous with its own have been expected to police them, with the assistance, since 2005, of the EU's own "co-ordinating" border agency, Frontex (from *frontières extérieures*). Between 2013 and 2016 the Frontex budget almost tripled, and in 2015, its mandate was extended. Germany, France, Austria, and Poland are among nations backing plans for a "standing corps" of up to 10,000 border guards.

Facts are hard to come by – the EU is oddly opaque about Frontex – but it looks as though the EU, having dismantled internal frontiers, has accepted that its outer ones must be harder. If so, it has taken a step towards a territorial definition of "Europe," and possibly, further down that road, towards a federal European State, or some other form of supra-national sovereignty. At a time of increasing worry over NATO, the idea of a European Army might re-emerge, as it has done, periodically, ever since the 1950s. The EU insists that its standing corps will be subject to its rules on human rights. It won't be an army, but some already find it reminiscent of the border guards of the DDR, the puppet state of Communist East Germany, where Angela Merkel grew up. Of necessity, these thoughts on the future of the EU are speculative, and of a scope commensurate with a project that took on the whole of European history, and is now at a turning-point in its own.

In late 2016 – not long after the Brexit referendum – Norcia was struck by a series of earthquakes registering up to 6.6 on the Richter scale. Two years later, much of the town still looks like a cleared-up war zone. Article 92 2(b) of the Treaty of Rome promises "aid to make good the damage caused by natural disasters or exceptional occurrences," and the rebuilding of Norcia is well under way, supported by a huge grant of 1.2 bn. euros from the European Solidarity Fund. This neighbourly helping hand is what the EU was originally *about*.

A young man said something that has stayed with me. He was describing what it's like to live in an earthquake-zone. "Our lovely, peaceful view of the Apennines," he said, "makes us forget that beneath the mountains the forces that destroy us are always gathering." I suggest that something similar is true of the EU. Absorbed in its vision, it overlooked its susceptibility to "exceptional occurrences" – the sudden end of the USSR, the migrant crisis, Brexit, a USA which, with Donald Trump as president, is as hostile to the EU as Putin's Russia.

The EU should stop its mission creep. Discussing the CETA Trade Agreement last year, the then deputy German chancellor, Sigmar Gabriel, said that "Canada is as European as some member states." Does that mantra also cover Germany's controversial gas-pipeline deal with Russia, which is no democracy, but in other ways is more "European" than Canada?

Gabriel also called the EU "the largest civilisation project of the 20th century," a description as high-handedly simplistic as Jean Monnet's Europe that has "never existed." Europe has always existed, and its "civilisation project," like any other, has always been precarious. Quiescent for decades beneath the lovely view, the old tectonic plates have begun to grind again, with seismic shocks all over the place – Hungary, Austria, Poland, Italy, Spain, the UK, Denmark, Holland, even Germany and France.

Some see the shocks as signs of the EU's imminent break-up, but geopolitical frictions, like those of geology, take time to reach breaking-point. Steps can be taken to alleviate them, and I hope that the breakaway movements will subside. I want the European Union to reform, but I don't want it to fail. The Europe of the EU, for all its faults, is a continent that still renounces unreason, a place of kindness and, yes, civilisation. It is the only Europe we have – we may not need it for the same reasons as before, but the world needs it more than ever.

This essay was the winner (selected by Roy Foster: see p.191) of the first annual Hubert Butler Essay Prize, organized by Europe House in London.

Nigel Lewis has reported for the BBC World Service, BBC Radio 3 and the Canadian Broadcasting Corporation, and has contributed to The Sunday Times, New Statesman, The Spectator *and BBC Radio 4. He has written the English libretto for Mozart's early* The First Commandment, *and is working on a novel,* Uncle Plato.

LAND OF HIDDEN HARMS

Ciarán O'Rourke

Motley crises.

THE RAID

Next to a clean, shopped shot
of Jeff Bezos's grinning head –

"top," once more, of the earth's
so-called list

of fish-faced, smiling rich –
wedged below

a line in bold, that
beacons the long

longed-for arrival
of this *boy who dreamed*

of colonising space,
news flaps in also

from dark-aged Sweden,
where fifteen

hundred summers past
a nameless

massacre occurred –
was schemed, that is,

and swung to gleeful,
throbbing motion –

in an island haven, walled
houses looking out

on the northern seas'
easy crash of light,

with, perhaps, the usual
fart-filled bustle

and settled ache of peace
we take

for ordinary living:
here, I learn,

some as yet unrealised
phantom gang

came slinking
with the tide

one day, and before
pickpocketing

the stock of bartered
jewels and laces, Roman coins,

along with every
shining thing, up-

turned their homely cup
of havoc

on the heads
of the island-folk,

whose now re-
surfaced bones

show signs of blunt
and subtle traumas, both:

the old man's axe-
opened skull, for instance,

dumped and singed
in the blazing hearth,

or the gentle, goof-limbed
body of a boy

who was stunned
and gnawed by sharpened clubs,

or a shapeless other, belted
clear out of time

to a mud-shattering death,
into whose

stopped mouth, after,
were shoved the teeth

of a ravenous bull.

THE TREE

A poem, which
as the bullets whinnied

through the night
and across the dreaming century

flittered from the cracks
of Fadwa Tuqan's singing heart,

and danced the wind,
and shook the years, eventually

to grapple here, unbesieged
but altered, an ever-changing sigh.

And so: *the tree* (she writes)
regains the blasted field at last,

like a shadow-torch
the ground ignit, that greens

the gravelled air in sun,
and celebrates the rain.

After the bone-dark
hurricane retreats, it lifts

a feast of light, this tree;
and after the ringing walls

break down, its leaves transmit
their murmurs, sounding

like the sea, to say:
the birds, if not the dead, return,

and with birds
the rising days begin,

the rage and ache
we call the spring,

a word for what
the carnage reckoned —

and still the birds returning.

WHAT STARLINGS DO

The starving starlings shoot
the noonday sun:

sporadic, flammering bursts
of flight

from wire-perch
to pavement cracks

that simmer black and grey.
Above the motley crisis

of the day, they swell
the sixteen winds of the city,

evict their secret
heart of song

with almost lexical aplomb,
pitching love-notes

with frail alarm
to the shifting, shuttered sky.

Below, street-bound,
they gutter the ground

for bits and scraps,
their scurry and hop

and bruise-blue sheen
equivocal as rain.

But when the governed air
 grows large,

they blend with every
sound and sight, like

the hidden children chirping
with the crowd – about

homes for all, and human rights.

THE SLEEPER

The boy who's chasing
pigeons round the green

is bright
as all the summer:

he edges the glassy grass
at a prowl, and plans

to stun their portly strut
to flight –

he leaps! and makes them
batter the light –

his rough staccato shouts
sing out, victorious!

And all the boarded
windows blink,

as the nearby
lady, rain-dark

hair pulled back
in a bun, a ripped

but double-bagged
black sack beside her,

slumps her shoulder
to the steel park-bench,

her two fists pressed
to the brow of her head.

MY POET FRIEND

My poet friend, in love again
with broken-

fingered, sleeting life,
swings one fist

behind him as he walks,
and crocks

a gun-like camera
with the other

close to heart –
to capture crows

that flare and squat
and strut the shore

with songless urgency,
their sin-grey heads

at work on sand
like him, he says, a proof

of brute unbeauty's
lasting charms

(on this, our isle
of hidden harms).

The misting sun
dilates and breathes

in beachy light
the crows have slung

across the wind
to snag his every step;

but he believes
the poetry

of hunger and debris,
and plants his feet

in the wake of their wings –
shouting to the shadows

unspeakable things.

Ciarán O'Rourke was born in 1991 and took a degree English and History at Trinity College, Dublin. He received a Masters in English and American Studies from Oxford in 2014, and is currently doing a doctorate on William Carlos Williams at his alma mater in Dublin. A winner of the Lena Maguire / Cúirt New Irish Writing Award, the Westport Poetry Prize, and the Fish Poetry Prize, his first collection of poems, The Buried Breath, *was published by The Irish Pages Press in late 2018. He lives in Dublin.*

I AM A DISILLUSIONED DISCIPLE
OF THE GOOD FRIDAY AGREEMENT

———

Andy Pollak

Bring 'em all on!

Disillusionment. That's the feeling these days among many people like myself who have been the most passionate advocates of the Good Friday Agreement. When I hear Arlene Foster's extraordinary choice of words ("the red line is blood red") in talking about the DUP resisting even the most common sense extra checks down the Irish Sea to keep Northern Ireland in regulatory and customs alignment with the EU, I wonder what has changed in unionism over the past 20 years. When I hear Sinn Féin describing the British government as the "main conflict protagonist" in the Northern Troubles, despite the IRA having killed nearly five times more people than the British Army, the RUC and the UDR combined, I wonder what has changed in republicanism over the past 20 years. When I hear that Catholic police officers – those who came into the PSNI as part of the 1998 Agreement's most successful element, policing reform – are once again not being posted to their home communities because of the dissident republican threat, I am close to despair.

Brexit, of course, is the main culprit. The voters of Britain barely spared a thought for the effect of their seismic 2016 vote on the sister island. Shockingly, a recent opinion poll appeared to show that the great majority of British Leave voters (along with their Northern unionist counterparts) even now believe that collapsing the Irish peace process is a price worth paying for leaving the EU. The result of that vote has been that the two Ulster tribes have returned to their traditional trenches with a vengeance.

In particular, Brexit has allowed the most fear-filled and eurosceptic elements in the DUP – led by its Westminster MPs – to take a hard-line anti-EU stance that is, while intrinsic to their psychological DNA, entirely at odds with the interests of the economically exposed province they purport to represent. In the longer-term, if a pro-EU Scotland eventually breaks away from the UK, it may also be seen to be at odds with their political interests. And do they not recognise that a hard Irish border following the UK crashing out of the EU is just the kind of development that will force moderate nationalists into the arms of Sinn Féin, and make the dissidents more attractive to disadvantaged young nationalists? It is very hard not to conclude that this is a classic example of "stupid unionism."

For its part, Sinn Féin, in true Pavlovian fashion, has seized the opportunity to push for "accelerated reunification post-Brexit." Just as the unionists are paranoid about the maintenance of the union, so republicans are obsessed with the holy grail of a politically united Ireland. The well-being of Northern Ireland rarely comes into the reckoning for either side.

For me the major miracle of the 1998 Agreement was the effective removal of the Irish border, while Northern Ireland stayed constitutionally part of the United Kingdom. In my 14 years heading the Centre for Cross Border Studies in Armagh (1999-2013) I was conscious of being part of an extraordinary experiment in bringing people together through practical cooperation projects, most of them funded by the EU, in business, agriculture, transport, health, education, local government, planning, the environment, tourism, waterways, the marine and a dozen other areas. For a decade and a half there was a benign window of opportunity that might, just might, have begun the process of taking the poison out of centuries of bad relationships on this island simply through helping the people of the two jurisdictions to get to know each other by working, learning and enjoying common pursuits together.

It might have not have been big or fast enough for some of us, but it was an important step towards a genuinely reconciled Ireland. As that wise man Sir George Quigley said just before his death in 2013: "The North-South relationship has been transformed. Someone, indeed, has referred to its unprecedented ordinariness and normality today. We seem to have been able to resolve North-South tensions in a way which still too often escapes us as far as the traditional divisions within the Northern Ireland community itself are concerned." Is all that good work now coming to an end?

And of course Brexit has poisoned the two relationships that were crucial to drawing up the Good Friday Agreement and to its relative success for many years. The decades of painstaking work to build good relations between the Irish and British governments, and between the former and the political representatives of unionism, appear to have come to naught. Relations between Dublin, London and Belfast are now frosty at best, toxic at worst. 20 years ago Ireland was led towards peace by genuinely courageous and visionary leaders (however flawed in other areas) such as Tony Blair, Bertie Ahern, John Major, Albert Reynolds, Mo Mowlem, David Trimble, John Hume, Gerry Adams, Martin McGuinness, David Ervine and from the US, George Mitchell and Bill Clinton. Later they were joined, after "road to Damascus" conversions, by Ian Paisley and Peter Robinson. If you think leadership doesn't matter, compare these major figures with their picayune equivalents today.

But if one looks more closely, is it just Brexit? I have recently been reading the Belfast-based political commentator Robin Wilson's 2010 book on the Good Friday Agreement and its implementation (*The Northern Ireland Experience of Conflict and Agreement: A Model for Export?*). Even given that Wilson was always a sceptic when it came to the Agreement, part of the school that thought it would institutionalise sectarianism, this provides some disturbing evidence for re-evaluation.

Wilson points out that the rot set in early, on the night before the Good Friday Agreement was signed, when Tony Blair gave David Trimble a side letter promising to review the exclusion of Sinn Féin from the Executive six months after the Northern Ireland Assembly was set up if the IRA did not begin to decommission its arms. This was a promise Blair was unable or unwilling to fulfil, and it planted the seeds for the eventual implosion (and electoral collapse) of the Ulster Unionist Party because of the IRA's failure to decommission, and its replacement by the DUP.

More importantly, there was a huge absence of trust there from the beginning: in the first few months of the new Executive the Ulster Unionists could not bring themselves even to speak to their Sinn Féin colleagues. By the time the first UUP-SDLP led government collapsed in October 2002, the atmosphere around the cabinet table was described by one civil servant as "poisonous." There was an almost complete absence of collective responsibility or joint decision-making. Sustainable power-sharing government just can't work like that.

As the late David Stevens of the Corrymeela Community pointed out, there was a "deep paradox in this: you have a deeply distrustful society and for government to work people have to trust each other." Yet MLAs being required to "designate" themselves as unionist or nationalist, allied to the ultra-complex D'Hondt voting system, effectively institutionalised this distrust.

Thirdly there was little sense of collective loyalty to the common institutions and the common place the four sectarian parties were governing: Northern Ireland. As former Taoiseach John Bruton said: "The Agreement itself, and the institutions it creates, must become the focus of a new loyalty. The Agreement is not the means to some other end. It must be seen as an end in itself. Unless that happens, every ordinary proposal from one side will be seen by the other through a prism of suspicion." In their very different ways, David Trimble, Seamus Mallon, Martin McGuinness - and latterly Peter Robinson - tried their best to forge a fragile loyalty to a new shared dispensation. But once we got to Arlene Foster and Michelle O'Neill that noble aim had been all but abandoned.

A senior Dublin official summed it up for Wilson in 2008, at a time when there was considerable optimism in the air after the resumption of power-sharing a year earlier. "I doubt if the current model is in the long term democratically desirable or a particularly good idea from an administrative point of view either. In other words, I would like to see the possibility in due course of evolution towards some form of voluntary coalition arrangement, with some sort of cross-community threshold of support. That would seem to me to make more sense in terms of accountability, the possibility of change, and avoidance of entrenchment of interests and corruption." 10 years on what we have is a blatant lack of accountability shown by the Renewable Heat Incentive scandal; the Assembly in suspension and thus deadlocked; sectarian "sharing out" between DUP and Sinn Féin interests rather than genuine power-sharing as the main characteristic of the latter years of the Executive; and numerous examples of corruption, particularly on the DUP side of the house. It was little wonder that the Executive was so unloved by the people of the North at the end: at one West Belfast meeting of broad nationalist opinion a year ago Sinn Féin could find only two people out of a crowd of over 150 to support them going back into that Executive.

Maybe the whole experiment was doomed once the reactionaries of the DUP became involved. The governments had decided to turn their backs on the middle ground sometime in the early 2000s, principally in order to get Sinn Féin and the IRA on board. After the St Andrews Agreement in 2006 this huge gamble appeared to have paid off. But as in Lebanon and other places where erstwhile bitter enemies go into government together, history has shown that it rarely lasts long. And the distinct impression now is that few people outside the two governments really want the North's institutions to be restored. Certainly nobody in the British or Irish political establishments is prepared for the ferocious horse trading and painfully negotiated compromises that this will once again require.

The moral and political core of the Good Friday Agreement as an instrument for peace and reconciliation has been hollowed out. Nobody seems ready for the hard graft needed to make a reconciled Northern Ireland work as the essential pre-requisite to what might happen next (in some medium-term future), whether it is a strengthening of the union with Britain (highly unlikely) or a move towards some kind of agreed Ireland. We are back again to the brutal binary choices that have blighted the North for the past century.

My personal hope (unrealistic as it may be) is that the non-unionist and non-nationalist "others," whom the Belfast researcher Paul Nolan recently identified as by far the fastest growing social group in the region, might keep growing until they offer a significant centrist/leftist alternative in Northern society and politics. Bring them all on: atheists and agnostics, Alliance supporters, greens and socialists and People Before Profit, foreign immigrants, hippies and gays and transgender people, sensible women of all persuasions, the alienated and marginalised and disabled and "plague on both your houses" people. Let Northern Ireland be taken over by oddballs and weirdos of every stripe. Nothing they could propose could be as stultifying and perilous as the drift towards the Border Poll that Sinn Féin are constantly demanding. For I believe that a 50% plus one vote for a (dis)united Ireland in such a poll will be just the thing to lead us to another recurrence of the ancient bloody conflict.

Andy Pollak was born in Ballymena, Co Antrim, and largely brought up in London. (His father, a Czech citizen of German-speaking Jewish descent, lost his editor's job and was forced to flee Czechoslovakia after the Communist takeover in 1948.) After graduation from the University of Sussex in 1969, he worked for the magazine Hibernia *and reported for BBC Northern Ireland and* The Irish Times *in the late 1970s and early 1980s. From 1981 to 1985, he was Editor of the important Belfast cultural and political magazine,* Fortnight. *He co-authored (with Ed Moloney) a biography of Ian Paisley,* Paisley *(Poolbeg, 1986). Between 1999 and 2013, he was the founding Director of the Centre for Cross-Border Studies, Dublin City University, with offices in Armagh and Dublin. He now publishes and blogs on* "Two Irelands Together."*

20-20

Glenn Patterson

The Freedom of the City – *45 years on.*

On the afternoon of Tuesday 10 April this year, the twentieth anniversary of the Good Friday Agreement, I was in Belfast's Ulster Hall, introducing a programme of music and readings to mark the granting of the Freedom of the City of Belfast to President Bill Clinton and Senator George Mitchell.

Up to the night of Monday 9 April I had been telling people I was introducing a programme of music and readings *for* Bill Clinton and Senator George Mitchell, but at rehearsals that evening it became clear that neither future Freeman would actually be in the audience for that part of the event. They would arrive after the interval when the stage had been re-set (something that seemed to require several dozen seats being brought up on to the stage.) The performers – many of whom were younger than the Agreement itself – were understandably disappointed. I (thirty-seven years older than it) was disappointed, truth be told. Still, being asked to take part was a big deal to them, and to me.

I put a lot of thought into my links. I was one of the 71.12% of the population of This Place™ who voted for the Agreement back in the spring of 1998. I thought it was worth remembering that feeling of exhilaration – well, exhilaration for something over seven in ten of us. I thought that it was worth recognising the contribution of the Senator and the former President in arriving at that negotiated Good Friday high.

As long as we didn't overlook the fact that almost from the get-go our politicians – and therefore the electorate who voted them in – did their best to fuck the whole thing up.

So in noting that the anniversary fell at a time of political stasis (as the majority of commentators admittedly did, though some of them made it sound as unlikely as hitting the bull's eye while standing with your back to the dartboard, blindfolded) I pointed out that stasis had in fact given momentum a pretty good – well *run* was clearly too active a word – grumpy-faced-arms-folded *squat* for its money in the two decades since 1998.

Talking of grumpy faces and folded arms, the young performer sitting next to me on stage returned to her seat after her turn and whispered that it was the worst audience she had ever played to, or at least one section of it was: right in the centre of the auditorium. I got up to do my next link and, right enough, a sourer looking bunch I never saw. Only later when the stage was re-set for the Freedom of the City presentations and that whole section of the audience moved en masse to occupy those several dozen seats newly installed on the stage, did I realize that that was our Belfast City Council.

Maybe they just needed to know their respective party positions on a gag before they cracked a smile. Or maybe it was just nerves.

Like I say, it was a big deal, this whole 20th anniversary business.

I wish I could say it was nerves that caused me to fluff my own lines that night. Or not fluff: just not fully deliver. I had wanted to say something about the ongoing paramilitary punishment attacks – more than ongoing, in fact: increasing in number in the weeks leading up to the anniversary – but I couldn't work it into any of my links and then the young performers were off-stage and the councillors and dignitaries were on (my own last act before retiring to watch from behind the piano was to announce the Freedom of the City party) and the moment was gone, and then the anniversary was gone, and then it was just Wednesday 11 April 2018 and then Thursday 12 April and day turned to night and in the west of the city republican paramilitaries were leading a young man on to a patch of waste ground at Ardmonagh Parade, forcing him down, and shooting him in both legs.

A neighbour told *The Belfast Telegraph* she was woken by his screams.

The victim was – you got there ahead of me –

20.

Glenn Patterson was born in Belfast in 1961 and studied on the Creative Writing MA at the University of East Anglia, taught by Malcolm Bradbury. He is the author of nine novels, most recently Gull *(Harper Collins, 2016) and two works of non-fiction,* Lapsed Protestant *(New Island, 2006) and* Once Upon a Hill: Love in Troubled Times *(Bloomsbury, 2008). He co-wrote the screenplay for the 2013 film* Good Vibrations, *about the music scene in Belfast in the late 1970s. He is the Director of the Seamus Heaney Centre, Queen's University Belfast, and still lives in Belfast.*

THE VIEW FROM THE LAGAN

Chris Agee

The vote was cant.

The vote, that is, for Brexit. But not, of course, for The Good Friday (or Belfast) Agreement. And therein – in the striking difference between those two votes – lies the potential of momentous change for all of Ireland "in the coming times."

The Belfast Agreement – it might truly be said – was the final result of a fitful 25-year negotiation (or "peace") process concurrent with the bloody and glacial denouement of the Troubles and their immediate aftermath – that is, from the Sunningdale Agreement in 1973; through the IRA ceasefire in 1994; to the final political-constitutional deal struck in the early hours of Good Friday 1998 (10 April) and announced and signed by the two Governments and eight parties, the latter on the steps of the old Stormont Parliament.

No wonder, then, that an Irish catchphrase for The Good Friday Agreement – "Sunningdale for slow-learners" – now has near iconic folk-status for that quarter century coming nearly full circle – and so bringing us (to tweak James Joyce at the start of his *Wake*) "by a commodious vicus of re-circulation back to Belfast Castle and Environs …"

Not that the parallel between the 1973 and 1998 Agreements is entirely justified.

Sunningdale emerged from the violent mayhem and freefall of the uber-sectarian Northern state in the early Troubles, prefigured and then milestoned symbolically by its clutch of escalating disintegrations: the Burntollet Bridge ambush by the RUC and loyalists (4 January 1969: "the spark that lit the prairie fire" – Paul Bew) and subsequent eclipse of the peaceful Civil Rights Movement; the intense rioting, fire-raising and ethnic cleansing in Belfast especially (August '69); the deployment of the British Army to protect Catholic areas and ostensibly to restore order; the massacre of 13 Derry civilians (including six children) by paratroopers on Bloody Sunday (31 January 1971), followed by an explosion of IRA recruitment; the introduction of internment for republicans and nationalists (August 1971); the proroguing of the Parliament of Northern Ireland and the establishment of Westminster Direct Rule, by the Heath Government (1972); the breakdown of talks between the British Government and the IRA (June-July 1972), and the latter's immediate answer on Bloody Friday (21 July: 22 bombs in 80 minutes, 9 dead, 130 wounded, in Belfast); and finally, the talks in Berkshire, England, involving the main unionist, nationalist and non-sectarian constitutional parties, and leading to the Sunningdale Agreement on 9 December 1973.

Sunningdale was an attempt to establish a power-sharing Northern Ireland Executive and a cross-border Council of Ireland (which had been envisioned in the Government of Ireland Act 1920 – that partitioned Ireland – but never instituted for sectarian reasons). The Sunningdale Agreement itself had been preceded in 1973, under the aegis of Direct Rule, by elections to the Northern Ireland Assembly and negotiations between the constitutional parties on the exact ministerial composition of the Executive – which quickly took power, just after the Agreement, on 1 January 1974.

Within five months, the Executive had been brought down by one of the regular wrecking-balls in the little Lilliput, with its deep-rooted cultural template of a four-strand politics: in this case, the hardline unionist-loyalist faction headlined with its stereophonic slogan, *No Surrender!* In this particular paramilitary-inspired incarnation, a quintessentially Irish faction (as in the eighteenth-century Irish "faction-fight") was manifested as the "Ulster Workers' Council Strike," a "popular" uprising (or *de facto* general strike) lasting two weeks and completely paralyzing the "Province." The British Government effectively capitulated due to the refusal to use military force at an early stage, the opposition to such strike-breaking by even the Executive unionists, and a likely fear of precipitating much worse.

It has often been claimed that this British-Irish strike was the largest in post-war Western Europe. The journalist Robert Fisk described it this way at the time:

> *The fifteen unprecedented, historic days in which a million British citizens, the Protestants of Northern Ireland, staged what amounted to a rebellion against the Crown and won … During those fifteen days, for the first time in over fifty years … a section of the realm became totally ungovernable. A self-elected provisional government of Protestant power workers, well-armed*

private armies and extreme politicians organized a strike which almost broke up the fabric of civilized life in Ulster. They deprived most of the population for much of the time of food, water, electricity, gas, transport, money and any form of livelihood.

The way was now well and truly open for the next two decades of accelerating stalemate.

So in comparison to The Belfast Agreement, Sunningdale now seems – to this writer at least – more provisional, *ad hoc* and "through-other", even a bit slapdash, the perforce product of pressing immediate circumstances and contending surrounding historical forces – more of an imperial Westminster political and security fix than a carefully-laid constitutional groundwork for a truly long-term settlement and dispensation.

And so too in comparison to its rough-and-ready prototype in Sunningdale, The Belfast Agreement also now seems to this writer more thorough and sturdy; but also more cautious, more tightly knit and embedded in politico-cultural terms, a *real tour de force* of constitutional and textual finesse that will bear up and endure. Above all, it dealt with a series of key issues not addressed by Sunningdale, for reasons as much cultural-intellectual as purely political: the recognition of the principle of self-determination; the parity of esteem accorded both national traditions; British-Irish intergovernmental cooperation; and the mandatory legal procedures and cross-checking political structures ensuring true power-sharing.

So between the metaphorical bookends of these two Agreements, one might say, a great deal of blood and treasure, suffering and experience, and so forth, had seasoned the North's collective learning curve. The role of poets, writers and artists of all sorts in this slow re-imagining of a shared future is as incontestable as it is well-known – and on full display in the pages of this striking issue.

Yet more than two decades between the two Agreements still had to be gone through before the promised land of Good Friday 1998. For those of us who "lived it bomb by bomb" (Derek Mahon), the exact recollection of the progression of events may (perhaps must) cloud and wane, since like a submerged sandbar "our own past is covered by the currents of action" (T.S. Eliot); nowadays, what seems more indelible, again to this writer, is the deep psycho-social watermarking of a whole society by the oppressive and funereal atmosphere of a "long period in which political stasis, cyclical violence and generalized social and economic stagnation became second nature to a riven culture" (1974-1998).

Even if the security situation slowly stabilized and improved from the late seventies, becoming more contained and almost choreographed in a cat-and-mouse fashion, the fundamentally violent dynamics of *The Troubles Without a Settlement* did not.

The decade after Sunningdale saw a seemingly interminable and gruesome unfolding of slow-motion crises and "spectacular" events: the Dirty Protest, the Five Demands and the Hunger Strikes; Thatcher's Pyrrhic prison victory and the counter-strike of the Brighton Hotel bombing; Sinn Féin's new and wily espousal of the strategy of "the Armalite and the ballot-box"; and, of course, beyond these global "highlights" and "milestones," a citizenry's pilgrim's progress through a relentless litany of political and sectarian murder and maiming, rioting and destruction, civil strife and cheek-by-jowl communal mayhem, in those areas that did not share the suburban or rural quietude that nonetheless characterized much of the rest of the North.

Then, midway into this quarter-century Slough of Political Despond, something more optimistic happened, given the grim political backdrop and the Thatcher Government's stridency: The Anglo-Irish Agreement (1985). It was opposed by republicans, but still more deeply loathed by almost all shades of unionism for its determination to assert, once again, the prerogatives of the United Kingdom over one of its (recalcitrant) constitutional constituents.

In retrospect, though opaque and almost quixotic at the time, the intermediate Anglo-Irish Agreement foreshadowed some of the consensual strands that would shape the negotiations leading to The Belfast Agreement: the British recognition of a military stalemate; the key use of treaty relations between the United Kingdom and the Republic, as a framework for a settlement; the establishment of an intergovernmental conference with an Irish advisory role; the requirement of majority consent in Northern Ireland for the island's unification; and the laying-out of the conditions for a future devolved-consensual government in the North.

As its hyphened name suggests, The Anglo-Irish Agreement was surely not just another political "milestone," internal to the North, on the often-tedious "peace-process" road: it was – looking back – a genuine watershed.

Yet it hardly dented or diminished the cavalcade of embittering violence over another decade. Frightful scenes rolled on unabated, intensifying memorably in the late eighties and early nineties, in the run-up to the first IRA ceasefire: the Loughgall ambush (May 1987), the Remembrance Day Bombing (November 1987); Michael Stone's attack on Milltown Cemetery mourners (16 March 1988); the mob-killing of the two hapless corporals on the Falls Road three days later; the massacres at Greysteel (October 1993) and Loughinisland (June 1994), the latter with likely police collusion; huge IRA bombings on the British "mainland" (Baltic Exchange, Docklands, Manchester, 1992-1996). *Et cetera,* and *et cetera* ...

The North's Book of the Dead, *Lost Lives* (1999), records it all bomb by bomb, bullet by bullet, atrocity by atrocity ...

Yet, at the collective corner of Everyman's eye, there were always the contacts, the conversations, the political manoeuvrings, the talks and finally the true negotiations – all of these shadowing this Troubled North like its better self. Violence and the drive to end violence – within Britain's overall, still-liberal democracy – were always two twins bound at the historical hip.

In short: The Belfast Agreement was the textual culmination of a long evolution of political, historical, cultural, intellectual, ethical, psychological and even artistical experience that this quasi-legal, foundational document both represented and incorporated. It was and is, quite literally, the bloody fruit of the Troubles. And its achievement, for many on this island and overseas, had something of the socially miraculous about it.

Such things *can* happen amidst "the nightmare of history" (Joyce). Hope and history *can* rhyme – at least for a comparative moment, however defined.

At a mere 30 pages, "The Agreement" (its formal name, *sans* adjective) is both surprisingly succinct and comprehensively dovetailed. Although obscured to a degree by the passage of time, this document is, in fact, two distinct but interrelated agreements signed on the same day: a multiparty agreement by most of Northern Ireland's political parties (known as *The Multiparty Agreement);* and a formal agreement, with legal status within international law as treaty lodged at the UN, between the British and Irish Governments (*The British-Irish Agreement*).

The Agreement opens with a political "Declaration of Support" from the participants in the multiparty talks, followed by an enumeration of "Constitutional Issues" vis-à-vis the two parts of Ireland, including the principles of majority rule, national self-determination, equality of rights and freedoms, cultural parity of esteem, and a permanent birthright bi-nationality for Northern Ireland in the matter of citizenship. The exact draft clauses for the incorporation of these principles into British legislation and the Irish Constitution are then laid out in two Annexes, A and B.

Three "Strands" and their enumerated provisions then follow. *Strand One* concerns itself with "Democratic Institutions in Northern Ireland," including detailed but concise sub-sections on "The Assembly," "Safeguards," "Operation of the Assembly," "Executive Authority," "Legislation," "Relations with Other Institutions," "Transitional Arrangements," and "Review." In short, Strand One covers the status and system of the government of Northern Ireland within the United Kingdom.

Strand Two, more amply adumbrated, deals with the "North/South Ministerial Council," outlining ministerial relations between Northern Ireland and the Irish Government, and is again followed by an Annex setting out precisely the 11 areas of cooperation and implementation. It deals, so, with the relationship of Northern Ireland and the Republic of Ireland.

Strand Three, the most substantial in terms of length, deals with the relations between the two sovereign states and the devolved institutions in Northern Ireland, Scotland and Wales. It comprises the "British-Irish Council," which includes the two states and three devolved British administrations (and whose aim is to promote "the harmonious and mutually beneficial development of the totality of relationships among the peoples of these islands"); the "British-Irish Intergovernmental Council" (for non-devolved state matters reserved to both Governments); and "Rights, Safeguards and Equality of Opportunity." This latter is further subdivided into "Human Rights," "United Kingdom Legislation," "New Institutions in Northern Ireland," "Comparable Steps by the Irish Government," "A Joint Committee" (on human rights), and "Reconciliation and Victims of Violence." Strand Three covers, in effect, the overall relationship between the Republic of Ireland and the United Kingdom and its constitutional constituents.

The Agreement then looks ahead with six further sections: "Rights, Safeguards and Equality of Opportunity (Economic, Social and Cultural Issues)," which deals with areas of promised future British policy (including a list of actions promoting the Irish language); "Decommissioning;" "Security;" "Policing and Justice" (including detailed Annexes on a "Commission on Policing" and "Review of the Criminal Justice System"); "Prisoners;" and "Validation, Implementation and Review." Taken together, the six codicils enumerate a series of commitments, pledges, objectives and Annexes in these soon-to-be highly contentious and stymieing areas.

In sum, the two opening sections, three *Strands* and six aspirational codicils constitute *The Multiparty Agreement*. Looked at as both a composite text and a political settlement with legal effects and annexes, it is really a quite extraordinary, nuanced, sophisticated and creatively structured document, particularly for politicians – even with bureaucrats, diplomats and mediators at their elbows.

Finally, the Agreement concludes with an Annex, pages 27-30, namely the "Agreement Between the Government of the United Kingdom of Great Britain and Northern Ireland and the Government of Ireland," the formal international agreement between the two governments – that is, *The British-Irish Agreement* simultaneous with, but distinct and inseparable from, *The Multiparty Agreement* (which the former seeks to copper-fasten at state level). It is this treaty agreement that Bertie Ahern and Tony Blair are putting their signatures to in the iconic photograph at a Stormont conference table.

Under The Agreement, both governments committed to organizing referenda in their jurisdictions; and these took place on 22 May, six weeks after the Agreement, about the length of a British General Election. But it is often overlooked, when the term "Belfast Agreement" is bandied about in political discourse, that the two electorates actually voted on the two different agreements, folded into one, that comprise the one document known as The Agreement, The Belfast Agreement or The Good Friday Agreement.

The Northern Ireland referendum was specifically to approve *The Multiparty Agreement*. The Republic of Ireland referendum was to approve *The British-Irish Agreement* and to adopt the 19th Amendment of the Constitution of Ireland, which permitted the State to comply with the Belfast Agreement as a whole and provided for the removal of the "territorial claim" contained in Articles 2 and 3.

Copies of the full 30 pages of the Agreement, without further comment, were distributed to all households in Northern Ireland. The cover simply bore the neutral exhortation: *This Agreement is about* your *future. Please read it carefully. It's* your *decision.* It cannot be said that any literate citizen in North, concerning himself or herself sufficiently, lacked access to the final text in question.

Debate in the Republic was also vigorous, serious and widespread, following the usual pattern in a republican polity, unlike Britain's, where the people can directly enact foundational law that the Irish Parliament is *obliged* to implement. For referenda there are never *advisory*.

The result of these two simultaneous referenda were large majorities, in both parts of Ireland, in favour of The Agreement. In the Republic, 56% of the electorate voted, with 94% in favour of the amendments to the Constitution. The turnout in Northern Ireland was 81%, with 71% in favour of The Agreement. It was thus overwhelmingly endorsed by the island of Ireland.

Whilst most of the Northern Irish population could not have described The Agreement with such forensic detail, the overall package in its main basic elements and dynamics was widely, thoroughly and empirically understood in the "hearts and minds" of the electorate on 22 May 1998 and, increasingly in application and action, thereafter. Moreover, the life-experiences and politico-economic-social-cultural transformations of the Northern Lilliput over the past two decades have deeply embedded many of its key ethical principles (e.g., "an agreed future," "parity of esteem," "equality and mutual respect", and so on) not only in common political discourse, but in the daily speech of "the people."

At the same time, over the same period – and above all since the Brexit Referendum – it has become increasingly clear that almost the whole of the political class in Great Britain (with some exceptions in Scotland) either never fully understood, or has (like an amnesiac) slowly forgotten, what it agreed to, across the Irish Sea, as the other larger part of the *United* Kingdom.

Of course, the fact that the political culture of Great Britain effectively scorns and shuns that of Northern Ireland, in all its sectarian works and antics, is hardly news. From "exclusion orders" to the refusal of the Brobdingnagian British Labour Party to organize in Lilliput (Britain's little contagious Gaza, it would seem), this political avoidance is patently self-evident; and as BBC viewers in GB get their pabulum of endless Royal photos, gilded carriages and emblematic processions and tattoos, their screens are suddenly, say, interrupted by chanting loyalists with gigantic Union Jacks smashing down the doors at the back of Belfast City Hall. That, as therapists are wont to say, is somewhat "incongruent" . . .

In particular, the striking constitutional implications of The Agreement have been slow to dawn generally, not just in the GB background, but in the NI foreground too.

The first of these implications is the general political and legal point that with a document as complex and "creatively ambiguous" as this, it is likely impossible to unpick one clause or dimension without the whole thing unravelling slowly, like an undarned sock – or even collapsing precipitously, like the proverbial house of cards. Very extensive British and Irish sovereign legislation, mandated carefully in the Agreement's various Annexes and Articles, has come into force and cannot legally be ignored for the sake of that new politico-economic project known as Brexit. For the existing law of the British Parliament is, of course, sovereign.

A second implication has to do with the cumulative nature of The Agreement. Most obviously, the international treaty dimension, *The British-Irish Agreement,* replaces directly the Anglo-Irish Agreement and its Intergovernmental Conference. But as illustrated above, the whole document is a complex algebra of various political, legal and cultural lessons a long time in coming. In this sense, one is reminded very slightly but unmistakably of the intellectual atmosphere of the American colonies just after independence (but before the United States), recorded famously in *The Federalist Papers,* as they sought a lasting constitutional dispensation that worked for them after Great Britain. They too had had trade issues, insurrection, Loyalists, a European power, and Lord North's imperious "Tory" administration . . .

Thirdly, The Agreement introduces a number of novel constitutional principles, outwith the legal norms in Great Britain, mainly concerning citizenship and human rights. It guarantees dual nationality (Irish as well as British citizenship) for anyone born in Northern Ireland (from 2004) who has a British, Irish or legally-resident parent – thus making Northern Ireland a *de jure* binational polity, unlike Great Britain, and possibly uniquely in the world, with the *de facto* exception of Kosova.

As one of the many trade-offs to major nationalist concessions, The Agreement also mandates (through subsequent British legislation) two guardian civil rights bodies – the Northern Ireland Human Rights Commission and the Equality Commission – in order to thwart any return to the previous sectarian state, so memorably described in Heaney's early poem, "The Ministry of Fear." To the same end, it also establishes a "Joint

Committee" between the two states to supervise human rights issues, and requires "Comparable Steps" from the Irish Government.

Very importantly, in Strand One under "Safeguards," the Agreement mandates the incorporation of the European Convention on Human Rights (ECHR) into the separate Northern Ireland legal system, as well as "arrangements to provide that key decisions and legislation are proofed to ensure that they do not infringe the ECHR and any Bill of Rights for Northern Ireland." In Strand Three, under "Human Rights," there is a kind of template for this optional Bill of Rights (never enacted), listing the eight main rights in question.

Although such aforementioned "legislation" was assumed to come from the Northern Ireland Assembly, it is now clear that Westminster Brexit legislation openly breaches this clause of The Belfast Agreement. Here is the relevant phrasing: "The British Government will complete incorporation into *Northern Ireland law* (italics added) of the European Convention on Human Rights, with direct access to the courts, and remedies for the breach of the Convention, including the power for the courts to overrule Assembly legislation on the grounds of inconsistency."

This clause, in fact, lay behind the adoption by Parliament of the ECHR for the whole of the UK (in the form of the Human Rights Act 1998). One of the courts to which the Irish and British citizens of Northern Ireland have direct access by right under The Agreement (without the possibility of a British court's "declaration of incompatibility") is, of course, the European Court of Human Rights. Brexit seems set to remove this right, so breaking The Belfast Agreement, unless it is preserved by "The Irish Backstop" in the longer term.

Regarding Irish unity, the Agreement includes two key constitutional principles. The first, well-known, is that Irish unity can only occur with the consent of the majority in the North, through a border poll called by the Secretary of State for Northern Ireland. The second, less remarked upon, is that the people of the Republic must agree, presumably (though this is unstated) through a vote on a constitutional Amendment.

These clauses on Irish unity – as well as those on "review" and "remedial action" "if difficulties arise" with The Agreement – illustrate with particular clarity one of the document's central realities: that it is a *fully binational settlement* in a variety of senses. In effect, the two Governments pooled sovereignty in limited but totally decisive ways, without which the Agreement could not have occurred. It is, therefore, not within the remit of British parliamentary sovereignty to fiddle with The Belfast Agreement unilaterally *if Westminster wishes to preserve its integrity.*

The British Government sought *The Multiparty Agreement* – in the first place, as a pressing national interest – in order to achieve a comprehensive and final settlement between all parties to a bloody conflict lasting four decades. In exchange, the Irish Government entered into an international treaty with "binding obligations" and "solemn commitments," amending several historically cherished Articles to its Constitution and permitting the State to be *bound* by The Belfast Agreement. It also amended Irish nationality law ("Irish Nationality And Citizenship Act," 2004) to make Northern Ireland fully and permanently binational. The Multiparty Agreement was not possible without The British-Irish-Agreement, and *vice versa* – and, despite all the flimflam of the Brexiteers, this must remain the case, since the Irish Government is a partner with a political veto, not a Brexit vassal.

Finally, The Agreement mentions the EU in passing at several points, notably speaking of the two states as "friendly neighbours and as partners in the European Union." In retrospect, the EU backdrop of the Customs Union and Single Market proved to be decisive to the success of The Agreement – for, with its various security installations dismantled, the Border became increasingly invisible, politically and psychologically, to both parts of Ireland. As the essayist Hubert Butler wrote 69 years ago, "either it will become meaningless and will drop off painlessly like a strip of sticking plaster from a wound that has healed, or else it will survive in some modified form as a definition which distinguishes but does not divide." Both scenarios were well under way when Brexit struck.

What sort of Northern Ireland, in a nutshell, has emerged from The Belfast Agreement over the past 20 years? The country could be said to be a devolved constituent jurisdiction, with dual nationality in perpetuity and a *de facto* binational written constitution, within a wider, successful and long-lasting multinational union *with a single passport nationality and an unwritten constitution.* (*Nota bene*: The Belfast Agreement is now a *de facto* part of the British Constitution but – totally exceptionally – one that is written and binational. That was the price of ending the Troubles.) Put this way, the coming struggle between Brexit and The Belfast Agreement, with truly unpredictable consequences, assumes its true meaning.

Of the many reasons for the transformation of the Irish Republic over the past four decades, the role of the EU has been paramount. It not only transformed the economy, but served as exemplar and benchmark for reshaping both popular *mores* and a more fully secular State. In return, the Republic is one of the most loyally pro-European of the 28 member states.

No wonder the Irish Government and the EU are fully aligned now on the necessity of The Irish Backstop, which guarantees that Northern Ireland would remain in the Custom Union and Single Market if no final Brexit trade arrangement is agreed between the UK and EU, after the proposed "transition period" ending in December 2020 – said Backstop being, after all, agreed to by the British Government itself in December 2017.

The highly impressive Irish diplomatic corps has clearly outmanoeuvred the exiting British Foreign Office; and made the case that insofar as The Belfast Agreement is a binational settlement, it is also a core Irish State matter and so equally a major instance of EU self-interest. Both the State and the European Union understand, therefore, that The Irish Backstop is the means by which The Belfast Agreement is to be preserved in its agreed form, against the usurpations of British sovereignty – for without the growing invisibility of the Border, guaranteed by the background Customs Union and Single market, a Hard Brexit will certainly open the old, sinuously winding 310-mile wound to some extent, and risk turning difference again into division.

So the Brexiteers have a point when they say that The Irish Backstop is not simply about the technological arrangements for monitoring the flow of goods across a new EU border. They correctly discern that this is a means of keeping Northern Ireland partly in the European Union; whilst failing to understand that the Customs Union and Single Market are the assumed and indispensable background for the end that is The Belfast Agreement itself. Given the free-trade and libertarian ethos (and animus) that characterizes much of English nationalism, they have an intuitive feel for Benedict Anderson's famous adage in *Imagined Communities* (1983): that *markets create nations*.

Nonetheless, the argument that The Irish Backstop creates, somehow for the first time, a "border in the Irish Sea" is patent tosh. That border has always been there and thus, since the Irish Union of 1801 put *United* in "The United Kingdom of Great Britain and Ireland" (as it was first known). (Much of the British political class appears to assume that *United* refers to the uniting of Scotland and England in 1706-1707). As the Belfast poet and all-Ireland Unionist Samuel Ferguson (whom Yeats greatly admired) put it at the end of a speech in Belfast in the 1880s: *Rule Britannia ... But not a colony of Great Britain!*

For what could have created more of a "border in the Irish Sea" than the autonomous sectarian statelet of Northern Ireland between 1920 and 1973, so divergent from Great Britain, in so many ways? Or the appalling Troubles themselves? Or the current sea-border between illiberal and liberal Britain in many new matters, such as gay marriage, abortion, bilingualism and Bible Belt creationism only one-step from the Moonies?

And so on – and on.

By now, it should be pretty clear that the political and textual processes, *inter alia,* leading to the two votes on The Good Friday Agreement and on "The United Kingdom European Union Membership Referendum" had, literally, *nothing in common.* Apart, of course, for the word *referendum.*

For the Brexit Referendum was finally cooked up in a backroom of Downing Street by David Cameron and a couple of aides as a national solution to the purely party political problem of intense Euro-scepticism (and submerged English nationalism) that had bedevilled the Tory party for more than three decades. Unlike the 30 Irish pages of The Agreement, it consisted of precisely 16 words, plus the *unofficial* name of the state (incompetence?) and an arguably missing comma: *Should the United Kingdom remain a member of the European Union or leave the European Union?*

This proposed referendum was included as pledge in the Tory Manifesto, *but the enabling legislation was never debated in Parliament.* The referendum itself was an advisory and pre-legislative plebiscite, not legally binding on the Government, since Parliament (or more precisely, the Crown in Parliament) is fully sovereign. Unlike, that is, The Belfast Agreement – where both Governments not only gave a "solemn commitment" to support and implement The Multi-Party Agreement, but jointly signed a "binding" international treaty agreement to mandate the legislation required of both states.

There was no serious previous demand for the EU Referendum by a wider British public, apart from the (then) "fruit-cake" fringe of UKIP, Farage and his ilk. After the vote, it was both impossible *and* deceitful to haruspex with certainty the causes of the result, given the sparseness of the question (i.e., whether these causes were immigration, economic decline, sovereignty, and/or hatred of European federalism, etc.).

In diametric opposition to The Agreement, like (dog-) whistling in the dark, the Brexit *vote* preceded (incredibly now) its assumed unknown *text*. It has taken most of three years to come up even with the first stage of this massive modern codex – with many more scrolls and codicils to come, if in fact Brexit does materialize.

Is this not the very definition of Tory *cant*, when speaking of the immutable Brexit vote: "a set form of words repeated mechanically … the secret or peculiar language or jargon of a class, party or subject …"?

We in the North cannot move backwards in any sense, large or small. The Belfast Agreement must not be damaged, deformed or broken in the pursuit of political ends by "intractable activists" (page 161), whether British-Irish Unionists, Irish Republicans, or English Tories. "The Agreement" is *an end in itself* – destination unknown. For it is actually both the *de jure* and *de facto* written binational Constitution of this troubled constituent of the United Kingdom – and so, for its true supporters, to be defended by *any democratic means necessary*.

Above all we cannot risk a return to "the ancient bloody conflict" (page 214) of the Troubles. Not one more dead child!

Surely the mere ideological aspiration for a thirty-two-county Republic is not worth that risk again.

But neither is – it *now* has to be said – a long-term dysfunctional Westminster Parliament and a failing, disunited "United Kingdom of Great Britain *and* Northern Ireland." So let us see what Brexit – "Quixotic Wrexit" – might bring.

For under The Agreement, this polity can be disassembled peacefully and legally through a legitimate poll guaranteed by the two states, specifically through *The British-Irish Agreement* – but only *responsibly* and so *crucially* (in successful and prudential terms) if this vote is proceeded by a long and careful period of discussion, debate, negotiation and possible consensus, not merely by the quasi-fossilized political parties, but the whole of civil society, its institutions and all its cultural formations – and including (as in this issue), perhaps decisively, its historically well-schooled poets, writers, artists, scholars and intelligentsia of all hues and stripes.

The two-year period of debate (2012-2014) before the Referendum on Scottish Independence might be something of a model – but, Ireland being Ireland, it might take a good deal longer than that. Everyone – but especially the remnant "Protestant people" in this "Province" of the Realm – must also needs feel, throughout such a period of prolonged debate, *respected and protected, protected and respected*.

Might there be a new Parnell adequate to the challenge? Time will tell.

For no state is eternal.

The Editor

NEW TITLES
FROM THE IRISH PAGES PRESS

The Buried Breath
By Ciarán O'Rourke
£12.00 or €18.00

Crann na Teanga / The Language Tree
By Cathal Ó Searcaigh
£28.00 or €42.00

Blue Sandbar Moon
By Chris Agee
£18.00 or €26.00

Balkan Essays
By Hubert Butler
£25 or €30

Order Online
www.irishpages.org